'Do you want to know why zebras don't get ulce. how we tackle (self-) sabotage in organisations? T essential answers to these questions. *The Saboteur* more timely as we live in a society with increasing ch Dr Drayton provides insights into themes we all nee .... keep ourselves and society safer from (self) saboteurs. He has the most captivating, vivid writing style, combining practical experience and science, historical and recent examples, including stories of success and catastrophe. A key piece of work for individuals and organisations alike.'

Elsine Van Os, *Founder and CEO, Signpost Six*

'*The Saboteur at Work* is a significant contribution to our understanding of how unconscious psychological processes can sabotage leadership, organisational behaviour and global politics. It's well written and researched, with stories that bring the research to life. The book is an interesting, absorbing and profound exploration of the unconscious in organisational and leadership behaviour.'

Professor Sue Dopson, *Professor of Organisational Behaviour, Saïd Business School, University of Oxford*

'A must read for anyone managing a team or striving to improve individual performance in the workplace. *The Saboteur at Work* brings to light the unconscious psychological processes that can obstruct our individual lives and impact our careers. Most importantly, Dr Drayton provides practical solutions to overcome these. Highly recommended!'

Ryan Wynch, *Global Head of Occupational Health, Novartis*

'This book could not have come at a better time, when individuals, groups and organisations seem to be imploding psychologically all around us. I love the way Mike moves from story or small detail to analysis. It reminds me of Erich Auerbach's classic work *Mimesis*. Drawing on dozens of psychologists, novelists and poets, the arguments build up magisterially, each chapter concluding with incredibly useful takeaways. It is also a deeply personal story, and brilliant on the stories we tell ourselves. Having a great interest in Alan Turing, I was delighted to see Bletchley Park as a positive organisational example at the conclusion. How could one resist turning the next page after an early line such as "I will also explain why zebras don't get ulcers"?'

Michael Gates, *Managing Director CrossCulture, and Associate Fellow, Saïd Business School, University of Oxford*

The Saboteur at Work

The Saboteur at Work describes how unconscious psychological processes can sabotage individual lives, the functioning of groups, teams and organisations, and even global politics.

Drawing on research in the fields of psychology and organisations, this comprehensive yet straightforward and accessible book enables you to understand how the unconscious can impact progress and performance and describes practical techniques you can use to overcome the saboteur, individually and at work. The book discusses the modern understanding of our adaptive unconscious, and you will learn about repression, imposter syndrome and other defence mechanisms. Ideas are brought to life using real-world examples and personal, organisational and national stories. The book explores the mind's capacity for self-deception by telling the story of Tony Blair and the invasion of Iraq and looks at unconscious processes in organisations, asking what role the saboteur played in huge corporate failures such as the collapse of Barings Bank and the Boeing 737 Max scandal. The saboteur also operates on a larger scale – governments and societies can be sabotaged by this unconscious force. In Nazi Germany, how did normal, decent people behave like monsters, colluding with or actively participating in the murder of innocent people? Why did big US corporates like IBM, Ford and Chrysler work with the Nazis to make the Holocaust possible?

If you manage a team or lead an organisation, you need to understand the role played by the saboteur in your workplace and in your own career and life. This book enables leaders and managers to develop their leadership skills by understanding how the unconscious impacts individual, group and social processes. It will also be of use to coaches and organisational consultants working in the areas of teams and performance.

Michael Drayton is an executive coach, organisational consultant and clinical psychologist. He is an expert in leadership, resilience and mental health at work. He is an Executive Coach on the Executive MBA programme at Saïd Business School (University of Oxford) and a Fellow of the Cabinet Office Emergency Planning College.

The Saboteur at Work

How the Unconscious Mind
Can Sabotage Ourselves,
Our Organisations and Society

Michael Drayton

Routledge
Taylor & Francis Group

LONDON AND NEW YORK

Designed cover image: Getty Images / S-S-S

First published 2023
by Routledge
4 Park Square, Milton Park, Abingdon, Oxon OX14 4RN

and by Routledge
605 Third Avenue, New York, NY 10158

Routledge is an imprint of the Taylor & Francis Group, an informa business

British Library Cataloguing-in-Publication Data
A catalogue record for this book is available from the British Library

Library of Congress Cataloging-in-Publication Data
Names: Drayton, Michael, 1960– author.
Title: The saboteur at work: how the unconscious mind can sabotage ourselves, our organisations and society / Michael Drayton.
Description: Abingdon, Oxon; New York, NY: Routledge, 2023. |
Includes bibliographical references and index.
Identifiers: LCCN 2022029116 (print) | LCCN 2022029117 (ebook) |
ISBN 9781032035871 (hardback) | ISBN 9781032035888 (paperback) |
ISBN 9781003188063 (ebook)
Subjects: LCSH: Self-defeating behavior. | Self-management (Psychology)
Classification: LCC BF637.S37 D83 2023 (print) |
LCC BF637.S37 (ebook) | DDC 158.1—dc23/eng/20220824
LC record available at https://lccn.loc.gov/2022029116
LC ebook record available at https://lccn.loc.gov/2022029117

ISBN: 978-1-032-03587-1 (hbk)
ISBN: 978-1-032-03588-8 (pbk)
ISBN: 978-1-003-18806-3 (ebk)

DOI: 10.4324/9781003188063

Typeset in Sabon
by codeMantra

Contents

Acknowledgements

This has been an emotionally tough book to write, especially the middle chapters. Without the support of my wife Angela, my daughter Jenny and my son Guy, I may not have made it to the end. I would also like to thank my editor Charlie Wilson for her patience, intellect and truly exceptional skill.

Introduction: The Rabbi Who Had a Brain Explosion

Our story begins on a warm, sunny day in Sydney, 13 October 2020. Elimelech Levy was driving around the suburb of Bondi Junction looking for a parking space. Mr Levy was a 36-year-old man with one child. He was also a rabbi of 14 years' standing and a well-respected figure in his community. People who knew him described him as a mild-mannered, peaceful man.

However, on 13th October 2020, he was feeling anything but mild-mannered. He had been driving around for ages trying to park and was becoming increasingly agitated. He was late. As he turned a corner, he saw it – an empty parking space. His heart leapt with joy and with a smile he muttered *'todah'*, the Hebrew word for 'thank you'. He slowed, indicated and stopped to reverse into the space. As he did so, another vehicle swerved, nosed in and quickly claimed the parking space. Mr Levy's smile turned to rage as he got out of his car to remonstrate with the driver – a man named Richard Georgeson.

'That was my space – what the hell are you doing?! Get your car out of my space now!'

'Tough', Mr Georgeson said, 'suck it up, buddy', and he sauntered off with a smirk on his face.

Mr Levy stood there for a moment staring at his car and the parking space. Then it happened. He went berserk. He snapped the windscreen wiper off Mr Georgeson's car and began smashing it against the bonnet. He then broke off a side mirror and kicked it hard down the street, before getting back into his car and driving off with a screech of tyres.

As Mr Levy drove, he began to calm down. 'What have I done?' he thought. 'What was I thinking?' He was eventually overcome with remorse and returned to Georgeson's car and left a note on the windscreen, confessing.

When he later appeared in court, Mr Levy attributed his behaviour to 'a brain explosion', saying he had deeply regretted his actions ever since. He was fined, but his lawyer and the magistrate acknowledged Mr Levy's behaviour as completely out of character (Parsons, 2020).

DOI: 10.4324/9781003188063-1

In some respects, this is a comical story. It's the story of a mild-mannered man being pushed just a little too far and losing the plot. It brings to mind the scene in *Fawlty Towers* where Basil's car breaks down and after a moment or two shouting at the car Basil disappears out of shot, only to return carrying a tree branch with which he starts to manically beat the car.

Have you ever found yourself in a similar situation to Elimelech Levy? Feeling so frustrated and overwhelmed that you behaved in a manner that was out of character for you? Maybe you were driving your car and another driver overtook and cut in too quickly, causing you to brake shapely. Then, overcome with fury, you tailgated the offending driver for a couple of miles until common sense returned and you backed off. You got home and thought about your reactions and the possible consequences. 'What if he'd braked and I'd gone into the back of him? All the hassle of the insurance claim, the car off the road... all for what? What was I thinking? He was an idiot – why didn't I just ignore him? I turned into a monster for those few minutes'. Indeed, you turned into a monster for those few minutes, or as Elimelech Levy would have said, you experienced a brain explosion.

This isn't just a story about individual road rage. It is about how this experience of not quite being in control of ourselves can impact our careers, our performance in teams and organisations and our place in society as a whole.

Enter the saboteur

These stories raise an interesting psychological and philosophical question. What happened to Elimelech Levy during those few minutes of brain explosion? It didn't seem like the peace-loving rabbi was in control, someone else, a monster, was. If you were the person tailgating the bad driver, then who was actually driving the car for those few minutes – who was the monster who had taken charge of the car? This book sets out to explore this question, to understand Mr Levy's brain explosion and the monster who was driving your car.

This book is about an unconscious psychological force that routinely sabotages our lives: our own brain explosion, our own monster. I call this force 'the saboteur' and it exists in all of us: in individuals, teams, organisations and sometimes even in whole nations.

The saboteur is what connects your own personal dramas, meltdowns and cock-ups with events such as the tragic suicide of Sylvia Plath, corporate failures such as that suffered by the Boeing Corporation and even global historical events such as the Holocaust and the disaster at the Chernobyl nuclear power station. The saboteur is a human phenomenon that has always been with us and will always be present, influencing our lives.

What this book is about

The Saboteur at Work describes how unconscious psychological processes can sabotage individual lives, the functioning of groups, teams and organisations, and even global politics. If you manage a team or lead an organisation, you need to understand the role played by the saboteur in your workplace and in your own career and life.

I set the scene in Chapter 1 by looking at self-sabotage – how, despite our best intentions, we often mess up in life. It is a common experience to set a goal, to want to achieve something, but fail to follow through on the behaviour that would reach that goal. The dieter who is desperate to lose weight eats chocolate; the person wanting a stable relationship turns a blind eye to the warning signs that their potential partner is probably already in a relationship; the person who wants a promotion at work sleeps in and is late for their interview. All these people genuinely want what they say they want. The problem is, there is another part of them – a part they are not consciously aware of – that does *not* want the desired goal. A part of the overweight person is terrified of being slim because of the attention it might bring. A part of the single person is terrified of commitment in relationships. A part of the person seeking promotion feels they are not competent enough to be in charge. This is the part I call the saboteur, and it is at the root of many problems in individuals, organisations and societies. The saboteur also embodies unconscious anger and destructiveness, as well as the fearfulness referred to in these examples. This can result in destructive behaviour wrapped up in the cloak of good intentions.

I draw on Sigmund Freud's concepts of the unconscious, defence mechanisms and repetition compulsion to explain how and why we self-sabotage. I bring these ideas up to date by relating them to current research in neuroscience; for example, Timothy Wilson's work on the adaptive unconscious. Throughout the chapter, I bring these ideas to life with stories from my experience as an executive coach and clinical psychologist.

Chapter 2 explores and sheds some light on our own dark cellar: our unconscious mind. I describe the evolution of ideas about the unconscious from before Freud to modern research in neuroscience. I establish that the human mind is an iceberg with most of its 'data' and processing power hidden beneath the surface of our consciousness. In terms of the information the human brain contains, consciousness is not in the ratio of one to a million but more like one to a billion. The things we are most frightened of, ashamed of and desire live in the unconscious and comprise the saboteur. This chapter discusses the unconscious and decision-making at an individual, team and organisational level.

Chapter 3 asks the question 'Why did I do that?' by exploring our psychological defence mechanisms. It's a common experience to deny the reality of a painful situation; for example, a smoker may deny the health risks associated with smoking. Defence mechanisms are unconscious coping strategies that protect us from thoughts that would otherwise overwhelm us with anxiety. The term was first coined by Sigmund Freud, and the theory was developed by his daughter, Anna. These defence mechanisms are how the saboteur shows itself to the outside world. I link self-sabotage with the phenomenon called repetition compulsion. This is where people compulsively repeat, time after time, upsetting or traumatising events. People find comfort in familiarity, even if that familiarity is deeply unpleasant. In exploring how defence mechanisms relate to self-sabotage, I describe the early psychoanalytic work on defence mechanisms and bring it up to date with more recent studies in neuroscience. I illustrate this by exploring the disastrous decision by Tony Blair and the British government to support the US invasion of Iraq in 2002.

Chapter 4 explores anxiety and self-sabotage. Anxiety is the emotion most associated with the saboteur. Most of us do our best to avoid feeling anxious, either by avoiding an anxiety-provoking event or doing something impulsive to end the anxiety. When we are anxious, our body is like a house with an oversensitive burglar alarm. If something harmless comes along – for example, a cat walking across the garden – the burglar alarm goes off, lights flash and sirens wail. When we are anxious, little things that are really no threat set off our physiological alarm, and just as if our house alarm has gone off, we pull the duvet over our heads in fear or grab the baseball bat to go and investigate. This chapter looks at the psychological and physiological roots of anxiety and how the saboteur interacts with this anxiety by either acting impulsively or avoiding problems. I explore how this can play out in decision-making in high-stress situations. I will also explain why zebras don't get ulcers.

Chapter 5 discusses the stories we tell ourselves and how we create our personal saboteur. Our reality is based on the stories we tell ourselves. This applies to individuals, organisations and nations. These stories become part of our unconscious and often part of our saboteur. The chapter discusses personal, organisational and national stories and how they can support or sabotage. I discuss the work of psychologists Kurt Lewin and Timothy Wilson on how changing stories changes behaviour. I tell the story of Nat Tate, David Bowie and the Author William Boyd. I also look at Sylvia Plath's most famous poem, 'Daddy'.

Chapter 6 looks at risk-taking and decision-making by discussing personality and the saboteur. I discuss the big five model of personality and how the five personality factors interact to either support or sabotage us at work. In particular, I look at personality and risk-taking in the financial services industry, considering the story of Nick Leeson and the Barings Bank scandal. I base the chapter on the neuroscience of risk-taking behaviour.

Having set the scene by looking at how the saboteur influences individuals, I move on and describe how the unconscious saboteur undermines the work of groups, teams and organisations, using the theories of Wilfred Bion and Kurt Lewin to explain why groups often perform terribly.

Chapter 7 examines how the saboteur is present in groups, teams and organisations. This chapter discusses the psychology of unconscious group dynamics and how these can affect decisions and behaviour in a positive or negative direction. People behave differently in a large group compared with when they are alone or with a few people. In groups, we consciously and unconsciously assess our and other people's position in the dominance hierarchy. Groups generate conformity. Groups create polarisation when people with similar views come together and make more extreme decisions than they would as individuals. If the group members are naturally risk averse, then the total group decision could be exceptionally cautious. If the group members include individuals who have a robust appetite for risk, then the final group decision could be a substantial gamble. To relate these theories to real life, this chapter looks at the unconscious group dynamics at play in the Stanford Prison Experiment, Chernobyl disaster and the Abu Ghraib scandal.

Chapter 8 discusses how the saboteur can grip not just individuals and groups but also entire nations – how the saboteur can shape large-scale social and political movements. This topic is a grim one – the role played by the saboteur in the rise of Hitler, the Third Reich and the Holocaust. I also tell the story of how IBM and Ford helped to facilitate the Holocaust.

Chapter 9 focuses on the practical steps that you can take to start to understand and manage your saboteur. The saboteur serves an important purpose, and it can actually help rather than hinder you. Feelings from the saboteur can compel you to behave unusually – perhaps even badly. But when you learn to stop, listen and reflect on what your saboteur is trying to communicate, you gain control over your actions. Noticing and reflecting on your feelings gives you lots of very useful information you can learn from. We all have an inner psychological team, and each character on that team needs to be heard. Then, your internal CEO can make an informed decision about whether and how to act. The saboteur has a collection of masks. It's important to recognise when the saboteur is at play in your life and use strategies to manage it. Working on 'levelling up' your ego will help you to build a better relationship with your saboteur.

Finally, Chapter 10 explores the far more complex problem of tackling the saboteur in organisations. I tell the story of how the saboteur in the Boeing Corporation contributed to two serious plane crashes and the deaths of 346 people. I contrast this with another organisation, one that was very successful. An organisation that, according to Winston Churchill, shortened World War II by two years, saving millions of lives. This organisation was Bletchley Park. The organisational culture at Bletchley Park was characterised by two factors that made it very difficult for the saboteur to operate: cognitive diversity and psychological safety. I then go on to unpack the various factors that create a culture that will inhibit the unconscious destructive parts of our unconscious – in other words our individual and collective saboteur.

Reference

Parsons, L. (2020). 'The "Brain Explosion" That Saw a Respected Rabbi Go Berserk After a Driver "Stole" His Coveted Parking Spot – As He Ripped the Windscreen Wiper Off a Stranger's Car and Used It to Smash the Bonnet'. *Daily Mail*, 4 December.

1 Our Own Worst Enemy: What Is Self-Sabotage?

The playwright Andrea Dunbar was born in 1961, a year after me. We grew up pretty close to each other on different council estates in Bradford, she on Buttershaw and I on Thorpe Edge. I never met Andrea, but I know something of her life because both estates were rough as hell. Andrea had a tough life of poverty and emotional deprivation. When she was in her early twenties, she was a single mother living in a refuge for 'battered women' (as such places were called in the 1980s). Andrea had always loved writing, and in 1982 she wrote a play, *The Arbor* (Dunbar, 1988). This was a brutally realistic and darkly comic portrayal of working-class life on Brafferton Arbor, a road on the Buttershaw Estate. Because of a fortunate series of events, her play ended up being staged at London's Royal Court Theatre. The play was a big success, and with some encouragement and support from the Royal Court's artistic director, Max Stafford Clark, she went on to write the play that would make her famous, *Rita, Sue and Bob Too* (Dunbar, 1988). The play was a massive critical and popular success and was made into a film, which was also a big success. It captured the atmosphere of the early 1980s. The poster advertising the film described it as 'Thatcher's Britain, with her knickers down'.

Andrea became a star overnight. Hollywood beckoned. Andrea Dunbar, the working-class lass from Buttershaw, had made it. She was respected and wealthy. And she had achieved this not by winning the lottery or appearing on Big Brother, but by producing a significant piece of literature that connected the world of Buttershaw to that of Sloane Square. In a rational world, you'd expect life to be good for Andrea from then on. She was a success, the Buttershaw girl who'd made it to the Royal Court through her talent. Unfortunately, though, that wasn't the path her life took. She returned to Buttershaw and started to drink heavily. Andrea didn't manage her money well and she ended up in debt.

On the 20th of December 1990, Andrea was drinking in The Beacon, the pub in Buttershaw that is seen in the opening shot of *Rita, Sue and Bob Too*. She had a terrible headache and sat with her head in her hands. She felt like she was going to be sick, and took herself off to the ladies, where she collapsed. An ambulance was called, and she was

DOI: 10.4324/9781003188063-2

taken to the Bradford Royal Infirmary, where she later died from a brain haemorrhage.

Andrea Dunbar was tough. You needed a certain amount of resilience to survive on Buttershaw. She was also extremely creative and talented. I would also speculate that she wanted to be happy – don't we all? Nobody consciously wants to feel miserable, lonely or unhappy. Nobody wants to end up living in a hell on earth. Andrea Dunbar was far from stupid, and I'm sure that returning to the Buttershaw Estate made sense to her – and seemed like the best option she had at that time. Andrea would have had at least a few options open to her following the success of *Rita, Sue and Bob Too*. There were a number of paths her life could have taken. She could have felt encouraged and validated by her success and followed the path of a successful playwright. Maybe she could have moved to London or perhaps a different, less deprived part of Bradford.

Andrea's dilemma was summed up in Adele Stripe's excellent fictionalised account of Andrea's life, *Black Teeth and a Brilliant Smile*. In the book, Andrea talks about Buttershaw:

> I like the area because that's all I've ever known. It's no better or worse than anywhere else, she continued. It certainly isn't as bad as some people make it out to be. You don't have to be hard to live around here. You've just got to have a knowledge of working-class life. Even from me moving to Buttershaw it's allus had a bad name. And I don't find it that bad at all. I moved away a few times, but I can't resist coming back. I dunno, I just like the people so much around here.
>
> (Stripe, 2017)

Later on in the book, Andrea is on a panel at an event about women writers at London's Riverside Studios. She is asked for advice on writing by a young, working-class woman writer. Stripe writes:

> … I stumbled on writing by accident. It found me. Like it's found you. But if you come from an estate then you will always be an outsider in this world. [She gestured to the stalls in the theatre.] As long as you're all right with that then there's no reason you won't succeed.
>
> As the event wound up Andrea answered the questions that other panellists struggled to complete. Her lucidity astonished the audience of television producers, commissioners and agents, so much so that by the time the event ended she was besieged by offers of work and representation. Well-heeled Londoners with middle-class accents shook her hand and told her how delightful she was. They pushed their business cards into her palm and offered to buy her drinks.
>
> (Stripe, 2017)

In the end, Andrea felt too much like an outsider and took the path back to Buttershaw and a chaotic life of heavy drinking and self-neglect – the life that was soon to kill her. How can we understand Andrea's decision? How can we get inside her head and see the world as she saw it?

Andrea Dunbar was in many respects a tough character and certainly a brilliant writer; but she had another side to her personality, an unconscious, self-destructive part – the saboteur. Andrea Dunbar was sabotaged from within, a victim of self-sabotage.

We all have an internal saboteur. The saboteur does not care whether you are talented, wealthy or clever; it affects us all. Members of the royal family, politicians, rock stars, actors and writers all do things that mess up their comfortable lives. You and I also make choices that sabotage our happiness. We act impulsively, lose control (like Rabbi Levy in the Introduction) or turn down opportunities because we feel fearful. Sometimes, like with Andrea Dunbar, the saboteur completely takes over and destroys the healthy, creative and hopeful part of us. It is very important to understand our saboteur, because if we don't understand it, the saboteur can get us into big trouble. If we do understand the saboteur and how it operates, then we can begin to control its influence. We can take a step back and think about the reality of our situation rather than just feeling compelled to act without thinking.

In this chapter, I begin by exploring a really common form of self-sabotage called imposter syndrome. This is when apparently successful people feel like they are a fraud and are terrified of being found out. Maybe this is how Andrea Dunbar felt when she met those well-heeled Londoners at the Riverside Studios? Finally, I finish up with some ideas that you can use to understand and manage any compulsion you may have to self-sabotage.

Imposter syndrome

Andrea Dunbar felt like an outsider in the literary world. Another writer who experienced this sense of being an outsider was the Nobel Prize-winning author John Steinbeck. In 1938, while he was writing *The Grapes of Wrath*, he recorded in his journal:

> I'm not a writer. I've been fooling myself and other people. I wish I were. This success will ruin me as sure as hell. It probably won't last, and that will be all right. I'll try to go on with work now. Just a stint every day does it. I keep forgetting.
>
> (Steinbeck, 1990)

John Steinbeck, one of the greatest writers of the 20th century, had a voice in his head – the saboteur if you will – telling him that he was fooling himself and he wasn't a writer. I wonder if Andrea had that same voice – that same saboteur – constantly telling her that she wasn't a proper writer, that she wasn't good enough? Thank God that Steinbeck was able to overcome his internal saboteur; otherwise, the world would have been deprived of *The Grapes of Wrath*. Maybe Andrea's saboteur had a stronger voice; maybe hers was a more powerful internal bully and her sense of herself as a worthy person was weaker than Steinbeck's. She fought back and wrote a couple of brilliant plays, but the saboteur won in the end.

Box 1.1: A brief history of imposter syndrome, and how it affects men and women

The term 'imposter syndrome' was first used back in the days of ABBA, punk rock and the Bay City Rollers, and soon after became a part of popular culture. In 1978, two psychologists at Georgia State University, Pauline Clance and Suzanne Imes, published their classic paper that introduced the world to imposter syndrome (Clance & Imes, 1978). They interviewed 150 high-achieving women. Despite the tangible and independent evidence of their abilities, the women consistently played down and generally minimised their accomplishments and attributed their success to luck or to other people overestimating them. The participants made external attributions for their success ('It was caused by factors external to me, like luck') and internal attributions for their failures ('I failed because I'm incompetent'). They felt that they had somehow managed to cheat their way to success or that success had been a lucky fluke and they were terrified of being found out.

Thus, the term 'imposter syndrome' was coined, and it really took off. It seemed to strike a chord with the experiences of many people. Imposter syndrome became one of those rare psychological terms (like 'denial') that pass into everyday language.

The Clance and Imes research focused on high-achieving women, but subsequent research found that both men and women can fall victim to imposter syndrome (Bravata et al., 2020). Interestingly, recent research demonstrated that imposter syndrome can affect men more than women in high-pressure situations (Badawy et al., 2018).

Rebecca Badawy and her colleagues recruited more than 500 undergraduate students, half of them male and half female. They measured their levels of imposter syndrome with a psychometric scale that included grading statements like, 'Sometimes I'm afraid others will discover how much knowledge or ability I really lack'.

In one study, the researchers gave the students two sets of five verbal and numerical tests. After the first set, the researchers increased the stress on half the students by telling them that they had answered all of the first five questions incorrectly. This fake feedback affected the male students with high imposter feelings much more than the female students. The men reported higher anxiety, made less effort and generally began to perform more poorly than those who were given accurate feedback. In essence, they started to give up. In contrast, the female students responded to the fake feedback by working harder and they showed improved performance.

The research showed that in high-pressure situations, the feelings and behaviours we call imposter syndrome are exaggerated in men but reduced in women. Women who experience imposter syndrome try harder when under pressure, but men with imposter syndrome seem to give up.

One of the defining features of all the successful business people I have coached is a pervasive feeling of not being good enough – a feeling that their self-evident success is due to luck rather than any talent on their part. Many feel like a fraud and fear that it will only be a matter of time before someone smarter sees through them and finds out the truth: that really they are nothing special.

Imposter syndrome is made up from this muddle of thoughts and feelings. I have yet to meet a successful person without some degree of imposter syndrome. In fact, those who don't have imposter syndrome usually have a much worse syndrome – narcissism.

At first sight, imposter syndrome doesn't make any sense. When presented with evidence of success, why would any reasonable person conclude that they are undeserving? Isn't there a lot of psychological research that shows most people think they are generally 'better' than everybody else? Most of us believe we are above-average drivers as well as being more ethical and compassionate than everyone else (Alick et al., 2005). In my experience, this is only true at a superficial level, because as soon as you scratch the surface of any human life, you quickly become aware of the pain, frailties, faults and weaknesses that lie within.

Imposter syndrome is a pattern of doubting one's accomplishments and fearing being exposed as a fraud. It's actually more common than you might think, with up to 82 per cent of people experiencing imposter syndrome at some point in their life (Bravata et al., 2020).

Imposter syndrome evolves from a specific psychological process. It begins when you are given a task you don't feel quite ready for. You start to experience feelings of anxiety, self-doubt and worry. These feelings can trigger a number of possible behaviours. You can either become obsessed with the task and over-prepare or avoid the task and procrastinate.

Let's say you get the task done and you experience relief and maybe even a brief period of accomplishment. This is usually short-lived for those of us with imposter syndrome. We start to think about the task and come to the perfectly reasonable (to us at least) conclusion that the outcome had very little to do with any innate ability we might have. If you over-prepared, the successful outcome was obviously a result of overworking rather than personal ability. You had to work twice as hard as an average person to get the same result. If you avoided the task and procrastinated, the success was down to luck and the fact that you winged it. So whether you procrastinated or over-prepared, any positive feedback is discounted. Success is attributed to luck or working twice as hard as anyone else, rather than your ability.

With every cycle of this psychological process, your feelings of being a fraud increase. Your self-doubt, low mood and anxiety grow. This is a self-reinforcing vicious circle: the more you succeed, the more you feel like a fraud, and the more you feel like a fraud, the more you fear being found out.

Real imposters

It's important to know that the world is full of real imposters. There are two types of real imposters: those who know they are imposters and those who are oblivious to their imposter-hood.

The Dark Triad

There are people who know that they are imposters and they don't care – in fact, they quite like the sense of power that comes with being able to pull the wool over people's eyes. These folk often have personality disorders like psychopathic personality disorder or narcissistic personality disorder.

Jimmy Savile is a dramatic example of someone who was not what he claimed to be. He was a real imposter and a real conscious saboteur. Savile was famous for being an eccentric TV personality who raised millions for charity. He was a friend of Prince Charles and Margaret Thatcher and was knighted for his charity work. Savile was also one of the UK's most prolific sexual predators: he physically and sexually abused vulnerable people from the late 1940s until his death in 2009. Savile exploited his fame and celebrity status to prey on hundreds of vulnerable people, mostly young women. He sexually assaulted and raped them in television dressing rooms, hospitals, schools, children's homes and his Rolls Royce. The scale of Savile's crimes was 'to the best of our knowledge unprecedented in the UK', according to a joint police and social services report into his activities (Gray & Watt, 2013).

Jimmy Savile is an extreme example of a real imposter and saboteur. He had what is known as the dark triad of personality characteristics: psychopathy, Machiavellianism and narcissism. This dark triad is common in famous or powerful people. Such people often have a glib superficial charm that masks the ruthlessness of their actions.

It's helpful to realise that real imposters, like Jimmy Savile, don't experience imposter syndrome. They think they're just great and simply don't doubt their abilities and wonderfulness. If someone doesn't experience any imposter syndrome, there's at least a chance that they may experience something much worse.

The Dunning-Kruger effect

Those with a dark triad personality know that they are imposters and they don't care. The other type of 'imposter' is the genuinely incompetent person who is so lacking in ability and insight that they don't notice their own ineptness. Consider for a moment the words of the philosopher Bertrand Russell writing about the rise of the Nazis in 1930s Germany, 'The fundamental cause of the trouble is that in the modern world the stupid are cocksure while the intelligent are full of doubt' (Russell, 2009). In other words, stupid people are too stupid to understand that they are stupid. That is the defining feature of imposter syndrome and of the Dunning-Kruger effect (Dunning, 2011).

The Dunning-Kruger effect is a cognitive bias that we have all experienced. Let's say you start a new job, and after the first week you think to yourself, 'Well, this isn't so complicated. It seems easy enough'. And then, as you slowly find out more about the job, you realise that it's quite difficult – in fact, it's really complicated. As you do this, your initial confidence quickly disappears. However, as time goes on and you progress with the job and learn more about it and practise, your confidence slowly returns.

The problem is that some people never experience that initial drop in confidence, and so they don't go on to learn and get better. They do become adept, though, at covering up their ineptitude by becoming experts in the great game of office politics, a topic that appears quite a bit in subsequent chapters of this book.

The Dunning-Kruger effect, then, is a cognitive bias in which people mistakenly assess their ability as being greater than it is. It's being ignorant of your own ignorance, or to put it more bluntly, being so stupid that you don't realise that you're stupid (Alicke & Govorun, 2005).

Our different selves

When we think about imposter syndrome or the saboteur, it's like we are talking about two separate beings living inside of us that have contradictory beliefs, desires and wishes. One is clever, competent and optimistic, and the other one is full of fear, doubt and worry. One desires stability, and the other desires something better – change, improvement. That is the dilemma of imposter syndrome and the dilemma of the saboteur: the choice between stability and change.

Why is this idea important to you and your life? Well, it's because the saboteur lives within all of us. We all experience anxiety when faced with new challenges. We might label it differently – some might call it anxiety or excitement, others call it terror – but it's essentially the same thing. It's an idea and a feeling that can get us into big trouble, either because we act impulsively, like Rabbi Levy, whose story I share in the introduction to this book, or we sabotage our lives, like Andrea Dunbar.

We all have a number of potential personalities (not just the two I describe in the preceding section). But when we are full of rage, like Rabbi Levy was, then just one of these personalities is in control – the angry one. When Andrea felt like a fraud, she was being controlled by her internal bully. Both of these constitute the saboteur. The saboteur is insidious because when it is in control of us, it blocks out access to the other, more capable parts of our personalities. It pushes away our other potential selves. When Rabbi Levy was angry and under the saboteur's control, that's all he was – angry. He wasn't able to access the more stoical and 'peace-loving' parts of his personality. He wasn't able to access the common-sense self that might have said, 'Just walk away; it's not important in the grand scheme of things'. That self was only able to get a look-in when the grip of the saboteur had loosened. When Andrea was feeling hopeless and like an imposter, she was being shouted at by her abusive internal bully and couldn't hear her other selves telling her how talented and successful she really was.

If we can begin to understand the saboteur better and understand the process by which the saboteur takes control of us, then we might be able to loosen its grip and regain access to the other, more capable parts of us. We might just be able to empower these more capable selves to have a voice and engage in a dialogue with the saboteur. This is how we can regain control over this psychological process that has the potential to compel our behaviour by taking control of us.

From our own worst enemy to our own best friend

Rule two in Jordan Peterson's book *12 Rules for Life: An Antidote to Chaos* is 'treat yourself like someone you are responsible for helping' (Peterson, 2018).

This is good advice for two reasons. First of all, it seems to me that many of us (not all) tend to put other people's needs before our own. This is a good thing, as long as you are also caring for yourself and valuing yourself. As the airline attendants say before take-off, 'In the event of an emergency, put your own oxygen mask on before attempting to help others'. This advice also applies, I think, to life in general.

Second, Jordan Peterson's rule encourages you to take an outside perspective, or at least a different perspective, on yourself and on your life. It suggests that you step outside of yourself and see yourself as others might see you. There is much research in psychology to show that other people have a more objective and balanced view of your personality, your emotions and your behaviour than you do (Kenny, 1994; Spain et al., 2000). I would bet that Andrea Dunbar's friends were constantly reassuring her and telling her how talented she was. I'd also bet that this reassurance and advice fell on deaf ears.

If you were able to metaphorically step outside of yourself when the saboteur was in control, then you would stand a much better chance of regaining some control of your feelings and behaviour. If Andrea had been able to see herself as others did, then she may not have felt like such an imposter and behaved in the self-sabotaging way that she did.

Here are a few ideas to consider that might help you to find this outside perspective of yourself and maybe come to a more accurate understanding of yourself and your life.

We see the world from the inside out

Always remember that you observe the world and other people from the inside out. When you do anything, let's say challenging, you are aware of what's going on around you. However, you are also all too painfully aware of all your faults, shortcomings and self-doubt. On the other hand, you only see other people from the outside – you see the face they choose to present to the world. It's easy to see other people as being confident and yourself as being full of doubt. But that isn't true.

If we think back to Andrea Dunbar's experience at the Riverside Studios, I would speculate that when she was talking to those 'posh' people who spoke to her with their 'Belgravia drawl', she felt in some way inferior. She may have associated their accent, mannerisms and attire with the teachers, social workers and bosses who had always had power over her. She felt like an outsider. It may also be interesting to speculate on how some of the 'well-heeled Londoners' there felt when they were speaking to Andrea Dunbar. Maybe they thought, 'Here's someone from a council estate in the north of England who's written a brilliant piece of literature. Look at me, with my private education and middle-class background. I've written nothing. I've had all these advantages and she's had no advantages. I'm a failure'. Behind the façade of the well-heeled Londoner was a person filled with self-doubt. But maybe the well-heeled Londoner was much better at hiding this and rationalising it than Andrea Dunbar was.

So the next time you are in a situation where you feel like an imposter or feel that you are not good enough, remember that you are only aware of your feelings and not the feelings and psychological states of the other people around you. Maybe they feel as scared as you?

Feelings are not facts

Towards the end of his life, Albert Einstein said to a friend: 'the exaggerated esteem in which my life work is held makes me very ill at ease. I feel compelled to think of myself as an involuntary swindler' (Holt, 2005). So if you sometimes feel like an imposter, you are in good company. Objectively, Albert Einstein was a genius, and yet he thought of himself as an involuntary swindler. How can you explain this? Well, maybe Einstein had temporarily abandoned the scientific method and based his conclusion on feelings rather than fact. Feelings aren't facts, and just because Albert Einstein felt like an involuntary swindler, that didn't make him an involuntary swindler. Similarly, just because you *feel* like an imposter, it doesn't necessarily follow that you are an imposter.

So when you find yourself feeling like an imposter, take a breath and think of some objective evidence that proves that you're not an imposter. Look at your CV, look at your qualifications, and remember that an interview panel appointed you to your job and chose you over other people. Assess whether you are really an imposter on this tangible evidence, not ephemeral emotions.

Listen to the saboteur

One of the dangers in personifying these personality factors as 'the saboteur' is that you might see them as something external. Most often, when the saboteur takes charge, that's how it feels. I'm sure Rabbi Levy felt that something had taken control of him when he was smashing up the car. However, it's important to hang on to the fact that the saboteur isn't external but is a part of you. It represents your fearfulness and anxiety and your freeze–flight–fight survival response (more on this in Chapter 4). All the saboteur really is, is a representation of your instinct to survive. The saboteur is warning you of the threat and advising you to either keep your head down (freeze), run away or avoid it (flight) or fight it (fight).

If someone close to you is trying to warn you of an impending threat, probably the worst thing you can do is ignore them. If you do, their warnings will become more insistent and urgent. It's the same with the saboteur. The more you ignore these unconscious thoughts and compulsions to act, the more insistent they will become.

Therefore, if you suspect that the saboteur is active, the best thing to do is to listen to the concerns of the saboteur. In other words, stop what you are doing and reflect deeply on the situation in which you find yourself. Reflect on what the saboteur might be frightened of or feel threatened by. Listen carefully and think about it – in other words, engage the rational part of your brain. You might feel like bashing up the car, but is it really the best course of action? You may feel like a failure and a fraud, but does reality confirm this? Often people don't do this; often they act on the compulsion or ignore it. Sometimes they do this by calling themselves names. How often have you said to yourself, 'You're such an idiot!' Instead, when you suspect a saboteur takeover attempt, just stop, take a deep breath and think about the situation and what the best response might be.

Aim for 'good enough'

Finally, the best tip for avoiding imposter syndrome is to strive to be good enough rather than perfect. Aim to be pretty damn good and not perfect.

When I first qualified as a clinical psychologist, I worked in a child and family psychology service. One of the problems we came across frequently was that of perfectionist parents. I remember one depressed teenager called Sarah saying to me that her mother would always describe herself as being her best friend. 'All that means is that I have a rubbish mother and a rubbish best friend', Sarah told me. In many respects, Sarah had the perfect mother. She was attentive and loving and seemingly could not do enough to make her daughter's life won-derful. She would buy Sarah whatever she wanted, and Sarah always turned up to sessions very fashionably dressed. Yet despite this almost smothering attention to making Sarah happy, both Sarah and her mother were quite depressed. Sarah's mother would always tell me that it was her aim in life to be the perfect parent. The irony was that by struggling for perfection, she sabotaged Sarah's life and her own. Perfectionism is one of the masks worn by the saboteur. One of the lessons I learnt working with disturbed families and children is that it's far healthier to strive to be good enough rather than perfect.

Donald Winnicott was a psychoanalyst and paediatrician who worked in London in the 1950s. He found that mothers who became depressed always aimed to be the perfect mother, whereas mothers who didn't experience depression just did their very best to look after their children and be a good enough mother (Winnicott, 1965). In other words, you need to strive to do the best you can for your chil-dren, but realise that at times you will get things wrong and that is okay. Winnicott also concluded that 'good enough' parenting was also very good for the child's development. This is because young children see their parents as infallible gods and themselves as dependent. He argued that the realisation that their godlike parents are in fact imperfect helps children to mature and see the world in a more realistic manner – not simply as black and white or good and bad. The child is able to see that someone who is good, their mother, can also make mistakes and be, in that sense, 'bad'. Winnicott concluded that perfectionism leads to depression, because ultimately perfection is impossible and aiming for perfection will always lead to disappointment because you will never reach the goal. He said that we should all just do the very best we can with the gifts we have and aim to be good enough, rather than perfect, which is good advice for life.

When discussing the tyranny of the Soviet regime, Alexander Solzhenitsyn said something very profound: 'the line separating good and evil passes not through states nor between classes nor between political parties either – but right through the centre of every human heart' (Solzhenitsyn, 2003). That is worth thinking about and remembering. Here is how I think that truth applies to imposter syndrome and self-sabotage: the line separating self-confidence from the imposter syndrome and the saboteur exists not between individual people or groups but through the centre of every human heart. In other words, it's not the case that only some people are disabled by the saboteur or imposter syndrome – we all have that potential deep within us.

Chapter takeaways

- The saboteur is at the root of problems in individuals, organisations and societies.
- Operating at an unconscious level, the saboteur undermines what we want to achieve.
- The saboteur wreaks havoc at work: due to imposter syndrome, many successful business people feel like a fraud and that they are not good enough.
- Understanding our saboteur is the key to diminishing its influence.
- We can take steps to stop self-sabotage:

  - Remember that everyone has a saboteur; you are not alone.
  - Look for evidence that you are not an imposter. Just because you feel like one, that doesn't mean you are one (feelings are not facts).
  - Listen to the saboteur: what is it trying to tell you, and how you can respond to this in a way that doesn't sabotage you?
  - Ditch perfectionism and aim for 'good enough'.

References

Alicke, M. D. & Govorun, O. (2005). 'The Better-Than-Average Effect'. In M. D. Alicke, D. A. Dunning & J. Krueger (Eds.), *The Self in Social Judgment: Studies in Self and Identity*, pp. 85–106. Hove: Psychology Press.

Badawy, R. L., Gazdag, B. A., Bentley, J. R. & Brouer, R. L. (2018). 'Are All Impostors Created Equal? Exploring Gender Differences in the Impostor Phenomenon-Performance Link'. *Personality and Individual Differences*, 131, 156–63.

Bravata, D. M., Watts, S. A., Keefer, A. L., Madhusudhan, D. K., Taylor, K. T., Clark, D. M., Nelson, R. S., Cokley, K. O. & Hagg, H. K. (2020). 'Prevalence, Predictors, and Treatment of Impostor Syndrome: A Systematic Review'. *Journal of General Internal Medicine*, 35(4), 1252–75.

Clance, P. R. & Imes, S. A. (1978). 'The Imposter Phenomenon in High Achieving Women: Dynamics and Therapeutic Intervention'. *Group Dynamics: Theory, Research, and Practice: The Official Journal of Division 49, Group Psychology and Group Psychotherapy of the American Psychological Association*, 15(3), 241.

Dunbar, A. (1988). *Rita, Sue and Bob Too; with The Arbor; and Shirley. Three Stage Plays by Andrea Dunbar; with an Introduction by Rob Ritchie*. London: Methuen.

Dunning, D. (2011). 'The Dunning-Kruger Effect: On Being Ignorant of One's Own Ignorance'. *Advances in Experimental Social Psychology*, 44, 247–96 (Elsevier).

Gray, D. & Watt, P. (2013). *Giving Victims a Voice: Joint Report into Sexual Allegations Made against Jimmy Savile*. London: Metropolitan Police Service.

Holt, J. (2005). 'Time Bandits: What Were Einstein and Gödel Talking About?' *New Yorker*, 28 February. Retrieved from: www.newyorker.com/magazine/2005/02/28/time-bandits-2.

Kenny, D. A. (1994). *Interpersonal Perception: A Social Relations Analysis*. New York: Guilford Press.

Peterson, J. B. (2018). *12 Rules for Life: An Antidote to Chaos*. London: Allen Lane.

Russell, B. (2009). *The Triumph of Stupidity in Mortals and Others*. Abingdon: Taylor & Francis

Solzhenitsyn, A. I. (2003). *The Gulag Archipelago, 1918–56: An Experiment in Literary Investigation*. New York: Random House.

Spain, J. S., Eaton, L. G. & Funder, D. C. (2000). 'Perspectives on Personality: The Relative Accuracy of Self versus Others for the Prediction of Emotion and Behavior'. *Journal of Personality*, 68(5), 837–67.

Steinbeck, J. (1990). *Working Days: The Journals of 'The Grapes of Wrath': 1938–1941* (reprint edition). London: Penguin.

Stripe, A. (2017). *Black Teeth and a Brilliant Smile*. London: Hachette UK.

Winnicott, D. W. (1965). *The Maturational Processes and the Facilitating Environment*. London: Karnac Books.

2 The Dark Cellar: The Unconscious from Freud to the Adaptive Unconscious

The 27th of November 2020 was a quiet night for the police in Brussels. The normally busy bars and clubs around the Grand Place were all closed because of the COVID lockdown. Then, in the early hours of the morning, a concerned resident of an apartment block called to report what sounded like a loud and raucous party in a neighbouring apartment. When the police turned up at the apartment to give the occupants a telling-off, the door was answered by a completely naked man. The police entered the apartment and were astonished to find a gay sex party in full swing.

As they began to detain the guests, one sharp-eyed gendarme spotted a man climbing out of a window and attempting to shin down a drainpipe to the street below and freedom. This man was chased, and when he was apprehended, he was found to have bloody hands and a backpack containing Ecstasy tablets. At first, he refused to give his name, but police eventually identified him as Hungarian MEP Jozsef Szajer.

Mr Szajer has been married to his wife for 25 years and is a founding member and leading light of the ruling Fidesz party, a conservative party that promotes traditional Christian family values and recently proposed a law to ban gay adoption in Hungary.

David Manzheley, the organiser of the party, told reporters:

> I always invite a few friends to my parties, who in turn bring some friends along, and then we make it fun together. We talk a bit, we drink something – just like in a cafe. The only difference is that in the meantime we also have sex with each other.
>
> (Walker, 2020)

He added that guests had been 'completely naked' at the time of the raid.

Following this incident, Jozsef Szajer resigned as an MEP and from the political party to which he had devoted 30 years of his life. He later said:

> I apologise to my family, to my colleagues, to my voters. I ask them to evaluate my mis-step on the background of 30 years of devoted

DOI: 10.4324/9781003188063-3

and hard work. The mis-step is strictly personal, I am the only who owes responsibility for it. I ask everyone not to extend it to my homeland, or to my political community.

(Banks & Hutchinson, 2020)

Here is another man – like Rabbi Levy – apologising for behaviour that seems completely out of character. The story of Jozsef Szajer is an example of the saboteur at work.

How can we explain the paradox of a man who campaigns for family values and opposes gay adoption, yet attends a gay sex party? We could, of course, just roll our eyes and laugh this off as yet another example of a hypocritical politician (which it is). However, there is also a more nuanced and interesting explanation that sheds light on how Jozsef Szajer was able to hold these wildly contradictory beliefs in his mind and act them out in a double life. That explanation draws on Sigmund Freud's theory of psychoanalysis with its focus on the unconscious life of the mind. The unconscious mind is where the saboteur lives.

The British psychologist Don Bannister described the mind as being 'a battlefield... a dark cellar in which a well-bred spinster lady and a sex-crazed monkey are locked in mortal combat, the struggle being refereed by a nervous bank clerk' (Bannister, 1966). He meant that we are all born with and continue to experience powerful biological drives. As we mature and become more socialised, we discover that such desires can get us into trouble and so we learn to deny, control or modify them so as to fit in with society.

In other words, we are constantly engaged in a dynamic struggle between what we'd like to do, what we ought to do and what we can get away with. This ambivalence is the essence of psychoanalysis.

It was the 'sex-crazed monkey' who compelled Jozsef Szajer to rush off to the gay sex orgy, while the 'nervous bank clerk' and 'well-bred spinster lady' informed his political views and day-to-day life as a husband, father and respected politician. More often than not, when the 'nervous bank clerk' loses control – when the monkey or spinster is in the psychic driving seat –trouble follows soon after.

Understanding the power of these unconscious forces helps you to understand why people often behave in ways that at first glance seem completely irrational. None of the people I have described in this book so far – Rabbi Levy, Andrea Dunbar and Jozsef Szajer – could be said to have behaved rationally; yet in many ways and in most situations, they were intelligent, reasonable and probably likeable people. Similarly, I am sure you can come up with many examples of intelligent, rational and nice people you know who have done stupid, or at least odd, things. And what about you? How many times have you done something, only to later think, 'Why on earth did I do that?'

When you have an understanding of the workings of the unconscious, it changes the way you see the world and even sometimes affects your decisions and how you behave.

The unconscious before Freud

When we think or talk about the unconscious, we are probably thinking of Sigmund Freud's formulation of the unconscious. However, people have been aware of the unconscious probably for as long as mankind has been able to reflect on themselves and their behaviour.

In the distant past, Szajer's aberrant behaviour might have been explained away as madness or even spirit possession. The ancient Greeks had a concept of the unconscious mind, as did philosophers who came before Freud's work in the 19th and early 20th centuries. Interestingly, Freud was a compulsive collector of antiquities. If you visit his preserved consulting room at the Freud Museum in London, you will find his desk crowded with statues of ancient gods, who would patiently watch over him when he saw his patients and wrote his books. Fittingly, his favourite was a statue of Athena, the Greek god of wisdom and war. 'The psychoanalyst', he said, 'like the archaeologist in his excavations, must uncover layer after layer of the patient's psyche, before coming to the deepest, most valuable treasures' (Freud, 1918). When Freud created the new science of psychoanalysis, he did so by collecting and analysing his patients' dreams and thoughts, and also ancient and modern ideas about the nature of consciousness (and the unconscious). Take a look at this quote:

> [In dreams] The beastly and savage part (of the mind)... endeavours to sally forth and satisfy its own natural instincts... there is nothing it will not venture to undertake as being released from all sense of shame and all reason. It does not shrink from attempting to have intercourse with one's mother, or with any man, god, or animal. It is ready for any foul deed of blood... and falls short of no extreme of mindlessness and shamelessness... there is in every one of us, even those who seem to be most moderate, a type of desires that is terrible, wild and lawless.
>
> (Buckley, 2001)

This is a quote that could have sprung from the pen of Freud (and could certainly apply to Jozsef Szajer). But it was actually written in 375 BC, two and a half thousand years before Freud, by the Greek philosopher Plato in *The Republic* (Plato, 2007). In another work, *Phaedrus* (Plato, 1952, Plato's Phaedrus. Cambridge: University Press), Plato describes the soul as being made up of three parts, two horses and a charioteer. One of the horses is noble, modest and honourable.

The second horse is insolent, full of pride and lacks integrity. Again, this observation describes well the dual nature of all human beings.

Freud not only drew on classical philosophy when creating his theory of psychoanalysis, he also had a good knowledge of contemporary philosophy about consciousness and the unconscious mind.

Box 2.1: Schopenhauer and the power of the unconscious mind

Arthur Schopenhauer was a hugely influential philosopher in the mid-19th century. Schopenhauer also drew on early Greek philosophy, and he argued that human intelligence and rationality are subservient to unconscious desire. He aggressively challenged the prevailing view of the mind as being purely rational and having no unconscious life. He argued that the conscious part of the mind is only the visible surface of the inner life, which obeys the often irrational drives of physical desire, overriding any conscious consideration. Like Freud, Schopenhauer emphasised the importance of sexuality in our life and the decisions we make. He thought that sexual drives invariably override our decisions without taking much account at all of our ultimate well-being. Also like Freud, Schopenhauer wrote about the meaning of dreams and the role of slips of the tongue in inadvertently revealing repressed thoughts and feelings (Ellenberger, 1970; Schopenhauer, 2010).

Sigmund Freud and psychoanalysis

Before Freud, most people (except philosophers and some psychologists) didn't give that much thought to the unconscious. The concept of the unconscious mind was neglected and languished in an obscure backwater of philosophy.

Freud's genius was synthesising these somewhat abstract philosophical ideas and transforming them into clinical and scientific theory. He took the ideas and tested them against the observational data he collected when he analysed his patients. The mapping of the unconscious was Freud's first and greatest achievement. His second was to give us a language we could use to understand and talk about concepts that were previously intangible. For example, he used the term 'repression' to describe the process of pushing to the back of our mind thoughts that are too disturbing for us to contemplate. Before Freud, if people behaved in uncharacteristic ways – particularly in uncharacteristically violent or sexual ways – their behaviour would have been explained as insanity, possession by evil spirits or the work of the gods.

Freud was a scientist in the way he viewed people and in his method of exploring the mind. He developed his understanding of the mind by collecting his patients' dreams, slips of the tongue (the famous Freudian slip) and puzzling behaviour and then carefully recording, studying and analysing them. He transformed philosophical concepts of the unconscious into scientific paradigms that have enormous explanatory power. As you will see, Freud's understanding of the unconscious provides a framework that we can use to make sense of human behaviour that seems at first glance completely irrational – like a politician shinning down a lamppost to escape police after taking part in a gay sex orgy.

Box 2.2: Freud's far-reaching influence

A fascinating aspect of Freud's science of psychoanalysis is that it wasn't simply confined to the consulting room. He likened the conflict in the unconscious to electricity (Tallis, 2020). This is a great metaphor, because electricity not only lit up Freud's consulting room but also theatres, office blocks and the centres of political power. In other words, Freud's ideas caught on and spread far and wide, heavily influencing the arts, politics and even the manner in which we view organisation. Freud was pointing out that the unconscious mind is not only present in a consulting room but everywhere where people live and work.

The following sections will be important in helping you to understand how the saboteur operates. Remember, the saboteur lives in the unconscious part of the mind. It is rarely seen by our rational conscious mind but always exerts a heavy influence on our behaviour. Freud's ideas about the unconscious and how it is constructed and how it relates to our conscious mind are fundamental. His theories are over a 100 years old and have been criticised. However, he was pretty much correct in all he said, and most of his concepts have been validated by modern neuroscience. He did get a few things wrong, but we'll come to that later.

Freud's structural model of the mind

In the earlier quote by Don Bannister, we were introduced to the idea of the mind as a dark cellar – a battlefield where a sex-crazed monkey struggles with an elderly lady, watched over by a nervous bank clerk as referee. This was Bannister's pithy, and some would say flippant, characterisation of the three parts of the mind in Freud's concept: the id, the ego and the superego.

Box 2.3: Id or it?

The terms id, ego and superego are translations of Freud's original descriptive words in German: *das Es, das Ich* and *das Über-Ich*. These translate more accurately in English as 'the it', 'the I' and 'the Above I'. To my mind, Freud's original terms better express their real meaning than the later English translations. The 'it' far better describes the cauldron of primitive desires that is the unconscious than does the more abstract term 'id'.

- **The id (the 'it'):** According to Freud, the id is not only the unconscious but is the source of psychological energy. It is made up of our most basic instinctual needs and drives of sex and aggression. The id is driven by what Freud called 'the pleasure principle', which demands immediate gratification of its desires. If these needs are not satisfied immediately, the result is a feeling of anxiety. The id is the only part of the personality that is present from birth. Freud described babies and toddlers as unrestrained and uninhibited ids. If a baby or toddler wants food or a nappy change, they will scream until they get what they need. There is no reasoning with the unrestrained id of a baby or toddler. The id is what we think of as the unconscious mind. It is big and powerful. The human mind is an iceberg with most of its 'data' hidden beneath the surface of our consciousness (see the next section). Our deepest fears, shame and desires reside in this vast unconscious, the id.
- **The ego (the 'I'):** The ego is the part of your mind that you think of as being 'you'. It is the rational and reasonable part of the mind. Its job is to mediate between the often unrealistic needs and demands of the id and the realities of the external world. It is the part of the personality that makes decisions. Freud described the ego as being dominated by the reality principle, constantly trying to come up with realistic ways to meet the id's demands and often having to compromise or postpone satisfaction in order to avoid the negative consequences of the society's social customs, rules and laws. The ego is absent in babies and young children and develops and gets stronger as we mature and are exposed to the civilising influence of the social world.
- **The superego (the 'above I'):** The superego is what we think of as our conscience. It consists of two parts. The first is a kind of psychic police officer that tells us what we should and shouldn't do. This is the part of the personality that experiences emotions such as guilt and shame. The other part is what Freud called the ego ideal and it is the idealised person we aspire to be. The superego is constructed from society's rules, attitudes and norms that become internalised and a

part of us. For example, most children are taught that it's wrong to steal and most adults experience a powerful emotional boundary to stealing. That's why shops can leave goods openly on display without their getting stolen. If children are brought up by overly permissive or overly strict parents, they develop into adults who have difficulties with rules and authority (either too rebellious or too compliant). The superego is the part of the mind soluble in alcohol.

You may recall the Plato quote earlier in this chapter that describes the soul as being made up of three parts, two horses and a charioteer. One of the horses is noble, modest and honourable. The second horse is insolent, full of pride and lacks integrity. In 1923, while describing the human mind, Freud wrote:

> In its relation to the id it is like a man on horseback, who has to hold in check the superior strength of the horse: with the difference that the rider tries to do so with his own strength while the ego uses borrowed forces. The analogy may be carried a little further. Often a rider if he is not to be parted from his horse, is obliged to guide it where it wants to go; so the same way the ego is in the habit of transforming the id's will into action as if it were its own. The ego represents what may be called reason and common sense, in contrast to the id, which contains passions. All this falls in line with the popular distinction which we are all familiar with…
>
> (Freud & Richards, 1923)

Jonathan Haidt uses a similar, and to my mind simpler, metaphor. Haidt likens our unconscious mind to an elephant and our conscious mind to a mahout riding the elephant. At first glance, the mahout, holding the reins, looks to be in control. However, if the elephant wants to turn left and the mahout wants it to go straight on, the elephant will always win. If this happens, the mahout may get cross or make up a post-hoc rationalisation to make sense of the outcome – 'I wanted to turn left anyway' (Haidt, 2016).

It isn't difficult to see how this applies to our own lives. Every day there are times when our own internal elephant goes in a different direction to our internal mahout. You've experienced this if you've ever eaten too much when you wanted to lose weight, slept in, procrastinated, tried to stop smoking, avoided a difficult conversation and so on. In Haidt's model, the elephant is the id, either looking for instant gratification or being skittish and shying away from threat. The mahout is the ego, with its ability to make long-term plans and goals and predict the consequences of behaviours. As we all know, in any serious battle between the elephant and the mahout – the ego and the id – the elephant always wins.

If we consider the contradictory behaviour and indeed attitudes of Jozsef Szajer, the words of Plato and Freud help us to understand what might have been going on beneath the surface of the face he presented to the world. He certainly sallied forth to satisfy his natural instincts without a sense of shame. And you can speculate that he did this with a sense of ambivalence: one part wanted to satisfy his instincts, while another part was terrified of getting caught, because he was more than aware of the consequences should his actions come to light. His conscious mind was the charioteer, and the two parts of his ambivalence were the horses.

I don't want to make any moral or legal judgements here – attending a gay sex party isn't illegal (except when it breaks rules on lockdown) and many would argue it is not immoral. However, Szajer's actions did have a catastrophic impact on both his career and his personal life. Therefore, I would argue that the 'horse' that took his 'charioteer' to the party was the saboteur. To mix a few metaphors, Szajer's nervous bank clerk failed to broker a compromise between his sex-crazed monkey and his well-bred spinster lady, and his elephant/id took him to the orgy. Sadly for him, his mahout/ego was left to deal with the consequences. Similarly, Rabbi Levy's elephant/id ran amok and trashed the car, and it was only later that his mahout/ego re-established some control.

The mind as an iceberg

The saboteur lives in the unconscious. Szajer's decision to attend the orgy and Rabbi Levy's decision to smash up the car were not considered decisions; they were impulsive. And the impulses were sexual in the case of Szajer and violent in the case of the Rabbi. As we have seen, these sexual and violent impulses are generated by the id, and the id is unconscious. In other words, its content is not directly accessible to our conscious mind. Let's pause there to consider this idea of what is unconscious and what is conscious.

Freud divided the mind into three levels of consciousness:

- **The conscious mind** is the part of the mind that you think of as being 'you'. It is where your personality is situated, along with the rational, problem-solving and planning parts of your mind. It is where the ego is. It is your mental mahout, to use Jonathan Haidt's metaphor. As we have seen, and as we will see, the conscious mind labours under the illusion that it is in control although much of the time it is not.
- **The preconscious mind** contains memories that we can retrieve if we choose to or if something in the outside world brings the memories to mind. For example, you might not be consciously aware of

the colour of your front door, the name of your first school or what happened on your first date. However, if I asked you to recall any of these facts, you probably could. There is a wealth of information floating around in our mind that feels as if it is on the tip of our tongue – we know it's there, but we just can't quite retrieve it. Often if we stop trying, it will emerge by itself.

Box 2.4: Stirring up emotional memories

I used to run a workshop on resilience for senior health service workers. As a part of the workshop, I would ask the participants to tell a story about a work incident that had had a significant emotional impact on them, good or bad. The stories were often very emotional and sometimes participants would appear to be full of feeling – tearful or joyful. What really struck me was that these stories triggered lots of memories for *me*, memories infused with emotion. More often than not, these memories were from a long time ago, but when I recalled them I experienced a similar feeling, as if it had happened yesterday. When prompted, stuff that I thought I'd forgotten – stuff that I hadn't thought about for 25 years – could return from my preconscious and unconscious mind as fresh as if it had happened yesterday.

- **The unconscious mind** is the home of the saboteur. It contains material that is too disturbing and anxiety provoking; in other words, things that are too hard to think about. These might be memories of something terrible that happened to you or thoughts that are too disturbing, such as wanting to murder somebody or maybe even thoughts about being worthless. The unconscious mind often contains our deepest fears – things we are ashamed of. Because such thoughts cause us overwhelming distress, they become repressed and find a home in the unconscious mind, which is not directly accessible by our conscious mind. Freud talked about how material from the unconscious will reveal itself to our consciousness in a disguised form through events like dreams or slips of the tongue (which Freud called parapraxis). These Freudian slips reveal our forbidden unconscious urges and fears. An amusing example is the unfortunate blunder made by journalist Jim Naughtie, who slipped up while pronouncing the then Culture Secretary Jeremy Hunt's surname on BBC Radio 4's *Today* programme. Another example can be found in the excellent poetry podcast of the comedian Frank Skinner. He was explaining how Alexander Pope was very disdainful of lesser poets, who would either be overly critical of him or suck up to him. 'Pope didn't like being pestered by second-rate comics', Skinner said, and then, realising his slip, he stopped and added, 'Damn you, Sigmund Freud!' (Skinner, 2020). This is a good example of how Freudian concepts have entered popular culture.

A popular and common way of understanding Freud's structural model of the mind is to think of it as an iceberg. The conscious mind is the tip of the iceberg, which can be seen sticking out of the ocean. Beneath this is the preconscious mind, which is the part of the iceberg you could see if you peered carefully beneath the ocean surface. However, the great bulk of the iceberg is largely invisible, and it is this that represents the unconscious mind. The ego is the visible tip of the iceberg, and the id is the unseen bulk of the iceberg. The superego straddles both the conscious and unconscious parts of the mind. It's interesting to note that Freud never actually used the iceberg metaphor in any of his published writings (Green, 2019). But I think it is a powerful idea that helps us to understand Freud's somewhat complicated theory of the mind. It's also interesting that research in modern neuroscience would see the conscious mind as being more like a snowball sat atop the iceberg, but more on that later.

Norman Dixon provided another interesting and creative metaphor to help us think about the unconscious (Dixon, 1987). He asks us to imagine the biggest university in the world. It has over a million students and 100,000 academic staff. This university is controlled from two small offices. The outer office is occupied by the university administrator. She is a formidable woman, and her primary task is to protect the university's vice chancellor (VC). In contrast, the VC is an introverted, agreeable and ageing professor of mathematics. He is most interested in his research, his orchids, and leading a quiet, stress-free life. Together, these two manage the university with a combination of delegation and defence. The VC delegates the practical tasks of running the university to the academic staff, and the administrator protects him from the staff members, students and incidents that might disturb his peace of mind. The administrator acts as a barrier against bad news.

Our conscious mind is a bit like the university VC delegating tasks. He can delegate all kinds of tasks, from high-level research delegated to professors, to building maintenance delegated to the janitorial staff. The university academic, admin and maintenance staff beaver away to keep the university running smoothly. In the same way, our unconscious is responsible for both complex cognitive tasks like decision-making and more automated tasks such as remembering to breathe. While all this is happening, the university administrator part of our mind protects us from being overwhelmed by the massive amount of information that is constantly impinging through our senses.

Carl Jung and the collective unconscious

It would be remiss to discuss the unconscious mind without mentioning Carl Jung. Jung was a contemporary and disciple of Freud. They later split and formed two schools of psychoanalysis. The split was caused by disagreements over two things: the nature of sexuality and the unconscious.

Like Freud, Jung acknowledged the importance of the unconscious mind in understanding personality. Jung built on Freud's theory by arguing that the unconscious consists of two layers. The first layer he called the personal unconscious. This is the same as, or at least similar to, Freud's concept of the unconscious. Jung believed that the personal unconscious contains our primitive and often socially unacceptable desires as well as repressed, often traumatic, memories.

The second layer of the unconscious is what Carl Jung called the collective unconscious. This is an innate, genetic (although Jung would not have used that term) version of the personal unconscious that is shared by every human being. The collective unconscious comprises basic imprinted instructions or maps of the world. According to Jung, the collective unconscious contains myths and stories that are common to all cultures and historical periods. Myths offer clues to universal human attributes, desires and fears.

These built-in predispositions have evolved, over millions of years, to promote survival. For example, we have a compulsion to move towards figures that offer nurturance and to experience fear of things that threaten existence, such as the dark or snakes. Jung called these imprinted predispositions 'archetypes', and they can be seen as repeated universal themes in different cultures and historical periods expressed through literature, art and dreams.

Jung's theory of the collective unconscious is complicated, but a more detailed explanation would go beyond the scope of this chapter. Nevertheless, it's important to be aware that the unconscious isn't just an individual phenomenon but occurs in groups and societies. We will return to this theme later in the book in Chapter 8 when I discuss the unconscious forces in societies and nations.

Modern neuroscience and the adaptive unconscious

The American social psychologist Timothy Wilson coined the term 'the adaptive unconscious' to sum up our modern understanding of the unconscious (Wilson, 2002). The adaptive unconscious acknowledges the contribution of Freud and his followers to our understanding of the unconscious. However, according to Wilson, the unconscious is made up of far more complex, sophisticated and helpful factors than

Freud realised. The modern adaptive unconscious is not the same as the Freudian or psychoanalytic unconscious. Freud believed that the unconscious mind was primitive, being concerned with sexual and violent impulses and desires, while the conscious mind, or ego, was the reasonable, rational and sophisticated part of the mind. Freud advanced our understanding of the unconscious enormously, but he did get a couple of things wrong.

First of all, Freud underestimated the ratio of information in the conscious and unconscious parts of the mind. In terms of the data stored, the ratio is not even a million to one but more like a billion to one (Dixon, 1987). If we think back to the iceberg metaphor of the mind, modern neuroscience would suggest a better or at least more accurate visual metaphor. We now know that the conscious mind in relation to the unconscious mind is more like a small snowball sitting atop a vast iceberg. Another metaphor is that the conscious mind is like a small rowing boat bobbing up and down on the surface of Lake Windermere, while beneath the boat, data flash through the 400,000 million neurons and 100 billion synapses that make up our nervous system.

Kristin Koch and colleagues found that the retina transmits approximately ten million bits of information per second to the brain (Koch et al., 2006). Other studies have found that our other senses (hearing, touch, smell and taste) provide an additional one million bits of information per second (Schmidt & Thews, 1989). Our mind has to process 11 million bits of information per second. Yet only about 40 bits per second reach our conscious mind (Sigman, 2017).

Therefore, in terms of both capacity to hold data and raw processing power, the conscious mind is tiny in comparison with the vastness of our unconscious mind. Most of the decisions you make are actually made in the unconscious mind, often before your conscious mind has even realised that a decision needs to be made. In decision-making, most of the processing takes place in the unconscious, which later reveals its outcomes to the conscious mind via thoughts, gut feelings and stronger feelings such as fearfulness or attraction.

In his erudite and fascinating book *Strangers to Ourselves*, Timothy Wilson describes the adaptive unconscious as being mental processes that are inaccessible to consciousness but that influence judgements, feelings or behaviour (Wilson, 2002). He argues that this adaptive unconscious has evolved to help us survive (and adapt to) an increasingly complex environment. Furthermore, he makes the point that most of the complexity of the world consists of the complexity of our relationships with other people, particularly groups, teams and society (our intimate relationships haven't changed that much over the millennia).

Our adaptive unconscious is invisible to us not, as Freud argued, because of repression but because of efficiency. The invisible processes that are taken care of by our unconscious mind include things we don't think of as being unconscious, such as judgements, feelings and motives. Already this goes a long way in helping us to make sense of the superficially puzzling behaviour of Rabbi Levy and Josef Szajer.

It's also more accurate to think of the adaptive unconscious as a number of parallel processes rather than a single entity. For example, our adaptive unconscious regulates physiological functions such as breathing, heart rate and temperature, and of course, these physiological functions are intimately connected, usually unconsciously, with psychological and emotional appraisals of what is happening in the world. When we feel threatened, our breathing increases, our heart rate goes up and we begin to perspire. However, what one person perceives as threatening (for example, public speaking or asking someone out on a date), another person will see as fun and thus non-threatening.

Our unconscious mind also takes care of tasks that might seem simple but are in fact unimaginably complex. Think for a moment of the complex processes involved in driving a car. The brain is constantly making decisions about speed, positioning of the vehicle in the traffic flow and the probability of various events such as traffic lights changing to red or a pedestrian about to step onto a crossing. All of the decisions are translated smoothly into arm and hand movements when steering and foot movements when braking. The manner in which we drive is also affected by such things as a sense of urgency if you are late or a bad mood or another driver cutting you up. Yet despite the cognitive complexity of this process, most drivers can carry out all of these tasks while happily chatting to a passenger, listening to the radio or planning dinner. It's a common experience to get into your car at work and then arrive home not even remembering the journey. All of this work is carried out by your unconscious mind.

To stay with the motoring analogy, modern science has lifted the bonnet of the brain and found something far more interesting, complex and useful than Sigmund Freud's id. The adaptive unconscious is, at least partly, a complex, sophisticated control mechanism that runs our lives. It has evolved over millions of years to keep us alive in the complex modern social structures within which we live.

The adaptive unconscious has many parallel systems all working together, and one of the systems is the Freudian unconscious – the id and the superego. When we feel under threat, or when we feel a strong emotional or sexual desire, it is the Freudian unconscious that has taken control of the mind; to use the motoring analogy, it is the Freudian unconscious sitting firmly in the driving seat. The Freudian unconscious is the saboteur. It was Rabbi Levy's saboteur that tore off the windscreen wiper of the car he attacked, and it was the saboteur that compelled Josef Szajer to put on his coat, leave his apartment and make his way to the gay sex orgy.

Chapter takeaways

- The saboteur lives in the unconscious mind.
- The conscious mind is absolutely tiny compared to the unconscious mind.
- While we think that we are in control, much of the time it is the saboteur in the driving seat.
- The saboteur makes decisions without your even realising it and can drive you to irrational behaviour.
- Understanding the power of the unconscious mind helps you to understand how you and others behave.

References

Banks, M. & Hutchinson, L. (2020). 'Hungarian MEP József Szájer Admits He Was Among Those Arrested at Party in Brussels'. *The Parliament*, 1 December. Retrieved from: https://www.theparliamentmagazine.eu/news/article/hungarian-mep-jzsef-szjer-admits-he-was-among-those-arrested-after-party-in-brussels.

Bannister, D. (1966). 'Psychology as an Exercise in Paradox'. *Bulletin of the British Psychological Society*, 19, 23–26.

Buckley, P. (2001). 'Ancient Templates: The Classical Origins of Psychoanalysis'. *American Journal of Psychotherapy*, 55(4), 451–9.

Dixon, N. F. (1987). *Our Own Worst Enemy*. London: Jonathan Cape.

Ellenberger, H. F. (1970). *The Discovery of the Unconscious: The History and Evolution of Dynamic Psychiatry*. New York: Basic Books.

Freud, S. (1918). *Case Histories II*. Penguin Freud Library, Vol. 9. Harmondsworth: Penguin.

Freud, S. & Richards, A. (1923). *The Ego and the Id, On Metapsychology*. Penguin Freud Library, Vol. 11. Harmondsworth: Penguin.

Green, C. D. (2019). 'Where Did Freud's Iceberg Metaphor of Mind Come From?'. *History of Psychology*, 22(4), 369–72.

Haidt, J. (2016). *The Happiness Hypothesis: Finding Modern Truth in Ancient Wisdom*. New York: Basic Books.

Koch, K., McLean, J., Segev, R., Freed, M. A., Berry, M. J., 2nd, Balasubramanian, V. & Sterling, P. (2006). 'How Much the Eye Tells the Brain'. *Current Biology*, 16(14), 1428–34.

Plato. (1952). *Plato's Phaedrus*. Cambridge: University Press.

Plato. (2007). *The Republic*. 3rd ed., trans. H. D. P. Lee & D. Lee. London: Penguin Classics.

Schmidt, R. & Thews, G. (Eds.) (1989). *Human Physiology*. 2nd ed., trans. M. Biederman-Thorson. Berlin: Springer.

Schopenhauer, A. (2010). *The Essential Schopenhauer: Key Selections from The World As Will and Representation and Other Works*. London: HarperCollins.

Sigman, M. (2017). *The Secret Life of the Mind: How Our Brain Thinks, Feels and Decides*. London: HarperCollins UK.

Skinner, F. (Host) (2020). 'Alexander Pope' (Audio Podcast). *Frank Skinner's Poetry Podcast*, 2 November. Bauer Media.

Tallis, F. (2020). *The Act of Living: What the Great Psychologists Can Teach Us about Finding Fulfillment*. London: Hachette UK.

Walker, S. (2020). 'Hungary's Rightwing Rulers Downplay MEP "Gay Orgy" Scandal Amid Hypocrisy Accusations'. *Guardian*, 2 December. Retrieved from: http://www.theguardian.com/world/2020/dec/02/hungary-rightwing-rulers-downplay-mep-jozsef-szajer-gay-orgy-scandal-amid-hypocrisy-accusations.

Wilson, T. D. (2002). *Strangers to Ourselves: Discovering the Adaptive Unconscious*. Cambridge, MA: Harvard University Press.

3 Why You Think You're Right, Even When You're Wrong: Denial and Other Ways the Saboteur Distorts Reality

On the morning of Wednesday 25th September 2002, readers of the *Sun* newspaper awoke to the alarming headline 'Brits 45 Mins from Doom. Cyprus within Missile Range'. The story went on:

> British servicemen and tourists on Cyprus could be annihilated by germ warfare missiles launched by Iraq, it was revealed yesterday. They could flood into the Mediterranean island within 45 minutes of tyrant Saddam Hussein ordering an attack. And they could spread death and destruction through warheads carrying anthrax, mustard gas, sarin or ricin. The terrifying prospect was raised in Downing Street's dossier on Saddam's arsenal, which also revealed he could be just 12 months away from having nuclear weapons.
>
> (Pascoe-Watson, 2002)

The story referred, of course, to the Iraq Dossier (later to be dubbed the Dodgy Dossier) about Saddam Hussein stockpiling weapons of mass destruction (WMD) in Iraq. The dossier was one of the principal sources of evidence used to justify the British invasion of Iraq in 2003.

Earlier in 2002, Tony Blair had asked Britain's intelligence agencies (the Joint Intelligence Committee) to put together a dossier containing all information available on the WMD that Blair believed were being stockpiled in Iraq. The dossier was prepared in the hope it would convince the public, Parliament and most importantly Blair himself of the existence of Iraq's WMD. The final draft of the dossier was a dog's dinner of old intelligence and some dubious new intelligence from one source ('Curveball', whom I discuss later in this chapter). The intelligence in the report was weak to say the least, and it contained no substantial evidence of the existence of WMD in Iraq. It was, according to Admiral Nigel Essenhigh, 'an over-long and rather poor cut and paste job' (Bower, 2016).

DOI: 10.4324/9781003188063-4

Later, the BBC journalist Andrew Gilligan claimed a source (Dr David Kelly, who later took his own life) had revealed that the dossier had been 'sexed up' – made more interesting – by Blair's head of communications, Alastair Campbell. Years later, the Chilcot Inquiry into the UK's involvement in the Iraq War concluded that the dossier had been more than just 'sexed up'; it had been wholly inaccurate (Chilcot, 2016).

The notion that Saddam Hussein had stockpiled WMD was the core argument that both the UK and the US desperately needed to justify the invasion of Iraq. The problem was that by 2002, there was no reliable evidence of any WMD in Iraq. Despite this, on 24th September, Blair made a statement to Parliament in which he said:

[Saddam Hussein's] WMD programme is active, detailed and growing. The policy of containment is not working. The WMD programme is not shut down. It is up and running...

The intelligence picture... concludes that Iraq has chemical and biological weapons, that Saddam has continued to produce them, that he has existing and active military plans for the use of chemical and biological weapons, which could be activated within 45 minutes...

(Guardian, 2002)

None of which was true.

The Iraq Survey Group was tasked with finding Saddam's WMD, but found nothing. In 2004, Blair again spoke at the House of Commons and said, 'I have to accept we haven't found them [WMD] and we may never find them. We don't know what has happened to them. They could have been removed. They could have been hidden. They could have been destroyed' (BBC News, 2004). In other words, in Tony Blair's mind, the lack of evidence did not mean a lack of WMD, but rather that the WMD did exist but had been moved, hidden or destroyed.

Despite no significant evidence of the existence of WMD, Tony Blair successfully campaigned for and then led the UK to support the US invasion of Iraq, an action that resulted in the deaths of over half a million people.

How can we explain this? Blair, for all his faults, is not stupid. His seemingly irrational behaviour in failing to properly weigh up the evidence can be, at least partly, explained as his being influenced by the part of his mind I label the saboteur.

Blair was not alone in falling foul of the saboteur at this time. Interestingly, we can see the same unconscious psychological processes at work influencing Blair's US counterpart, George Bush. Bush and the US administration's decision to prosecute the war in Iraq was similarly based on very shaky intelligence, which they then passed on to the UK, which in turn was included in the Dodgy Dossier.

In 2000, a former Iraqi chemical engineer called Rafid Ahmed Alwan al-Janabi turned up in a German refugee camp claiming that he had top-secret information about Saddam Hussein's biological warfare capability. Alwan was assigned the codename 'Curveball' and was feted by the German intelligence agencies who enthusiastically debriefed him. The resulting intelligence was then shared with the US and the UK intelligence communities. Curveball claimed that since 1997, Saddam had been developing and building mobile biological warfare production units. These units were trucks that had been converted to deploy biological weapons. Curveball even made a crude diagram of one of these adapted trucks. This was included in the US presentation to the UN Security Council arguing for the invasion of Iraq.

It subsequently emerged that these mobile biological warfare units had been a complete figment of Curveball's imagination – he had made up the whole story. Journalists from the *Guardian* newspaper interviewed Curveball years later. He admitted to lying, telling the *Guardian* that he had made up his accounts of the mobile biological warfare units and hidden biological warfare factories because he wanted to bring down Saddam's regime. He also expressed his amazement that his fabrications had been not only believed but used to justify the invasion of Iraq (Chulov & Pidd, 2011).

Again, we have a situation where seemingly intelligent and sophisticated people – the US government – seized upon a piece of information and magnified it, while turning a blind eye to the possibility that it was unreliable. They saw what they wanted to see, not the uncomfortable reality.

The mind's capacity for self-deception

To understand the processes that both Blair and Bush went through, we need to briefly set the scene. The invasion of Iraq had its genesis in the 9/11 attack on the World Trade Centre. This was a terrible event and an unimaginable shock for the US administration, particularly US military and security agencies. This incident initiated the hunt for Osama bin Laden, who had planned the attack; the invasion of Afghanistan; and the war on terror agenda.

Somewhere along the way, the US administration had made links between the regime of Saddam Hussein in Iraq and the funding of Al Qaeda. Saddam also had a history of using chemical weapons against his own people. The US administration had come to the understandable conclusion that Saddam Hussein was a bad person who was hostile to the US and thus an enemy and, in the wake of 9/11, a threat that needed to be addressed. This strongly held belief triggered an a-priori and obsessive hunt for evidence to justify the belief and military action against Iraq.

In 2001, UN weapons inspectors were sent in to Iraq to look for evidence of biological and chemical warfare installations. While this was going on, and eight months before the invasion of Iraq, Tony Blair had written to George W Bush to offer his unqualified backing for war, saying, 'I will be with you, whatever' (Booth, 2016). This was well before the UN weapons inspectors had completed their work. So even before the evidence of the UN weapons inspectors was available, Blair had committed himself to supporting Bush and the invasion. He had already made up his mind and, just like Bush and the US administration, he began gathering post-hoc evidence to support the decision. He sought out the evidence he needed to show he was right and ignored evidence that suggested he might be wrong.

In his book on intelligence analysis, *How Spies Think*, David Omand, a former director of GCHQ, writes:

> The errors in the intelligence assessments of Iraq were not the result of conscious politicisation of intelligence by the analysts to please their customers. They resulted from the great capacity of the mind for self-deception and magical thinking, believing we are seeing what deep down at an emotional level we want to see. It is then natural to find reasons to rationalise that belief.
>
> (Omand, 2020)

It is this capacity of the mind for self-deception, as Omand puts it, that strongly influenced the decision to invade Iraq. It is evidence of how our unconscious psychological processes become the saboteur at work.

To summarise, before the invasion, Blair made a passionate speech to Parliament using words that conveyed absolute conviction. He described Saddam's WMD programme as being active, detailed and growing. He declared that the UN policy of containment wasn't working and concluded that Iraq had chemical and biological weapons which could be activated within 45 minutes. But this was his *perception* – in *reality*, there were no WMD and, crucially, there wasn't even any substantial evidence to suggest they had ever existed.

Nevertheless, the invasion of Iraq went ahead. This was when reality really began to contradict the message and Blair's conviction. The most obvious question that emerged was: if Saddam did possess WMD, why didn't he deploy them against the coalition forces?

Following Saddam's defeat and execution, UN weapons inspectors reported that they were still unable to find any evidence of WMD. As a result, Tony Blair did not conclude that he had been wrong all along. He again spoke to the House of Commons and boldly asserted that the WMD could have been removed, hidden or perhaps destroyed. In short, he maintained his belief that the WMD did exist when all of the evidence conclusively pointed to the fact that they had never existed.

We could, of course, conclude that Blair was simply lying. In other words, he was consciously aware of the absence of WMD and for whatever reason decided to proceed with the war in any case. However, to explain Blair's actions, I am more inclined to go with David Omand's hypothesis about how the mind deceives itself. This is because it wasn't just Tony Blair who had been taken in by the flimsy evidence of WMD, but all the US and the UK intelligence and military communities. These experienced and clever people seized upon the evidence that supported a decision they had already made and turned a blind eye to any evidence that disconfirmed that decision.

In the years following the Iraq War, Tony Blair was heavily criticised for his decision and actions. He was called all kinds of pejorative names such as psychopath and narcissist, and of course, he was accused of lying ('Bliar'). But I'm sure as I can be – having never spoken to Tony Blair – that he doesn't think of himself as, let's say, a bad person.

About ten years after the Iraq War, the writer Matthew Syed interviewed Alastair Campbell (Blair's communications chief who had allegedly 'sexed up' the Dodgy Dossier) and asked him what it would mean for Tony Blair to admit that he was wrong in his decision to support the invasion of Iraq. Campbell replied:

> It would overshadow everything he had ever worked for. It would taint his achievements. Tony is a rational and strong-minded guy, but I don't think he would be able to admit that Iraq was a mistake. It would be too devastating even for him.
>
> (Syed, 2015)

The way in which Tony Blair maintained his psychic equilibrium and avoided thinking about something that would have been 'too devastating' for him was by deploying his own psychological weapons of mass destruction: in other words, psychological defences that destroyed his capacity to see the world as it is.

Nobody, not even the worst person in the world, thinks of themselves as being bad, wrong or evil, or even 'a malignant narcissist' (as Tony Blair's former friend, the writer Robert Harris, once called him). Hitler, Stalin, Mao, the most tyrannical, murderous and destructive people, were all completely convinced they were doing the right thing for the best of reasons. They experienced themselves as being on the side of righteousness as they tortured, murdered and destroyed.

Alexander Solzhenitsyn said: 'the line separating good and evil passes not through states, nor between classes, nor between political parties either – but right through every human heart' (Solzhenitsyn, 2003).

This is a fact that our defence mechanisms – our saboteur – blind us to. The saboteur persuades us to instead see a distorted reality, one in which issues are black and white and people are wholly good or wholly bad. And so if you (and your in-group) are all good, then the opposition (the out-group) must be all bad. It is the same psychological process that you can see in football supporters and very strongly in political activists. Jung made the profound point that before we start fixing the world or other people, we should look at our self, when he wrote,

> The acceptance of oneself is the essence of the whole moral problem and the epitome of a whole outlook on life. That I feed the hungry, that I forgive an insult, that I love my enemy in the name of Christ -- all these are undoubtedly great virtues. What I do unto the least of my brethren, that I do unto Christ. But what if I should discover that the least among them all, the poorest of all the beggars, the most impudent of all the offenders, the very enemy himself - that these are within me, and that I myself stand in need of the alms of my own kindness - that I myself am the enemy who must be loved -- what then?
>
> (Jung, 1965)

How the saboteur distorts reality: denial, cognitive dissonance and confirmation bias

Not for a moment do I argue that the Iraq War was caused by psychological factors alone. Wars are complex events. However, the decision to go to war is ultimately made by individuals who have the task of sifting through and weighing up information and competing vested interests. There is much value in looking at the psychological processes involved in how we make important decisions when we are under extreme pressure.

We have already seen in preceding chapters how the part of our mind that I call the saboteur can influence us to behave in ways we ordinarily would not. The saboteur is most influential when we are experiencing strong emotion; in other words, when our internal 'elephant' is determined to go one way when perhaps our more rational 'mahout' would prefer to take a different route (this metaphor is explained in Chapter 2). Defence mechanisms evolved to protect us from being overwhelmed by anxiety, and they usually do a good job of this. However, these defences sabotage our effectiveness in some situations – usually, critically important ones that require us to process (think about) distressing material rather than avoid it.

Sometimes we need to struggle to see reality as it *is*, not how we would prefer it to be.

Tony Blair's decision to support the US invasion of Iraq was influenced by three distinct but overlapping psychological processes: denial, cognitive dissonance and confirmation bias.

Denial

Box 3.1: General Gamelin and his denial of the evidence

It wasn't only Tony Blair and George Bush who had a saboteur at work influencing them to ignore important evidence that contradicted their strongly held beliefs. In the spring of 1940, the supreme commander of the French land forces, General Maurice Gamelin, was feeling confident, some would say complacent. He was convinced that the Germans were planning to invade France in the north. It was an accepted fact that they would not invade through the Ardennes Forest, which the French believed was too dense to allow German tanks through. However, as time went on, intelligence trickled through that the German army was indeed planning to invade in the Ardennes. The most striking evidence was provided by a French air force colonel who was returning to base and spotted a column of German tanks 60 miles long advancing through the Ardennes. Gamelin ignored this.

On 10th May 1940, Hitler launched his attack on France through the Ardennes Forest, and by 22nd June, it was all over. The defeat was overwhelming, humiliating and confusing for the Allies. The French army was well trained and strong and possessed as many men and tanks as did the Germans, and the French capitulation arguably allowed Germany to prosecute the war for another five years, costing upwards of 30 million lives (Dixon, 1987). The saboteur was hard at work in the mind of General Gamelin and indeed the French military command in 1940. Gamelin *denied* the reality of the situation and instead saw what he wanted to see.

Denial is not just a river in Egypt. It is also a psychological defence mechanism. The term was first coined by Sigmund Freud in the 19th century. The essence of the idea is that when people, organisations, governments or even societies are presented with information that is too disturbing, threatening or in conflict with existing beliefs, the new information is disavowed, ignored or reinterpreted. Sigmund Freud first came up with the theory, and it was later developed by his daughter, Anna Freud. They described denial as an unconscious mechanism for coping with anxiety, memories of past trauma or unpleasant aspects of reality in which the unconscious erects a barrier that prevents the distressing thought from reaching the consciousness. Tony Blair turned a blind eye to all the evidence contradicting his strongly held belief that Saddam was stockpiling WMD.

Like so many things, the concept of denial is more nuanced than you might think at first sight. In his book *States of Denial*, Stanley Cohen discusses three subtle types of denial (Cohen, 2013):

- **Blatant denial:** Blair's denial was literal and blatant. A bit like a wife confronted with evidence of her husband's infidelity saying, 'That couldn't have happened; my husband would never have done such a thing'. In other words, the fact, or knowledge of the fact, is denied. In a social or cultural context, individuals, groups and governments might deny an atrocity, saying there was no massacre, those who say there was are lying, we didn't notice anything, and it couldn't have happened without us knowing. In blatant denial, the facts are simply denied. This can occur in good or bad faith, using unconscious defence mechanisms or conscious deliberate lies.
- **Interpretive denial:** This is a slightly different form of denial. An example might be Bill Clinton's sexual relationship with Monica Lewinsky. Clinton first explained this using blatant denial, saying, 'I did not have sexual relations with that woman'. Then he used interpretive denial, conceding that he had had oral sex with Miss Lewinsky, but described it as an 'inappropriate behaviour' rather than a 'sex act'. In other words, he conceded the act had taken place, but denied it was sexual, reinterpreting it as an inappropriate behaviour, which sounds a lot less damaging than the facts suggest.
- **Implicatory denial:** This is where there is no attempt to deny the facts or a straightforward explanation of those facts. However, what is denied is the obligation to do anything about it – and the psychological and moral implications of the act. For example, you might see a person collapsed in the street but deny having any responsibility to do something to help that person. You might say, 'They must be drunk', 'It's got nothing to do with me' or 'What can I do? I don't have any medical training'. An example of implicatory denial is the story of 28-year-old Kitty Genovese, who in March 1964 was brutally stabbed to death outside her apartment building in Queens, New York. When the police investigated, they discovered that 38 people had witnessed the various stages of Kitty's murder. When the detectives asked the witnesses why they didn't step in to help or call the police, most replied with a variation of the phrase, 'I thought somebody else must have'. This dreadful crime and the response of the witnesses were the inspiration for decades of research in social psychology into how normal, well-adjusted and intelligent people are able to turn a blind eye to others in distress. This phenomenon came to be known as the bystander effect or diffusion of responsibility (Sanderson, 2020). Of course, bystander effect is another form of denial.

We often think of denial as a personal act. It usually is, but it can also occur at organisational, social and cultural levels. I explore this later in the book, when I describe the rise of the Nazis in Germany, but let's briefly look here at how denial can manifest in these different contexts:

- **Individual denial:** This is the type of denial written about by Sigmund and Anna Freud. It is Jozsef Szajer denying his sexual identity by joining a Conservative political party. It is Rabbi Levy denying his rage and sense of injustice and indeed behaviour by blaming it on 'a brain explosion'.
- **Systemic denial:** Often, denial is public, organised and systemic. This is where whole societies, or groups in society, publicly espouse views which privately they know are wrong, and wrong in the sense of being incorrect and morally wrong. This is best seen in totalitarian societies such as the Soviet Union and Nazi Germany. Systemic denial is far more than just putting a gloss on unfortunate events. It is the active manipulation of information and historical records to construct a reality that fits in with the ideological needs of the state. Furthermore, it becomes a crime against the state to deny this falsified version of reality. In the Soviet Union, if a person spoke out against the 1930s show trials, for example, or against the Soviet regime, they and most likely their family, friends and associates would be arrested and tortured until they publicly recanted and declared the state to be correct. They would then face either execution or deportation to a Siberian gulag. Another tactic was to diagnose people who spoke out against the reality of the regime as being insane and confine them to psychiatric institutions. Denial became a part of the ideological machinery of the state and the truth ceased being merely a personal matter. Denial was enforced by the secret police, and if you didn't participate in the big lie, something terrible would happen to you.
- **Cultural denial:** This is also systemic but far more subtle and nuanced. It happens where people are bombarded with messages from the media, from those in authority, and peer pressure to turn a blind eye to the reality that they can clearly see. It becomes an unwritten agreement not to talk about, or even think about, events that people know to be wrong. An example is the Rotherham grooming gangs scandal in which more than 1,400 children in Rotherham were systematically groomed and sexually abused, mainly by men of Pakistani Muslim heritage. The authorities – social workers, child protection workers and police – were criticised for turning a blind eye to the abuse because they feared being thought of as racist (Hall, 2014). In effect, those tasked with the protection of vulnerable children colluded with the abusers in a process of cultural denial. Many people in Rotherham knew that vulnerable young girls were being

sexually exploited. Certainly, the abusers knew this very well, social workers knew and the police knew. Many members of the public strongly suspected what was happening. However, this process of cultural denial became the saboteur at work and very effectively sabotaged the very system that had been put in place to protect vulnerable children.

Cognitive dissonance theory: how cults survive encounters with reality

In the autumn of 1954, the social psychologist Leon Festinger was reading a newspaper when he came across a story about a woman who claimed that the world was about to be destroyed by a massive flood. Mrs Mariah Keach explained that she had been receiving messages from the Guardians of the planet Clarion warning her that on 21st December 1954, the planet would be flooded by God and only a chosen few would survive. At the time, Festinger was studying the psychology of belief change, and he thought that Mrs Keach and her followers might be good subjects for a social psychology experiment. Back in the 1950s, university ethics committees weren't quite as strict as they are now, and so Festinger and two research associates approached Mrs Keach posing as potential believers in her prophecy. They joined her group of followers in order to carry out some covert participant observation.

Of course, 21st December came and went without either the prophesied flood or the Guardians manifesting to rescue the true believers. You might think that this would have weakened the beliefs of Mrs Keach and her followers. Not a bit of it. Mrs Keach explained that she had received word from the Guardians that thanks to the goodness and light created by the believers, God had decided to spare the world and not go ahead with the flood after all. This allowed the believers to see themselves as saviours of the world rather than just gullible or foolish.

Interestingly, those believers who were on the edges of the group and had not made much commitment dropped out when the disaster failed to occur. However, those who had made a strong commitment, such as by resigning from their jobs and selling their houses and possessions, actually became *more* convinced of the truth of Mrs Keach's revelations. These committed followers had experienced a strong and psychologically disturbing conflict between what they believed and reality. In order to avoid this conflict (or cognitive dissonance as Festinger termed it), they were forced into modifying their belief in a manner that cast them in a good light and in a way that allowed them to sidestep the discomfort of feeling foolish when their initial belief was proved to be wrong.

Festinger concluded:

A man with a conviction is a hard man to change. Tell him you disagree and he turns away. Show him facts or figures and he questions your sources. Appeal to logic and he fails to see your point...

Suppose an individual believes something with his whole heart; suppose further that he has a commitment to this belief, that he has taken irrevocable actions because of it; finally, suppose that he is presented with evidence, unequivocal and undeniable evidence, that his belief is wrong: What will happen? The individual will frequently emerge, not only unshaken, but even more convinced of the truth of his beliefs than ever before. Indeed, he may even show a new fervor about convincing and converting other people to his view.

(Festinger et al., 1957)

When we are shown hard evidence that contradicts a strongly held belief, we are far more likely to either ignore or reinterpret that evidence to support the belief than we are to change our belief. According to Festinger, this is a universal human characteristic and not just confined to cults.

Box 3.2: Misinterpreting facts to support beliefs

Recent research showed how cognitive dissonance influences our political beliefs. Brendan Nyhan, a political scientist from the US, set out to answer the question: do facts matter when people decide whom to vote for? The answer is no. Not only are facts irrelevant to people's voting decisions, but when people are given grossly wrong information, giving them the correct information later only makes them cling even more tenaciously to their beliefs.

In Nyhan's research, Republican voters in America who strongly disagreed with Obama's economic policy were shown a graph that showed employment had increased over the previous year – the graph clearly showed a rising line. They were then asked whether unemployment had increased or decreased. Many, looking straight at the graph, said that employment had decreased.

In another experiment, people were asked to interpret a table of numbers about whether a skin cream reduced rashes. Some were asked to interpret a different table – containing exactly the same numbers – about whether a law banning citizens from carrying concealed handguns reduced crime. When the participants did the maths in the skin cream table, they got everything right. However, when they were asked to do the maths in the gun-control table (and when numbers conflicted with the person's attitude to gun control), they managed to get the sums totally wrong and in a way that supported their belief.

> What this means is that when you are attempting to persuade somebody of a particular course of action and they seem to have made their mind up, the more you present facts that demonstrate their opinion is wrong, the more tenaciously they are likely to cling on to that opinion (Flynn et al., 2017).

Confirmation bias

As soon as we have developed even a tentative belief, our mind begins to frantically search for evidence that confirms this belief. Any evidence that we encounter that suggests we are perhaps wrong, we angrily reject. That is confirmation bias, one of the many cognitive biases described by Daniel Kahneman in his classic text *Thinking, Fast and Slow* (Kahneman, 2011). We don't perceive circumstances objectively but actively choose data that confirm our pre-existing beliefs, because this makes us feel wise and good about ourselves. Thus, we become hostages of our assumptions.

How to become more aware of these processes

Blair and Bush assumed and desperately wanted to believe that Saddam was stockpiling WMD, and they became hostages of that incorrect assumption. And, as in many actual hostage situations, people ended up dying.

Using this as a metaphor, what was being held hostage was Tony Blair's ability to think and perceive the world in a more or less accurate manner. How do you resolve a hostage situation? Well, you do this through negotiation.

The process of hostage negotiation starts with understanding what the hostage taker wants and being clear about what you want. In order to free the hostage, you need to find a compromise between what you want (or your existing belief) and opposing data. This isn't easy and requires both cognitive and emotional strength.

You are prone to believing what you want to believe. Seeking to confirm your beliefs comes naturally, and it feels stressful and counterintuitive to actively seek out evidence that contradicts your beliefs. However, if you want an accurate (or as accurate as possible) understanding of a situation, then you have to struggle and make the emotional and cognitive effort to look for evidence that suggests you might be wrong.

Denial, cognitive dissonance and confirmation bias sabotage our ability to think, to see the bigger picture and to make informed decisions. On the other hand, you probably formed your opinion for good reason. The skilful, thoughtful approach is to listen to your saboteur and give your beliefs due respect, but at the same time give an equal amount of thought and respect to contradictory beliefs. By doing this, you will minimise the cognitive dissonance and the probability that confirmation bias will sabotage your decisions.

Why is this important to me?

So far, I've talked about how defence mechanisms like denial and cognitive biases such as cognitive dissonance have played out in historical events and unusual situations (like Mrs Keach's cult). It's always easier to see evidence of these phenomena in other people – especially in hindsight. It's easy to speculate on and infer unconscious motivations behind other people's actions. An interesting question to ask ourselves might be: what would I have done in that situation?

We like to think that had we been in the situation Tony Blair found himself in, or if we had been in charge of the French armed forces and somebody had pointed out they had just seen a 60-mile column of tanks advancing through the Ardennes Forest, then we would have done something about it. However, given what we know about ourselves as human beings, chances are we'd have done the same.

The processes that I've described in this chapter don't just apply to historical figures like Tony Blair and General Gamelin. They are universal human characteristics and are just as active in ourselves. We all have an internal saboteur living inside of us. When we think about great events in history, we invariably see ourselves on the right side. We see ourselves as people who are wise and would more often than not do the right thing. We find it very difficult to see ourselves making stupid mistakes, like the mistakes made by Tony Blair, General Gamelin or indeed the followers of Mrs Keach. The problem is that none of these people were stupid. At the time they acted, they honestly believed that they were doing the right thing.

When we see old newsreels from 1930s Germany, it's comforting to think that we would never have supported Hitler and the Nazis. We might even identify with the victims of the Nazis. However, the uncomfortable truth is that statistically speaking, you would probably have been one of the Nazis – most people in Germany supported Hitler (I discuss this in more detail later).

Let's say that you're a young man growing up in Munich. You feel resentment about how Germany was treated following World War I, you feel frightened of the increasing economic uncertainty, you enjoy the positive messages Hitler espouses and you're looking for someone else to blame for your problems. All of these seem like good reasons to be a big fan of Hitler and the Nazis.

Of course, you only see history backwards – if you are that person, you can't know what will happen in the future. So you gradually get sucked into the Nazi party, and then, five years later, you find yourself deployed as a guard at Auschwitz. You have the uniform, all your friends have similar views, and that role has become part of your personality. Then you look around and see what's going on, and you are asked to do something terrible. Let's say a woman has just arrived at the camp and she's hysterical because she's been separated from her children, and your commanding officer orders you to put a bullet through her head. What do you do? How would you behave? Well, chances are that you would pull the trigger. That's what everybody did.

So then it's worth asking the question: why did you do that? There are lots of reasons. The most obvious is that if you refused to follow an order, you might have faced a gun at your head. However, there are also far more subtle reasons, which I will discuss later.

Once you've carried out the act, how then do you think about it? Well, that's when your defence mechanisms of denial, cognitive dissonance and confirmation bias start to kick in. You might say to yourself, 'Well, what choice did I have? It's not my responsibility. I have to follow orders'. You could have added, 'She was only a Jew – not really a human being'. Or if you are feeling compassionate, you could even say to yourself, 'It's probably better for her that she died quickly and avoided the suffering of the camp'. You have committed a terrible act and your internal saboteur colluded with that and now seeks to protect you from the unbearable reality of what you have just done.

Hannah Arendt, the political scientist, observed the trial of Adolf Eichmann in Jerusalem. Before encountering Eichmann at the trial, she expected to see a monster. To her shock, she in fact found him to be an unprepossessing and rather boring bureaucrat. This led her to coin the phrase 'the banality of evil'. In her 1963 book about the trial of Eichmann, she wrote:

> The trouble with Eichmann was precisely that so many were like him, and that the many were neither perverted nor sadistic, that they were, and still are, terribly and terrifyingly normal. From the viewpoint of our legal institutions and of our moral standards of judgement, this normality was much more terrifying than all the atrocities put together.

> (Arendt, 1963)

It's important to you in your life that you know that we all have the capacity for evil, not just impulsive violence but cold calculated evil. Understanding this terrible fact helps you to resist the influence of the saboteur, step outside of situations that are difficult and maintain some perspective.

Chapter takeaways

- The saboteur can distort reality. It's a defence mechanism that protects us from dealing with a truth that the conscious mind would find distressing.
- We can think adamantly that we are right when, in truth, we are not.
- Presented with evidence that suggests we are wrong, the saboteur rejects it. We often ignore or reinterpret this evidence.
- Denial can be blatant ('There's no way that happened!'), interpretive ('I may have done this, but I didn't do *that*') or implicatory ('Okay, I did it, but I'm not responsible').
- To avoid being sabotaged, you need to listen to the saboteur *but also* consider that opposing beliefs may be valid. Challenge how you think and feel in order to get perspective, and then you can make an informed, balanced decision.

References

Arendt, H. (1963 (1994)). *Eichmann in Jerusalem: A Report on the Banality of Evil*. London: Penguin.

BBC News. (2004). 'WMD May Never Be Found – Blair'. *BBC News*, 6 July. Retrieved from: http://news.bbc.co.uk/1/hi/uk_politics/3869293.stm.

Booth, R. (2016). '"With You, Whatever": Tony Blair's Letters to George W Bush'. *Guardian*, 6 July. Retrieved from: http://www.theguardian.com/uk-news/2016/jul/06/with-you-whatever-tony-blair-letters-george-w-bush-chilcot.

Bower, T. (2016). *Broken Vows: Tony Blair – The Tragedy of Power*. London: Faber & Faber.

Chilcot, J. (2016). *The Report of the Iraq Inquiry. Executive Summary*. London: Her Majesty's Stationery Office, pp. 128–35. Retrieved from: https://www.gov.uk/government/publications/the-report-of-the-iraq-inquiry.

Chulov, M. & Pidd, H. (2011). 'Curveball: How the US Was Duped by Iraqi Fantasist Looking to Topple Saddam'. *Guardian*, 15 February. Retrieved from: http://www.theguardian.com/world/2011/feb/15/curveball-iraqi-fantasist-cia-saddam.

Cohen, S. (2013). *States of Denial: Knowing about Atrocities and Suffering*. Hoboken, NJ: John Wiley & Sons.

Dixon, N. F. (1987). *Our Own Worst Enemy*. London: Jonathan Cape.

Festinger, L., Riecken, H. & Schachter, S. (1957). *When Prophecy Fails: A Social and Psychological Study of a Modern Group That Predicted the Destruction of the World*. Minnesota: University of Minnesota Press.

Flynn, D. J., Nyhan, B. & Reifler, J. (2017). 'The Nature and Origins of Misperceptions: Understanding False and Unsupported Beliefs about Politics: Nature and Origins of Misperceptions'. *Political Psychology*, 38, 127–50.

Guardian. (2002). 'Full Text of Tony Blair's Statement to Parliament on Iraq'. *Guardian*, 24 September. Retrieved from: http://www.theguardian.com/politics/2002/sep/24/foreignpolicy.houseofcommons.

Hall, K. (2014). 'Real or Imagined: Racism "Fear" Over Rotherham Child Abuse'. *BBC*, 27 August. Retrieved from: https://www.bbc.co.uk/news/uk-england-south-yorkshire-28951612.

Jung, C. G. (1965). *Memories, Dreams, Reflections*. New York: Random House.

Kahneman, D. (2011). *Thinking, Fast and Slow*. London: Penguin Books, p. 499.

Omand, D. (2020). *How Spies Think: Ten Lessons in Intelligence*. London: Penguin UK.

Pascoe-Watson, G. (2002). 'Brits 45 Mins from Doom'. *The Sun*, 25 September, p. 4.

Sanderson, C. (2020). *The Bystander Effect: Understanding the Psychology of Courage and Inaction*. New York: William Collins.

Solzhenitsyn, A. I. (2003). *The Gulag Archipelago, 1918–56: An Experiment in Literary Investigation*. New York: Random House.

Syed, M. (2015). *Black Box Thinking: Why Most People Never Learn from Their Mistakes – But Some Do*. London: Penguin.

4 The Oversensitive Burglar Alarm: Stress and the Saboteur

When you're feeling under a lot of stress, it can really help to understand that your reaction – let's say your anxiety – is there to protect you from a threat. That threat could be really serious, like getting a tyre puncture when you're doing 80 miles per hour in the fast lane of the M1. Or it could be a serious but less immediate threat, like being diagnosed with a life-threatening illness. It could even be an event that you find threatening at the time but objectively is trivial, like being criticised by your boss. Your mind and body will react in almost the same way to these events, activating your threat response.

One aspect of your threat response is that your unconscious mind – your saboteur – partially disables your ability to think. It compels you to focus on the threat and ignore things around you that might distract you. For example, if you're crossing the road and you suddenly notice a bus heading towards you at 40 miles an hour, you need to get out of the way fast. You don't want to be thinking about why you didn't notice the bus in the first place or the consequences of the bus hitting you – you just want to move fast and get out of the way. You have to respond to the threat of the bus automatically.

However, what if the threat isn't so immediate, like the diagnosis of a serious illness? What if the threat isn't a real threat but an instance of you worrying too much or being a bit paranoid, like those critical remarks from your disagreeable boss? Well, the problem is that the same psychological and physiological processes will kick in. In other words, your attention will narrow in on what you see as the threat and you'll feel compelled to act quickly, either by freezing, trying to escape from the threat or fighting the threat. This is the fight or flight reaction that most people have heard of.

Think of your threat response and your feelings of anxiety as being like a physiological burglar alarm. When the burglar alarm in your house is working well and is adjusted correctly, it only goes off if someone tries to break into your house. However, let's imagine for a moment your house burglar alarm starts to malfunction and becomes oversensitive. Let's say, for example, that when your neighbour's cat walks through your garden, it triggers the alarm, and all of a sudden the siren goes off and lights start flashing. It might even alert the local police or a security

DOI: 10.4324/9781003188063-5

company. If you are under a lot of stress and are overly anxious, you possess the human equivalent of an oversensitive burglar alarm. You perceive something in the world that seems threatening (but in reality isn't threatening), and it sets off your internal burglar alarm. You might feel an increasing sense of panic and a need to escape from the threat. Sometimes you might just freeze and don't know what to do. And sometimes you become very volatile and aggressive and want to fight the threat. This oversensitive internal burglar alarm is the saboteur.

Sarah's story

Many years ago when I was working as a clinical psychologist, a woman was referred to me because out of the blue she began experiencing panic attacks in the workplace. Sarah was a senior executive with a very big company and was very capable, confident and, for the most part, level-headed. She had no history of panic attacks or indeed any other mental health difficulties. Seemingly, she had had a pleasant and uneventful journey through life, until now. I asked her to tell me about what was troubling her.

'Well', Sarah told me,

> I was at work and I had to go to a meeting. It was nothing special or stressful or anything like that, but when I walked into the meeting room, I panicked. I couldn't breathe. I thought I was having a heart attack. It felt like every fibre in my body was screaming at me to get out of that room. I just fled.

Sarah told me that she literally ran out of the room, followed by a couple of her alarmed colleagues. She sat down on a chair in the outer office gasping for breath. An ambulance was called and she was taken to casualty. The doctor there told her that there was nothing wrong with her and she'd probably had a panic attack.

'Me? Panic attack? I've never had a panic attack in my life. I'm not the sort of person who panics – I've never panicked!' Sarah told me. Nevertheless, she did concede that she must have experienced some kind of anxiety or panic attack in that meeting room.

During the course of our first few therapy sessions, we explored what might have triggered this panic attack. Was it a stressful meeting? No. Did she have any strong feelings about any of her colleagues in the meeting? No. Was anything else going on in her life at the time that was causing her to feel anxious? No. When had she last experienced a panic attack? Never; this was the first. How was her childhood? Happy and settled. Current relationships? Happy and settled. And so we went on with nothing apparently amiss. I was running out of questions. Eventually, I asked if she had any physical health problems.

'No', she said. Then she paused for a moment. 'Oh. There was something three years ago – I nearly died. I was in intensive care in the US for three weeks'.

Sarah went on to explain that she had been on a ranch holiday in the USA with her family. They decided to go on a cowboy camping weekend trip, where they rode horses, camped out and ate sausages and beans from a tin plate. During the weekend, Sarah was walking in the Nevada Desert when she noticed something in her peripheral vision. It was a snake, and she was about to stand on it. She glanced down and saw, to her horror, that the snake was about to strike her. It bit and latched on to her ankle, chewing her flesh. Sarah was terrified and screamed. Eventually, the snake let go and disappeared. She was left with the wound on her ankle, which quickly swelled. She returned to the camp and sought help. The guide was worried, and a trip to the hospital was quickly arranged. Sarah was admitted for observation. A few hours later she began to feel strange. Her condition deteriorated and she found it hard to breathe. She was transferred to the Accident and Emergency department and then the intensive care unit, where she was put on a ventilator. Sarah looked very panicky just telling me this story.

'I recovered', she said, 'but it was a big shock in my life. I thought of myself as being fit, healthy and strong. It showed me how fragile life can be. God, I hate snakes'.

We were both struck by how terrifying her experience had been, and in the following sessions, we kept coming back to it. As we talked about it, the connection appeared. We wondered: in the room where the panic attack occurred, were there any trailing leads? We thought perhaps it had triggered Sarah's fear of snakes. She went away to investigate and returned to tell me that there was indeed a short lead connecting the desk plugs with an overhead projector. This lead had brightly coloured stripes on it, a bit like the coral snake that had bitten Sarah.

Our understanding of what had triggered the initial panic attack was this: Sarah had walked into the room feeling preoccupied with work stuff. But her unconscious mind – let's say her saboteur – always on the lookout for threats, had spotted this stripy lead. It had immediately connected this with the experience that had nearly killed her – and triggered her threat response. Although her rational mind knew she was safe, her unconscious mind – her saboteur – triggered her flight response, and every cell in her body compelled her to escape the danger, which was the lead/snake. Of course, her rational mind knew that it wasn't a snake, but her saboteur did not want to take the risk.

Interestingly, when Sarah went back to the room and saw the lead, she didn't experience any panic. That was the moment her panic attacks – and, more importantly, her fear of panic attacks – stopped. Once Sarah had made that connection, her rational mind was in a position to reassure her unconscious saboteur, and then the threat disappeared.

Anxiety is the emotion that drives and gives executive power to our saboteur. If we want to understand our own saboteur – that is, the fears, phobias and worries that disrupt our lives – we need to understand our own anxiety: how that anxiety works and what triggers the anxiety. That is what we will explore in this chapter.

The history of your saboteur

You are the end point: the product and the fruition of the lives, adventures and tragedies of many thousands of people. Thousands of people have lived, formed relationships and had children so you could live. Think for a moment of your ancestors. Think what the lives of those people must have been like. Probably far tougher than your life. All those people going back to prehistory managed to survive, reproduce and pass on their genes – to little old you. All this genetic knowledge lives in you now, as you sit and read this book.

Consider for a moment what your ancestors have survived. Two World Wars to begin with. If you are Jewish, your ancestors may have survived the Holocaust. Think back to the harshness of life in Victorian Britain. My ancestors survived working in the textile industry in Victorian Yorkshire. Your ancestors survived the harshness of life in Mediaeval Europe – did you know that the Black Death killed somewhere between 30 and 60 per cent of the population of Europe? Your ancestors were in the minority, in the 40 per cent that made it. If your family is from London, consider that 20 per cent of the population of the city was killed in the Great Fire of London. If you go back even further to prehistoric times, how hard was it to survive in that environment?

The main factor that enabled all these people, your ancestors, to survive was their ability to anticipate and escape from threats. Making rapid decisions and moving quickly can be the secret to survival.

A lion sprinting at 50 miles an hour from a 100 feet away will bring you down in just over one second. In that one second, you will have had to decide what action to take to evade the lion. These are the decisions many of your ancestors would have had to have made – and at the time they were the right decisions otherwise you would not be here.

In his powerful novel about the First World War, *All Quiet on the Western Front*, Erich Maria Remarque describes how soldiers reacted and dived for cover before they were consciously aware of an incoming shell:

At the sound of the first droning of the shells, we rush back, in one part of our being, a thousand years. By the animal instinct that is awakened in us we are led and protected. It is not conscious; it is far quicker, much more sure, less fallible, than consciousness. One cannot explain it. A man is walking along without a thought or heed; – suddenly he throws himself down on the ground and a storm of fragments flies harmlessly over him; – yet he cannot remember either to have heard the shell coming or to have thought of flinging himself down. But had he not abandoned himself to the impulse he would now be a heap of mangled flesh. It is this other, this second sight in us, that has thrown us to the ground and saved us, without knowing how.

(Remarque, 1958)

The sound of the incoming shell reached the unconscious mind, and the unconscious mind made a decision and triggered action before the sound had even registered with the conscious mind. The factor that flung the soldiers to the ground and saved their lives is called *preconscious processing*.

To survive these situations, our ancestors needed fast reactions. These reactions developed and were honed over thousands of years, and they remain with us today.

It is this phenomenon that makes great sportsmen and sportswomen. It allows cricketers to accurately strike a ball that they haven't even consciously seen yet and allows goalkeepers to occasionally dive the correct way and save a penalty. In his book *The Hour Between Dog and Wolf*, John Coates explains that most of the behaviour of athletes in modern sporting events happens at an unconscious or preconscious level. He writes:

> A cricket ball bowled at 90 miles an hour covers the 22 yards to the batsman's wicket in about 500 milliseconds; a tennis ball served at 140 miles an hour will catch the service line in under 400 milliseconds; a penalty shot in football will cover the short 36 feet to the goal in about 290 milliseconds; and an ice hockey puck shot halfway in from the blue line will impact the goalie's mask in less than 200 milliseconds. In each of these cases, the less than half a second travel time of the projectile gives the receiving athlete about half that time to make a decision whether or not to swing the bat, or return the serve, or jump to the left or right, or reach for the puck, for the remaining time must be spent initiating the muscle or motor response.
> (Coates, 2012)

He goes on to make the startling point that our visual system is just not up to the job of processing such fast incoming information. He writes,

> once an image hits the retina, it takes approximately 100 milliseconds – that is a full tenth of a second – before it consciously registers in the brain. Pause for a moment and contemplate that fact. You will

soon find it profoundly disturbing. We tend to think, as we survey the world around us or sit in the stands of a sporting match, that we are watching a live event. But it turns out that we are not – we are watching news footage. By the time we see something, the world has already moved on.

Preconscious processing is both our saviour and our saboteur.

This preconscious processing plays a major part in our decision-making. Your ancestor hears a rustle in the bushes that could be food or very well might be a predator. The probability is that your ancestor was overcautious and reacted to the rustle in the bushes as if it were a predator, running like hell to escape. Let's say that nine times out of ten the rustle in the bushes wasn't a predator but was high-protein food. Your ancestor missed out on the food, but nevertheless they survived and passed on their genes. They sacrificed a high possibility of food to mitigate a low risk of danger. That is the gene that got passed on, the gene that says if there is even a hint of a threat, you should treat it as being serious and run like hell.

We can now think of that predisposition as our negativity bias. In our lives today, we are far more likely to see possible risks and threats in a situation (in other words see a 'predator') than the opportunities of the situation (in other words the 'food'). Furthermore, our threat response is constantly being triggered. Now, however, the threats we see are not threats in the sense of predatory wild animals, but take the form of disagreeable managers, unreasonable deadlines, competitive colleagues and complaining customers.

Thinking, fast and slow

Have you ever reacted to a situation quickly because it seemed to be a threat, but then it turned out to be nothing? Or have you ever made a decision quickly and then later realised that the decision was rather irrational (a bad thing)? Let's look at these in turn.

The psychologist Daniel Kahneman, along with his colleague Amos Tversky, has done the most to throw light on these complex mental processes (Kahneman, 2011). His work dovetails nicely with that of Timothy Wilson on the adaptive unconscious (Wilson, 2002). Kahneman won the Nobel Prize for economics for his work on unconscious processing and unconscious bias. He developed the dual process theory, which is enormously helpful in making sense of how our brain processes information and makes decisions.

According to Kahneman, our brain has developed two parallel processing systems to cope with the complex demands of modern life. He called these System 1 and System 2. These are their defining characteristics:

- System 1:
  - Fast
  - Unconscious
  - Automatic
  - Emotional
  - Reactive
  - Effortless (doesn't use much energy)
  - Naïve (takes everything at face value)
  - Responsible for about 98 per cent of our day-to-day thinking

- System 2:
  - Slow
  - Conscious
  - Effortful
  - Controlled
  - Rational/logical
  - Responsible for 2 per cent of our day-to-day thinking

System 1 is fast, intuitive, associative, automatic and impressionistic, and it's completely unconscious – rather like the systems that control our temperature and heart rate. When we refer to having a gut feeling about something, we are talking about System 1. If I ask you to finish the phrase 'bread and…', what word immediately pops into your head without you even trying? 'Butter', I would guess. Similarly, if I ask you 'What's 2 + 2?', you can't help but think '4'. If you've ever had the experience of driving home on a familiar route and not being able to remember the journey, it was System 1 that was driving you home. You didn't have to think about turning left or taking the second exit from the roundabout; it was all done automatically by your unconscious.

Now, extending that metaphor, imagine you're on holiday in France and have to drive on the right – the side of the road you're not used to driving on. You have to concentrate hard to make sure you don't drift onto the wrong side of the road, and you have to be really careful that you don't navigate a roundabout the opposite way to all the other traffic. If you have to drive through Paris, you certainly can't do it automatically; you have to focus and have your wits about you. In Kahneman's theory, it's System 2 driving you around Paris.

System 2 will also take over your driving in the UK if you're faced with an emergency. Let's say you're listening to the radio and chatting to a friend when you see a ball roll out into the road in front of your car. Immediately, your attention will be on the road and what you're doing, and you won't hear the radio or your friend. Even if you're driving around an unfamiliar area or a complex road system that you're not used to, your System 2 will take over. Imagine driving around Trafalgar Square for the first time: you are unlikely to have the radio on, or at least if you do, you'll be unaware of the noise.

System 1 can easily answer the question 2 + 2, but if I ask you 'What's 374 × 97?', then you'll have to stop and concentrate and focus, and it will be System 2 answering that question. System 2 is slow and deliberate and gets tired very quickly. System 2 is focus and concentration, and it hogs your brain's CPU. To see how System 2 monopolises brainpower and attention, do the online selective attention test at http://www.theinvisiblegorilla.com/videos.html.

The brain resists using System 2, because it burns so much energy. To use a different motoring metaphor, System 1 is a bit like the Tesla Model 3, which goes very quickly and burns little energy. In contrast, System 2 is more like a Bentley: very nice, but returns 12 miles to the gallon.

For Kahneman, System 1 is the star of the show, whereas System 2 is more like an understudy who has deluded herself into thinking that she's the star and has very little idea of what is really going on.

System 1 is efficient and very good at what it does. As we know from the preceding pages, it's highly sensitive to subtle environmental changes, particularly signs of danger or threat, and is quick to respond to avert potential trouble. When the threat is real, this system is unbelievably efficient. However, if the threat isn't real, then System 1 can sabotage our thinking and ability to respond appropriately to the event that it has mistakenly seen as a threat.

Furthermore, System 1 is hopeless at the kind of logical and rational thinking that is needed for well-considered decisions. It will jump wildly to conclusions, and it's prone to a bunch of extraordinary and often unbelievable-sounding (but true) cognitive biases. In that sense, System 1 can lead us astray in two ways: first, by overreacting to a situation that it sees as threatening but in reality isn't a threat and second, by making decisions very quickly (a good thing) but often irrationally (a bad thing).

Decision-making under extreme stress

On the whole, we see ourselves as being civilised, intelligent and rational people. If you have read the book so far, you will realise that we're all of the above things – but only part of the time. This rational, civilised and intelligent person is in fact a small part of the human being we are; let's say it occupies a small room, perhaps the attic, of a large house that is our brain and indeed our mind.

All animals, including you, respond physiologically to external threats in exactly the same way. In other words, your body reacts to threats in exactly the same way as does a rat, lion or zebra. This response can be summed up in a phrase that almost everyone is familiar with: freeze, flight or fight. If a rat sees a large cat prowling around in a garden, its threat response is activated and it tells the rat to freeze, in the hope the cat won't see it. Let's say the cat does see the rat and begins to sprint towards it. Then the rat goes into flight mode and runs. But then the rat finds itself trapped and the cat launches itself, going for the kill. That's when the rat begins to fight for its life.

Imagine you're sitting on a tube train minding your own business when a group of rowdy drunks boards the train. You inwardly groan and look down. 'Whatever you do', you think, 'don't make eye contact'. Then one of these very aggressive-looking men sits next to you and grabs your newspaper. You quickly get up and run, trying to make it to the next carriage, but your way is blocked by another member of the group, who grabs you by the throat. You immediately lash out, punching his face to try to escape his grip...

In the presence of great physical danger, you have only three options: try to make yourself invisible (don't make eye contact) so the predator doesn't notice you, run away (move to a different carriage) or fight back. This behaviour is instinctive rather than rational. The entire purpose of these instinctual responses – the freeze–flight–fight mechanism – is to ensure the survival of the species, to ensure your survival so you are able to pass on your genetic material to the next generation.

When we reflect on this example, it's also worth making the distinction between emotion and feeling, because they are very different things:

- *Emotion* is a visceral sensation whose purpose is to motivate action in order to achieve the primary goals of evolution: to survive and reproduce. Emotions are physiological and they are in the body.
- A *feeling* is our rational interpretation of that emotion. A feeling lives more in the mind than in the body. It's a label we attach to an emotion; it's how we consciously name our physiological responses.

If you're riding on a rollercoaster, you experience a particular physiological and emotional response. Your heart starts to race, your breathing becomes fast and shallow, you start to perspire, and your stomach feels a bit queasy. Now, you can label that as a feeling of 'excitement' and love it and want to repeat the experience (as many rollercoaster aficionados do). Alternatively, you could label the same physiological and emotional responses as a feeling of 'terror' and think to yourself, 'That is the first and last rollercoaster I'll ever ride on'.

The actual physiological response to an event is the emotion, and our interpretation of that emotion is a feeling. You can probably see how important it is to make this distinction because our feelings – how we label external events – will determine to a large extent our future behaviour.

Why zebras don't get ulcers

Let's return to the discussion on the threat response. If you're a lion and you're attacked by another lion, you might be a similar size and be of similar status in the dominance hierarchy, and so your instinctive response is probably to fight rather than run.

However, let's say that you're not a lion but you're a zebra, and you happen to notice a lion lurking in your vicinity. Well, you certainly aren't as strong, and you're certainly lower down in the dominance hierarchy, so what do you do? You run like hell – you run for your life.

The primatologist and neurologist Robert Sapolsky shows how this fantastically efficient biological mechanism is great when we're under real threat – let's say we're being chased by a lion – but can kill us when the threat is not real (Sapolsky, 2004). Sapolsky demonstrates that for animals such as a zebra, stress is generally episodic (e.g. running away from the lion), while for humans, stress is often chronic (e.g. worrying about losing your job). Therefore, animals on the whole don't experience chronic stress-related disorders such as ulcers and hypertension (with the notable exception of some higher primates; Sapolsky found chronic stress responses in baboons). These chronic stress-related disorders are becoming increasingly common in humans, particularly those at the bottom of the dominance hierarchy (Marmot, 2015; Peterson, 2018). In the modern world of work, threats tend not to be lions but micromanaging bosses, disagreeable work colleagues and overwhelming workloads. All of these things ultimately lead to burnout (Drayton, 2021).

Whether you fight or run, your body needs to very quickly deliver energy to your muscles so that you're able to run as fast as you can or fight to the death. This means that your liver and your fat cells pump blood into your muscles at a massive rate. At the same time, your breathing and heart rate increase dramatically to deliver more fuel and oxygen to your muscles. Because of this, your blood pressure also rises significantly.

If you're being chased by a lion and your life is under threat, probably the last thing you want to do is stop and eat something, or have sex. In this life-threatening situation, your body is attempting to conserve all the energy it has and put that energy into surviving. As a result, it shuts down both your digestive and reproductive functions. The threat response also narrows your attention, because you need to focus on the threat – and the lion. You don't want to be distracted by anything else. One of the functions that use a lot of energy in our bodies is our immune system. This more or less stops working when we're experiencing an existential threat. In short, your freeze–flight–fight response shuts down any physiological functions that waste energy and narrows attention so you aren't distracted by information that would slow you down.

The freeze–flight–fight response works great for the zebra and even works well for you in specific high-threat situations. However, the obvious difference between you and the zebra is that you possess the intellectual capacity to think about the future and remember the past. In other words, you are much better at worrying than the zebra.

Sapolsky makes the point that the stress response in animals, like the zebra, switches on very quickly and then, once the danger has passed, switches off again. One minute our zebra is grazing; the next minute it notices the lion, the alarm sounds and its stress response kicks in. The zebra runs and either survives or is killed and eaten by the lion. If it does escape and survive, within a few minutes it is peacefully grazing again and not worrying about what might happen in the future. As we all know, it doesn't work like this in humans. We frequently experience events that are not particularly threatening, such as a job interview, as being life or death. All the time, we project ourselves into the future and imagine things going wrong for us. The physiological consequences of this are that all of the systems I have just written about, such as our heart rate, digestion, sexual responses and immune system, become disrupted by the threat-response hormones generated by the brain.

In the presence of physical danger, our bodies react in a similar manner: they release vast amounts of energy and direct it to the most important centres to prepare us to either fight back or flee. However, you can react in much the same way even in the absence of danger, even if you're merely thinking about it. This is unpleasant in itself. However, stress is implicated in causing and certainly exacerbating many of the chronic illnesses that are common in modern life, such as cardiovascular disease, diabetes and obesity, and even general susceptibility to falling ill (because of the reduction in effectiveness of our immune system).

This is why our saboteur is both good and bad. It's an incredibly effective system for protecting us from immediate and life-threatening threats. But it's not well adapted for modern life, and because it's triggered, like an oversensitive burglar alarm, by events that are not really that threatening – not threatening in the short term at least – it can make us chronically ill.

How our unconscious sabotages decision-making

By definition, the most important decisions we are required to make are most likely to be made in stressful situations. Even the act of making an important decision is stressful in itself, because the consequences of a wrong decision may be serious. People such as politicians, CEOs and even airline pilots can least afford to be unwell, yet are the very ones most likely to be impaired by the saboteur when attempting to do their job.

I have already described how the freeze–flight–fight system is activated by external and internal threats (that is, a perception of threat when in reality no threat is present). Our threat response operates on the assumption that the best way to counter threatening situations is by running away or fighting. In other words, by physical action. However, most of the threats we come up against in modern life are best responded to by thought rather than intense physical activity – by calm reflection, not impulsive reaction.

In our day-to-day lives now, the kinds of things that threaten our well-being are feeling overwhelmed with work, having to deal with difficult people or having to react to aggressive or just plain bad drivers during our commute to work. We have to deal with conflict in our personal relationships, ideological and political disagreement and worries about the future. In all of these situations, our threat response – gearing up the body for intense physical activity – is not only ineffective but harmful to our ability to come up with an effective response. If you are stopped by the police for speeding, your racing heart, raised blood pressure, muscular tension and sweating – which would have enabled you to escape from a wild animal in the olden days – are not going to reassure the police officer.

You can see the threat response in action very clearly in the examples I gave earlier in this book. For example, when Rabbi Levy's parking space was 'stolen', he went straight into 'fight' mode and began destroying the miscreant's car (see the Introduction). When poor Andrea Dunbar felt threatened by the posh literary types in London, she took flight back to the Buttershaw Estate in Bradford (see Chapter 1). Both felt threatened but responded to the threat in ways that made their situation much worse rather than solving the problem. If Rabbi Levy and Andrea Dunbar had engaged their System 2 thinking, their responses may have been far more adaptive. The Rabbi may have shrugged and thought, 'What the hell? This isn't really important.' and driven on. Maybe Andrea could have reflected on the great success of her writing and thought, 'I'm just as good as they are'.

Chronic stress: ageing faster and dying younger

Up to now, we have looked at how threats in the environment affect our immediate responses, in particular our ability to make decisions appropriate to the situation. In other words, we've considered the effects of *acute* stress. To use the burglar alarm metaphor, for most modern-day threats the alarm not only doesn't help but actually hinders an effective response.

I'd now like to pose a different question. What if the burglar alarm is going off almost constantly, like the annoying neighbour whose burglar alarm is very sensitive and goes off every couple of nights? What happens then? Well, if it's just a house burglar alarm, it's annoying but gets ignored. But what happens if it's your threat response, your physiological burglar alarm? What long-term effects might this *chronic* stress have on you and your health?

Box 4.1: The toll of continued self-sabotage

In 2021, Mark Borgschulte and colleagues studied the effects of modern corporate culture on the health of 1,605 company executives, most at the 'c-suite' level, at large publicly listed US firms over the past 50 years (Borgschulte et al., 2021). Borgschulte had decided that this was an important topic to research after reading about the case of Oscar Munoz, the chief executive of United Airlines, who suffered a heart attack 37 days after being appointed CEO. Mr Munoz was, apparently, the picture of health, being a keen cyclist and tennis player, yet he keeled over with a coronary a month after getting the big job. Five months after his heart attack and subsequent surgery, Mr Munoz returned to work. Despite being very ill, he continued to work during his recovery.

Borgschulte found that overworked and highly stressed chief executives age faster and die younger than those of the same age and health status in less stressful occupations. In particular, the researchers found that executives faced with industry downturns and the threat of takeovers were more likely to die earlier. The report tells the story of James Donald, chief executive of Starbucks, who was fired in 2008 after Starbucks' stock fell by more than 40 per cent in a year. The report shows shocking photographs of Mr Donald with analysis indicating that he aged by almost seven years in the four and a half years from December 2004 and May 2009. The researchers discussed the tremendous pressure that senior executives, particularly CEOs, are under in modern corporate America. The estimated lifespan of a CEO increases by two years when they are insulated from corporate stress; for example, with antitakeover laws. They also found that a CEO's life expectancy decreases by 18 months when they have to deal with industry-wide downturns.

There is overwhelming evidence that being exposed to chronic stress makes us very ill – both physically and mentally. The Borgschulte research also shows that it accelerates the ageing process and consequently shortens our lifespan. The physiological and psychological effect of chronic stress long outlasts the events that triggered the stress response in the first place. Chronic stress causes a wide variety of physical disorders, such as cardiovascular disease, including heart disease; stroke; and an increase in general ill health due to suppression of the immune system.

This is the paradox of the saboteur – of our threat response. Evolution gave us the saboteur in order to help us to survive, to get out of trouble. Unfortunately, it has not adapted well to modern life, and rather than helping us to survive, it actually threatens our survival. The more stressed we are and the longer we feel stressed, the less capable we are to deal with modern life and its stresses.

Think back for a moment to Tony Blair and the decision to support the invasion of Iraq (see Chapter 3). I think that it's reasonable to assume that he was under an enormous amount of stress at that time. His saboteur – his threat response – would have been hyperactive both psychologically and physiologically. It is ironic that people in positions of great responsibility, such as prime ministers, CEOs and military leaders, are frequently put under enormous external stress, and this stress is perhaps one of the biggest obstacles to their functioning efficiently and rationally.

In a grimly amusing experiment, David Beaty looked at how stress impairs memory and cognitive ability. In a military aircraft full of servicemen, he 'inadvertently' left the pilot public address system on, allowing the poor servicemen to hear a conversation between the pilot and co-pilot about a serious mechanical problem that was going to result in the plane having to ditch into the ocean. With this alarming news fresh in their minds, the servicemen were asked to carry out some simple mental tasks including recalling the emergency escape sequence they had previously learned. These stressed servicemen were unable to remember the escape sequence, let alone manage the cognitive tasks (Beaty, 1969). This probably explains why following most air crashes rescuers find the dead are still strapped into their seats, because in the stress of an aeroplane emergency, people forget how to open the lap seat belt. Just at the time when we most need to think clearly, our saboteur disables our thinking.

This also applies to you. Let's say you're being interviewed for a new job, or maybe you're doing a job that you hate or a job you're not very good at. You might do a job where you're responsible for the well-being of other people and you know that if you make a mistake, others will suffer. What about if you feel unfairly – or even fairly – criticised, or maybe you're being threatened with the sack? All of these situations will trigger your threat response and generate anxiety, fear or even outright terror.

However, the freeze–flight–fight mechanism not only is useless in dealing with these situations but actually hinders an effective response. Your saboteur, in its desperate effort to help you survive, makes your situation a whole lot worse. A dry mouth and a red face leaking sweat and a pounding heart aren't going to look good when you're being interviewed by a potential employer. You already feel apprehensive, and then your threat response makes things worse by priming you to run away or fight, while you're sitting in an office chair trying your best to look cool and in control. Your saboteur piles misery upon misery. It's like being kicked when you're already down.

Here are a few things you can do to better understand and, let's say, recalibrate your burglar alarm so it doesn't go off when you don't want it to.

The keys to managing anxiety are:

1. Control your breathing
2. Reframe your beliefs/thinking.

Breathe

In anxiety, a negative feedback loop develops between mind and body. Due to past experience, your mind perceives threat when none actually exists (like an oversensitive burglar alarm). This catastrophic thinking triggers your freeze–flight–fight system. This gets your body ready to hide, run or fight. Your heart rate goes up, and your breathing becomes rapid and shallow. This physiological response reinforces the catastrophic thinking ('I'm going to faint/can't breathe', etc.), and that's the feedback loop.

The easiest and most effective way to disrupt the negative feedback loop is to take control of your breathing. Take slow deep breaths with slight pauses between inhalation and exhalation think – 'slow and low'. Try this:

1. Breathe in for 10 sec
2. Hold for 5 sec
3. Slow exhale for 10 sec
4. Hold for 5 sec
5. Repeat × 3

Reframe

Public speaking is a situation that many people feel anxious about, so I will use it as an example.

Reframe catastrophic thoughts as:

- My feelings are excitement not panic.
- I am a bit anxious, but everybody gets a bit anxious when speaking in public.

- These are my colleagues, and they want me to do well.
- I am quiet and thoughtful, not brash – aim for Tom Hanks/early Henry Fonda/Nicola Walker rather than Leonardo DiCaprio or Madonna – avoid trying to be a glib motivational speaker. Most people prefer kind and thoughtful to brash and flashy.
- Focus on the 'audience' not on yourself. It's about them not you.

Chapter takeaways

- The saboteur is always looking for threats, and it takes charge of protecting us from them, though in fact it's really not the best person for the job.
- The saboteur's quick reactions can save us – but often they sabotage us. We may wrongly interpret something as a threat; we may react in an inappropriate way.
- While the conscious mind can think rationally and logically, the saboteur jumps to conclusions and is influenced by a whole host of cognitive biases.
- The saboteur deals with threats as if they are physical: it makes us run or fight when this is not at all helpful and can make the situation much worse.

References

Beaty, D. (1969). *The Human Factor in Aircraft Accidents*. London: Secker & Warburg.

Borgschulte, M., Guenzel, M., Liu, C. & Malmendier, U. (2021). *CEO Stress, Ageing, and Death*, Working Paper 28550. Cambridge, MA: National Bureau of Economic Research. Retrieved from: https://doi.org/10.3386/w28550.

Coates, J. (2012). *The Hour Between Dog and Wolf: Risk-taking, Gut Feelings and the Biology of Boom and Bust*. London: HarperCollins UK.

Drayton, M. (2021). *Anti-burnout: How to Create a Psychologically Safe and High-performance Organisation*. Abingdon: Routledge.

Kahneman, D. (2011). *Thinking, Fast and Slow*. Harmondsworth: Penguin Books.

Marmot, M. (2015). *Status Syndrome: How Your Social Standing Directly Affects Your Health*. London: Bloomsbury Paperbacks.

Peterson, J. B. (2018). *12 Rules for Life: An Antidote to Chaos*. London: Allen Lane.

Remarque, E. M. (1958). *All Quiet on the Western Front*. New York: Fawcett Crest.

Sapolsky, R. M. (2004). *Why Zebras Don't Get Ulcers*. Revised and updated edition. London: St. Martin's Press.

Wilson, T. D. (2002). *Strangers to Ourselves: Discovering the Adaptive Unconscious*. Cambridge, MA: Harvard University Press.

5   The Stories We Tell Ourselves

Our reality is based on the stories we tell ourselves. This applies to individuals, organisations and nations. These stories become a part of our unconscious and often a part of our saboteur. This chapter discusses stories and how they can support or sabotage, and how changing stories can change behaviour both at work and outside of work.

Your personality has been at least partly constructed from the stories you have told yourself over the years – stories about yourself, others and how you fit into the world. This includes the part of your personality we are calling the saboteur. You use stories to make sense of your life, to weave together the often chaotic events we experience into something coherent – something that makes sense. These stories become a part of you and define the sort of person you believe yourself to be.

The stories you tell yourself help you cope with day-to-day life. Most of them are trivial, mundane and fleeting. For example, another driver cuts you up and you immediately start telling a story about how they are stupid and aggressive (when, in fact, the person might be very mild-mannered and just made a mistake). Other stories are far less trivial, and they are deeply ingrained. When I worked as a clinical psychologist, I would interview criminals to prepare psychological reports for the court. Almost without exception, the offender would tell a self-serving story to explain their crime: 'Well, I wouldn't have stabbed the security guard if he hadn't tried to stop me. If he'd just got out of my way, he'd have been fine – so it wasn't really my fault. It was his fault for getting the way!'

You use these hastily constructed stories to structure an often nuanced and complicated reality into a simple, often black-and-white story. You make up the stories without consciously thinking about it. If you didn't, you would just experience the world as noise and chaos and a mess of overwhelming data.

Box 5.1: The life and death of Nat Tate

In April 1998, a glittering party was held in a Manhattan art gallery to launch a biography of the American painter Nat Tate. The party was attended by David Bowie and Gore Vidal, as well as gallery

---

DOI: 10.4324/9781003188063-6

owners and art critics from influential papers such as the *New York Times*. Many of these experts in modern American art spoke enthusiastically about Nat Tate, warmly remembering aspects of his life and exhibitions of his works they had attended, and reflecting on the sadness of his premature death.

Nat Tate had an interesting life. He was born into poverty but was adopted by a wealthy couple who supported his interest in art. He went to art school and later studied with Picasso and Braque in Paris, before returning to New York to produce a body of work in the Abstract Expressionist movement. Tate, however, was beset with self-doubt, constantly comparing himself to his mentors. One day he collected up his paintings and made a bonfire of them, before leaping to his death from the Staten Island ferry, into the freezing waters of the Hudson River. His body was never found.

However, perhaps the most interesting thing about Nat Tate's life is the fact that he never actually existed. Nat Tate was a figment of the imagination of the British novelist William Boyd (the name was inspired by the National Gallery and the Tate in London). The launch party in New York was an elaborate publicity stunt conceived by David Bowie, who had published the fictional biography *Nat Tate: An American Artist, 1928–1960* (Boyd, 1998).

This is an amusing story. However, it also poses an interesting question: why didn't the experts spot the hoax? The answer is that they had internalised this fictional story and made it a part of themselves.

Victims, heroes and villains

Stories can define how you think of yourself (I'm a shy person), other people (people are usually kind) and the world (the world is safe; if you behave decently, nothing bad will happen to you). We use these stories to predict the future. You might tell yourself, 'If I work hard and try to get along with people, I'll be okay'. Or, conversely, 'I've always been a failure and I always will be'. It's easy to see how stories can start to construct our unconscious saboteur.

When you think about your past, it is always a series of connected stories. In my work as a clinical psychologist, a story I frequently heard was a variation of 'The reason I'm like this is because of the way my parents treated me'. Often, psychotherapy works when the therapist helps the patient to re-examine their past and tell a different story – usually recasting themselves as a hero rather than a victim.

It's impossible to understand your past – your autobiography – without constructing it as a story. Of course, you are the main character in this screenplay, and because you are the main character, you must be the hero or the victim. Some people even cast themselves as the villain, and that is usually the result of other people consistently describing them as being bad in some way.

If you are the hero of your story, you will tend to ignore the role that chance has played in your life. There is a cliché that says that success breeds success, and this is partly true, but often more from circumstances than talent. 'Heroes' overestimate the role their personal attributes have played. For example, about half of the differences in income across people worldwide are explained by their country of residence rather than intelligence, hard work or other personal attributes (Milanovic, 2015).

The self-fulfilling prophecy

To understand how people use stories to explain their life, let us look at how writers – professional storytellers – distil their experiences. The writer thinks about random events and imposes and magnifies meanings and connections. And that's what we are looking for: the meanings attached to the event (which form the essence of the story) rather than just a chronology or document of the event (which would be journalism). In our personal stories, we almost always cast others in the role of hero, victim or villain. We are the central character in our personal novel, and we portray ourselves as the hero or the victim. The villain is always played by the other. Of course, we are sometimes the 'villain' in other people's narratives. Our 'villain' is our unconscious saboteur and is largely invisible to us.

What better writing in which to find this distilled and concentrated meaning than poetry?

Let's take a look at the life of Sylvia Plath, one of the greatest and best-known poets of the 20th century who, tragically, took her own life at the age of 30. We can find clues in her relationship with her husband Ted Hughes and in her poem 'Daddy' as to the stories that Sylvia might have constructed to make sense of her feelings – unwittingly creating a self-fulfilling prophecy.

When Sylvia first met fellow poet Ted at a party, they had an instant connection. Sylvia wrote in her journal:

> he kissed me bang smash on the mouth and ripped my hair band off, my lovely red hair band scarf which had weathered the sun and much love, and whose like I shall never again find, and my favorite silver earrings: hah, I shall keep, he barked. And when he kissed my neck I bit him long and hard on the cheek, and when we came out of the room, blood was running down his face...
>
> (Plath & Kukil, 2000)

The meeting was prophetic because it foretold a relationship that was very stormy. Sylvia's sometimes poor mental health was made worse by

Ted's serial infidelity. When, after several years of marriage, Ted left Sylvia for another woman, Sylvia committed suicide. Had her relationship led her to that precipice? In part; but in fact her unhappiness and death had roots further back – in her relationship with her father, Otto Plath.

Just before her death, Sylvia wrote one of her most famous and moving poems, 'Daddy'. The poem is a powerful account of her relationship with her father and the devastating impact his death had on her. In 'Daddy', Sylvia wrote:

> I was ten when they buried you.
> At twenty I tried to die.
> And get back, back, back to you.

Her suicide was a serious attempt but unsuccessful:

> And then I knew what to do.
> I made a model of you,
> A man in black with a Meinkampf look

The man in black – the model she made of her father – was Ted Hughes, and much of the emotional instability in their relationship resulted from Sylvia confusing her feelings for Ted with those resulting from the loss of her father. She told herself a story, deeply embedded within her consciousness, that described a world where the only man she could love would have to be clever and dominant, like her father – and, just as her father did, would eventually abandon her. Sylvia's unconscious saboteur led to unstable and sometimes volatile provocative behaviour, which contributed to her being abandoned and thus recreating the past in the future.

At first sight, this seems fantastic or irrational, but it is more common than you might think. This process, which Freud called repetition compulsion, goes a long way to explaining similar situations to that of Sylvia Plath. For example, when I worked as a clinical psychologist, I would talk to women who had had multiple partners, all or most of whom had been violent towards them. Often, they would have a number of children from different partners and were contemplating moving in with a man who all the available evidence would suggest was at best unreliable and at worst abusive. I would be charged with making a decision as to whether this future relationship might place the woman's children at risk. Often, I would point out to the woman that her prospective partner had convictions for violence, had an addiction problem and was generally a rootless individual. She would counter that he was different and only needed to be loved to bring out the best in him. She would purposefully ignore all the objective data indicating risk. I might ask if she had ever met a man who might be more stable, perhaps be kind to her and maybe even have a job. She would say that she had met such men but considered them to be boring, or if not boring, too good to be interested in her. Her story was along the lines of, 'Violent men are exciting, and their worst excesses can be tamed by the love of a good woman. Stable men are boring, and because of that, my love is of no value to them'.

So, stories have a certain amount of predictive validity – in other words, we use them to make guesses about how particular situations might turn out in the future. These guesses then determine our expectations and, if we're not careful, become self-fulfilling prophecies. Our stories not only explain our lives but can go on to create our lives.

Life scripts

The story of Sylvia Plath is an extreme one; however, we all make sense of our lives using stories. Many of the stories we tell ourselves are largely unconscious and have been constructed from the life scripts handed to us by others when we were young (Erskine, 2010). The life scripts are the stories we tell about ourselves that were shaped by our parents or caregivers, whose life scripts were in turn shaped by their parents and so on. Sylvia Plath's story is an example of this. Philip Larkin memorably described this process in his poem 'This Be the Verse':

> They fuck you up, your mum and dad.
> They may not mean to, but they do.
> They fill you with the faults they had
> And add some extra, just for you.

(Larkin, 2003)

Larkin goes on to describe how misery gets passed down in families because the mum and dad in the poem had inherited a faulty script from their own parents.

Box 5.2: A story I told myself

I grew up thinking that my father didn't really want me. He wasn't particularly mean to me, but he was very cold and detached. I told myself a number of stories to explain this. The more reasonable ones were that in 1960s Yorkshire at the time I was growing up, this was what men were like. Another story was that he was probably tired because he worked hard. However, the most damning story was that the reason he was cold towards me was that I wasn't worthy of being loved. Like all children, I was the centre of the universe and anything that happened, good or bad, was caused by me. Therefore, my father's emotional detachment was my fault in some way.

That was the story I told myself for probably 40 years. Then my wife started researching her family tree, which prompted me to do the same. I discovered my father had actually been married before he met my mother. He and his first wife had had a child – a daughter called Judith – who died in infancy. Soon after Judith died, my father's marriage seemingly broke down and they divorced. A few years later he met my mother, and I came along.

This news was, in many ways, a profound shock for me because it caused me to re-evaluate our relationship and rewrite the story of that relationship. My new story was that my father was emotionally devastated by the loss of Judith – his first child, my half-sister. And when his second child came along – i.e. me – he didn't want to get too emotionally close in case I were to die young. The idea that my father did not love me, which had troubled me throughout my adult life, had been wrong – well, probably wrong.

This story about not being wanted by my father has, for good or bad, made me the person I am. When I changed the story, I also changed the way I feel about myself. The new version engenders a sense of compassion for my dad and for myself. It's a common belief that your past is wholly responsible for how you behave now. However, if we think about it, your past is just a story you are telling yourself about something that no longer exists – something that is no longer real.

Our life scripts are also hugely determined by social and cultural influences such as our peer group ('boys don't cry'), religion ('homosexuality is wrong') and politics ('the rich are bad, greedy and avaricious'). These deep-seated and often barely conscious stories form templates or themes that we repeatedly use to order and even arrange our lives. We fit the random events of life into an overarching theme to reinforce our stories. This is also an example of confirmation bias at work (see Chapter 3): we notice things in the world that confirm and fit in with our stories and turn a blind eye to things that contradict them.

Stories as the foundation for the saboteur

We all tell stories about our lives, the organisations within which we work and society in general. Most of the time the stories don't feel like 'stories' to us because we experience them as reality – as 'This is just the way things are'. Because of this, we never think to question them. If your stories – the stories you tell yourself – are reasonably congruent with reality, then this isn't much of a problem. However, if your stories are more at the extreme end of the normal distribution, then these unconscious stories form the philosophy and beliefs that filter your perception of reality and evolve into your unconscious saboteur.

Let me give you a couple of examples. First, imagine that you are the apple of your mother's eye, and from birth, she told you how wonderful/brilliant/clever/competent you are. But in fact you're average or even below-average in these attributes. Well, when you venture out into the real world and your bosses, colleagues and friends tactfully, or not so tactfully, point out your faults, mistakes and the myriad of reasons why you are not wonderful, this will create a disconnect between your experience of yourself and what the world is telling you. There are two obvious ways of bridging this gap: (1) you accept that your self-image is distorted and think about how you can change or (2) you feel angry and resentful at all these people who don't understand or appreciate your talents (which are obvious to you). You can see how this might cause problems.

Alternatively, you might be like Andrea Dunbar (see Chapter 1) and experience a life where people have told you that you are, let's say, worthless, lacking talent, no good. And yet, because of a combination of your actual innate talent and circumstances that allow you to express that talent, you become a success. Other people start to tell you how talented and brilliant you are – but, like Andrea Dunbar, you don't *feel* talented and brilliant. You feel like an impostor, hence impostor syndrome. Again, you can accept this feedback from the world and think about changing your view of yourself, which is terrifying because it disrupts your whole sense of who you are as a person. Or, you can conclude that other people are not seeing the real you because they are either stupid or insincere, and this allows you to stay as you are: comfortable but denying your own competence, talent and glory. It is this denial of, and perversion of, reality that grows into the saboteur.

Stereotype threat: how stories sabotage whole groups of people

Many of the stories we tell about ourselves aren't so much individual stories but stories created about the particular social group to which we belong, and that very belonging results in us soaking up the stories and they become integrated into our perception of who we are. It's important to note the word 'perception' here. The perception we absorb may be true, but it might be a distorted perception that comes from a socially held but crude stereotype based not on us as an individual but on the general characteristics of the group to which we belong. This social perception – or, as it is more commonly known, stereotype – influences how others see us, how we see ourselves and how we behave – especially how we behave in particular social situations. Such stereotypes can be silly and trivial, or they can have a devastating impact on people's lives.

In the 1990s, the African-American social psychologist Claude Steele began studying how negative racial stereotypes of African-Americans not only result in overt discrimination but also become absorbed into the individual psyche of African-American people and can sabotage their performance, particularly in academic tasks (Steele, 1997). His work shows how able and competent African-American students can actually reduce their performance in a way that confirms a stereotype of African-American students as being less able than white or Asian students. Steele called this process 'stereotype threat'.

In the past, the observation that generally African-American students perform more poorly on tests of standard aptitude than white or Asian students has been explained in terms of genetics or cultural influences. (Similar explanations have been given as to why women seem less attracted to STEM[1] subjects in comparison to male students.) However, the research of Claude Steele and his colleague Joshua Aronson showed that a subtle cognitive bias was contributing to this disparity in performance. The prevalent negative stereotype of black students not being as intellectually able as white students triggered a high level of anxiety among African-American students, and this inhibited their ability to think clearly and thus perform to the best of their ability in academic tests. Even a subtle reminder of the stereotype was found to have a catastrophic impact on test performance. In effect, these internal psychological processes acted to sabotage the African-American students' performance (Steele & Aronson, 1995).

Stereotype threat also sabotages the performance of women, as shown by Stephen Spencer and colleagues (Spencer et al., 1999). In a study, two groups of women students took a maths test. The first group were told that in the past the test had shown no gender differences; the second group were told the opposite. The first group performed as well as a similarly able group of men; the performance of the second group was significantly poorer.

Other research shows that stereotype threat occurs and can be triggered in all groups for which a negative stereotype exists. Stereotype threat seems to kick in only in specific contexts where the individual is measured against specific comparison groups. For example, studies have shown that white students who are told that Asian students tend to perform better on maths tests will underperform. White athletes underperform when competing against black athletes when researchers trigger stereotype threat in the white athletes ('white boys can't jump') (Steele, 2010).

Another very interesting and counterintuitive finding of stereotype threat research is that people experiencing stereotype threat do not even have to believe in the negative stereotype for the threat to impact their performance. It is enough to simply be aware of the negative stereotype (Steele, 2010).

Beating the saboteur with story editing

So far, I have discussed how stories can sabotage people's lives. How can we prevent this? It's too easy to say, 'Just change your story'. Stories run deep and are all around us in society, and telling people to change the story is a bit like telling a depressed person to cheer up. It tends not to be that effective. We don't think of the stories as 'stories'; we think of them just as being how life is. We say to ourselves, 'It's just how I am' or 'This is how things are'. We perceive the stories we tell ourselves not as stories but as reality. Therefore, to change our perception of reality, we have to find a way of editing our stories. This was the approach taken by the American social psychologist Timothy Wilson in his story-editing research (Wilson, 2011).

Let's look at two examples of the role of stories in real human problems. These problems are very different, but what unites them is that they are, at least partly, caused by the same psychological process: quite simply, the stories that we tell ourselves about the world.

Example 1: story editing to stop self-sabotage at college

Imagine that you are undertaking a course of study at a university or college. You don't think of yourself as particularly academic and you haven't studied seriously before – only at school. You are very apprehensive about the course and wonder whether you will measure up. The first term of the course is very hard, much harder than you expected. At the end of the term, you sit an exam and you do badly. What story do you write to explain this situation?

You could write a self-sabotaging story about how you are not really cut out for academic study. You say to yourself, 'I did find the course much harder than expected and I performed poorly on the exam, and that was just the easy stuff in the first term. I'm really not looking forward to the second term'. These thoughts are at the forefront of your mind when you begin the second term and you feel even more anxious and apprehensive than you did when you started the course. Every time you look at the coursework, you feel anxious, and so you tend to avoid it – procrastinating. Towards the end of the second term, you have to do another exam, an exam that you haven't prepared for. Predictably, you do poorly – even worse than you did on the first exam. You think, 'Well, what's the point? I tried, didn't I?' And you end up dropping out of the course.

However, what might happen if you were able to tell yourself a slightly different story? What if, for example, you tell the story of yourself as a person who enjoys pushing themselves and trying something new? What if after doing badly in the exam, you say to yourself, 'Well, that was a wake-up call. If I'm going to do better, I'll need to think about better ways of studying, and I need to work harder'. Let's say that this story spurs you on to make more effort, and by the end of the second term, this has paid off and your exam performance and results improve.

But as we have already discovered, our stories are deeply rooted in our family history – so how can we possibly hope to change or edit the stories?

Timothy Wilson and Patricia Linville wondered whether it is possible to edit our stories and whether this might help reduce the level of college dropout in poorly performing students. They felt that if they could somehow help these struggling students to change their perceptions about college – in other words, edit the stories they told about themselves and about college – then their performance might improve. They carried out a very interesting and effective piece of research to test out this idea.

They took a group of first-year college students who were performing poorly and considering dropping out. The students were at a critical stage where they could tell themselves either a story of persisting through adversity or a story of giving up. Wilson and Linville set up a very simple intervention in an effort to help these students edit their internal stories. They gave them some information and statistics that suggested that many college students struggle in the first year and do poorly but often do better and improve as time goes by. They also showed them videotaped interviews of students saying things like, 'Oh yeah, I found the first year really tough. I did really badly on the exam. But I got some help and worked hard, and now I'm in the third year and I'm doing well. I'm really glad I stayed'.

Wilson and Linville also had a control group of randomly assigned students who did not get the intervention. This allowed them to accurately track whether the information and videotapes had made a real difference to whether the students dropped out or not.

This simple 30-minute intervention was very effective. The researchers found that the students who had been prompted to edit their stories had significantly improved grades and were significantly less likely to drop out of college than the students who had not received the intervention. In a sense, the intervention nudged the students into a self-maintaining optimistic mindset (Wilson & Linville, 1982).

One of the remarkable things about this study is that the intervention only took 30 minutes. Traditionally, changing people's perceptions of the world – the stories they tell themselves about the world – might take many hours of psychological therapy. This study shows that using very quick and simple interventions can make a massive difference to people's lives.

Example 2: story editing to prevent child abuse

Wilson's work on story editing convincingly shows that it can help improve academic grades and reduce dropout rates in higher education. But what about a far more serious and dramatic problem – child abuse? Could this story-editing approach help to minimise the risk of children being mistreated?

For a number of years, I worked as a clinical psychologist in a child and family service. One of the reactions that I frequently (almost always) encountered in parents who had been physically abusive to their children was that they blamed the child. The abusive parent would tell themselves a story about their child being constitutionally 'bad' in some way. They would say, 'He's got a bad personality – he was born that way' or 'She's just stubborn, she does it on purpose'. or 'He's evil, he has the devil inside of him'. Contrast this with the average parent, who attributes their child's difficult behaviour to environmental or situational factors that could easily be put right. They say something along the lines of, 'Oh, don't worry. He's just hungry/overtired/needs a cuddle/is having a tantrum'. They wouldn't think of describing their child as 'evil' when they misbehave; the word wouldn't even cross their mind.

Essentially, the average, 'good enough' parent tells themselves a different story to explain their child's behaviour than the abusive parent. The story told by the abusive parent is one of the unconscious factors that sabotage their parenting. (The academic literature strongly suggests that these attributions, both positive and negative, are largely unconscious; Bugental et al., 2002.)

I will just pause here to make the point that not for one moment am I seeking to explain child abuse as being a result of this single psychological factor. It's a complex problem and multifactorial in its cause. Be that as it may, these unconscious stories, unconscious narratives, do play a causative role in child abuse. If we accept this, then surely helping these potentially abusive parents to change, or edit their stories about why their children behave as they do, would be helpful.

This was the hypothesis that Daphne Bugental and colleagues at the University of California set out to investigate in their groundbreaking 2009 research. They targeted parents who had been assessed as being at high risk of abusing their children. In this sample, 50 per cent of parents had said that they had been physically abused when they were growing up and another group were parents of children with medical problems.

Just over 100 parents were randomly assigned to one of the three groups. The first group, the control group, were given information about services that were available, but no visits or hands-on practical help. The second group took part in the standard parental support programme, which included an average of 17 home visits from childcare professionals over the course of a year, along with interventions such as parental education, anger management training and parenting advice.

The third group, the group that we are interested in, received the standard parenting support programme and, in addition, a story-editing intervention with the goal of changing or reducing the extent to which parents blamed their children for their perceived 'bad' behaviour (e.g. crying) and instead explained their children's behaviour as a result of external causes that could be changed. This was a very active intervention, so rather than just telling the parents that this was what they should do, the home visitors actively encouraged them to come up with alternative explanations for their child's behaviour. The parents were asked to think of concrete examples of situations when their children had behaved badly and how they had explained that to themselves. For example, was the reason a baby cried inconsolably in the evening not to provoke his mother, but because he had indigestion – not the child's personality, but an environmental factor that could easily be changed?

The programme lasted for one year, and at the end, the three groups of parents were assessed on how frequently they had used harsh or even abusive parenting techniques, such as shouting, shaking or smacking. What the researchers found was interesting. The first two groups were not significantly different in terms of their use of harsh or abusive parenting styles. The figures are still shocking, though: 23 per cent of children in the standard parenting support group were the victims of abusive parenting, compared with 26 per cent in the no-intervention control group. However, in the group that received the story-editing intervention, only 4 per cent of children were abused. In addition, there was a dramatic reduction in the use of corporal punishment: approximately 42 per cent of parents in the first two groups reported slapping or spanking their children; in the story-editing group, only 18 per cent of parents reported doing so.

The parents and children were followed for a number of years, and it emerged that the children in the story-editing group had lower levels of the stress hormone cortisol as well as improved cognitive functioning (Bugental & Schwartz, 2009).

Why is all this important for you?

Timothy Wilson's work on story editing is not only interesting but highly applicable to your life, especially your career.

Consider Wilson's work with students who were failing and considering dropping out. Essentially, he prompted them to take a longer-term strategic view of their college career. His work helped the students not to become overwhelmed by short-term stresses and setbacks and to persist in the face of adversity.

This story-editing approach also helps people not to underestimate the difficulty of tasks or indeed life. Some people, especially young people, have a rather distorted view of life as a result of social media. They check their Facebook and Instagram accounts and see their friends living happy, successful lives. Of course, their friends are just sharing the positive, enjoyable aspects of their life and keeping the worries, failures and disasters to themselves. This can develop into a problem, where you see everyone else seemingly having a great time while you are only too aware of your doubts, inadequacies and failures. It's all too easy to divide the world into successes and failures – heroes or zeros. And of course, being aware of our own deficiencies, we put ourselves in the failure category.

Wilson's story-editing technique helped the students he worked with to get some perspective. They were able to see people whom they perceived as being successful – those in the final year of college – as once being like them: struggling, fallible human beings.

If you are at work feeling overwhelmed or struggling with something, try to remember this. Everybody finds life difficult at times, but with persistence and a bit of support, most people get through. And the very act of struggling to overcome the difficulty will make you stronger – with, of course, the right mindset. And the right mindset consists of telling the story of yourself as a hero who overcomes adversity, rather than a failure who only just manages to scrape through.

Similarly, if you are in a position of authority and somebody beneath you in the hierarchy seems to be struggling, it might be helpful to them if you empathise and normalise their struggles. Tell them that when you started out you also found things very hard. Tell them you might seem older, wiser, more senior than them, but you still struggle and occasionally feel overwhelmed.

Also think about how you can apply the mindset described in Daphne Bugental's work with abusive parents to your own life. When things are not going well for you, do you tend to view these life difficulties as having internal, stable and global causes? In other words, do you believe that your problems are caused by factors that are specific to you (internal), apply to every situation (global) and will never change (stable)? This way of looking at the world, known as the depressive attributional style, is one of the main factors that contribute to clinical depression (Seligman et al., 1979). This mindset is characterised by Sylvia Plath's story, in which her father's death and her relationship with Ted Hughes were intrinsically linked. When you face a difficulty, try to see it as being more systemic than just 'internal'. In other words, life problems, and organisational problems, are always multifactorial: it's not just one thing (i.e. you) that leads to difficulties, it is always a combination of many things.

Another characteristic of stories that sabotage our lives is the idea that because we fail at one thing, we will fail at everything. Because we are rubbish at maths, we must be stupid, i.e. rubbish at everything. This is the 'global' part of this depressive attributional style, the idea that our performance in one area of life will generalise to all areas of life: if you have had one or two bad relationships, then *all* your relationships will be bad. In the stories we tell, we often characterise ourselves and other people as being wholly good or wholly bad, and this is always a mistake. You, like everybody else, have the capacity for good as well as evil. Remember the quotation from Aleksandr Solzhenitsyn in Chapter 1:

> If only there were evil people somewhere insidiously committing evil deeds, and it were necessary only to separate them from the rest of us and destroy them. But the line dividing good and evil cuts through the heart of every human being. And who is willing to destroy a piece of his own heart?
>
> (Solzhenitsyn, 2003)

The only constant global thing in life is change. Stories that sabotage our lives often have a theme that 'things will always be like this'. If you're having a bad time, if you feel fed up, if you're very worried about something, at that moment it feels like this is how you will always feel. But that is never the case. Situations change and people change. We feel bereft, terrible and inconsolable when a loved one dies, but with time, most people overcome this. One of the helpful factors in overcoming such events is remembering that all emotions and situations are transitory. None of us feel happy all the time and all of us feel miserable some of the time. Problems arise when we start to tell stories that make these feelings and situations concrete, and we feel determined to hang on to them. You might say to yourself, 'I will always feel like this; nothing will ever change'. A more helpful story is perhaps one that draws on the old Persian saying, 'This too shall pass'.

Think carefully about the stories you tell about yourself and your place in the world. They can either help you to navigate life's difficulties or sabotage your life.

Chapter takeaways

- We live according to stories we tell ourselves. They can help us or sabotage us.

- We tell stories in order to make sense of the past, the present and the future. Without them, we would be overwhelmed by the chaos and complexity of life.
- The stories are largely unconscious – we don't think to question them – and they can distort reality, which feeds the saboteur.
- The saboteur can take a story and turn it into a self-fulfilling prophecy.
- The saboteur is affected by stories that are bigger than us: stereotypes.
- To avoid self-sabotage, we need to edit our stories. That means:
  - Taking the long view and getting perspective
  - Seeing an issue as multifactorial rather than just specific to you
  - Challenging the idea that just because something has happened, it will keep happening
  - Knowing that 'this too shall pass'

Note

1 Science, technology, engineering and maths.

References

Boyd, W. (1998). *Nat Tate: An American Artist 1928–1960*. Harmondsworth: Penguin.

Bugental, D. B., Ellerson, P. C., Lin, E. K., Rainey, B., Kokotovic, A. & O'Hara, N. (2002). 'A Cognitive Approach to Child Abuse Prevention'. *Journal of Family Psychology: JFP: Journal of the Division of Family Psychology of the American Psychological Association*, 16(3), 243–58.

Bugental, D. B. & Schwartz, A. (2009). 'A Cognitive Approach to Child Mistreatment Prevention among Medically At-risk Infants'. *Developmental Psychology*, 45(1), 284–88.

Erskine, R. G. (2010). *Life Scripts: A Transactional Analysis of Unconscious Relational Patterns*. London: Karnac.

Larkin, P. (2003). *Collected Poems* (A. Thwaite, Ed.). London: Faber & Faber.

Milanovic, B. (2015). 'Global Inequality of Opportunity: How Much of Our Income Is Determined by Where We Live?' *The Review of Economics and Statistics*, 97(2), 452–60.

Plath, S. & Kukil, K. V. (2000). *The Unabridged Journals of Sylvia Plath, 1950–1962*. New York: Anchor Books.

Seligman, M. E., Abramson, L. Y., Semmel, A. & von Baeyer, C. (1979). 'Depressive Attributional Style'. *Journal of Abnormal Psychology*, 88(3), 242–47.

Solzhenitsyn, A. I. (2003). *The Gulag Archipelago, 1918–56: An Experiment in Literary Investigation*. London: Random House.

Spencer, S. J., Steele, C. M. & Quinn, D. M. (1999). 'Stereotype Threat and Women's Math Performance'. *Journal of Experimental Social Psychology*, 35, 4–28.

Steele, C. M. (1997). 'A Threat in the Air: How Stereotypes Shape the Intellectual Identities and Performance of Women and African-Americans'. *American Psychologist*, 52, 613–29.

Steele, C. M. (2010). *Whistling Vivaldi: How Stereotypes Affect Us and What We Can Do*. New York: Norton.

Steele, C. M. & Aronson, J. (1995). 'Stereotype Threat and the Intellectual Test Performance of African-Americans'. *Journal of Personality and Social Psychology*, 69, 797–811.

Wilson, T. (2011). *Redirect: The Surprising New Science of Psychological Change*. London: Penguin UK.

Wilson, T. D. & Linville, P. W. (1982). 'Improving the Academic Performance of College Freshmen: Attribution Therapy Revisited'. *Journal of Personality and Social Psychology*, 42(2), 367–76.

6   The Saboteur in the System

To begin, let us explore how one of Britain's oldest and most venerable banks was sabotaged. Our story begins in January 1990, when this bank offered one of its junior employees the opportunity to work in Singapore. The bank was Barings Bank and the employee was Nick Leeson.

Box 6.1: A prestigious and reputable merchant bank

Barings Bank opened its doors in 1762. In Georgian and then Victorian Europe, Barings was a big name in banking. An example of its power was that in 1803 Barings helped to broker the deal and provided the finance for the purchase of Louisiana by the US government from France. This is still the biggest land deal in history. The Barings family boasted five separate hereditary peerages, and Barings was the banker of royalty. Arguably, it became the most respected bank in the City of London.

Barings had survived over 200 years of ups and downs in Britain's financial markets and considered itself invulnerable, as much a part of the British establishment as Earl Grey tea, cucumber sandwiches and umbrellas. Unfortunately, however, Barings was invulnerable in the same way that the *Titanic* was unsinkable. Nick Leeson was the iceberg that sank Barings. And just like the iceberg, the part of Nick Leeson that did the damage was hidden beneath the surface of his affable, hard-working and competent demeanour. It was his unconscious saboteur.

To paraphrase Alexander Solzhenitsyn,[1] the line between integrity and dishonesty cut right through the middle of Nick Leeson, the senior managers (and owners) of Barings Bank and the very culture of the financial services industry. The collapse of Barings resulted from a failure in the whole system rather than simply a single rogue trader. Leeson lied and cheated partly for financial gain, but mainly to impress his bosses and fit in. In turn, the Barings senior management were happy to turn a blind eye to his activities, because they liked the

DOI: 10.4324/9781003188063-7

profits he generated. And it all happened in the wider political and economic context of the deregulation of the financial markets and the 'Big Bang' of the early 1990s. Nick Leeson's unconscious saboteur drove his dishonesty. The organisational saboteur at Barings made sure that nobody looked too closely at Leeson's 'too good to be true' revenue. Finally, the 'Loadsamoney'[2] culture of the 1990s financial markets sabotaged oversight and compliance in favour of greed. Nick Leeson's story is an interesting and enlightening one because it's the story not only of a flawed individual but also of a flawed institution and flawed society.

Who was Nick Leeson?

Nick Leeson was an outsider. He was very different to most of his contemporaries on the trading floor. Leeson grew up in humble circumstances in Watford. His father was a plasterer, and his mother a nurse. The family lived in a small council flat before moving to a modest three-bedroomed house on a council estate in Watford. He went to a state school and then a grant-maintained comprehensive. This was Nick Leeson's first contact with the financial services industry, because his school was an offshoot of Parmiter's Grammar School in Bethnal Green, London. Parmiter's had links with the City, providing candidates for City of London back office and clerking jobs.

Nick Leeson's headmaster described him as a 'thoroughly dependable member of the school. Of perhaps 120 pupils in his year he was one of the 30 prefects selected by staff. He was an asset to the school' (Rawnsley, 1995). Similarly, friends and neighbours painted a picture of Leeson as being a likeable, dependable and, well, average person. Nick Leeson wasn't particularly academic at school, leaving with a C grade in English literature and a D in history at O level, but failing his maths A level. After leaving school, Leeson found a low-level clerical job with the Queen's banker, Coutts, where he stayed for two years learning the ropes. He then moved to Morgan Stanley as a futures and options settlement clerk. This is where he was first introduced to the dark arts of the investment banking world.

In 1987, Leeson applied and was accepted for a job at Barings as a lowly stockbroker's clerk. He worked hard, was personable and made a good impression. Eventually, as a reward for his hard work, Leeson was promoted and offered a plum posting to the bank's offices in Singapore.

A few months before he was offered this job, Leeson had applied to the Securities and Futures Authority for a City of London trading licence. This was declined, because he had a county court judgement against him for an unpaid debt. Leeson's managers at Barings were informed of this but turned a blind eye and proceeded with his posting to Singapore. I'd speculate that their reasoning was that his job in Singapore was managing the back office rather than actively trading. This early warning sign, both of Nick Leeson's attitude to boundaries and of his manager's tendency to ignore this, was to become a recurring theme in this story.

Leeson did well in Singapore. He and his wife lived the high life: he was well paid, and the couple lived in a luxury flat in a nice part of Singapore, all paid for by Barings Bank. Leeson quickly rose through the ranks, promoted to the point where he was managing the settlements and accounting department of Barings' futures trading department.

A big part of Nick Leeson's job was managing client accounts and generally looking after clients. He came up with the idea of applying for a trading licence for the Singapore International Monetary Exchange (SIMEX). He justified this by saying that he didn't want to trade but thought it would be good public relations for him to be able to show potential clients around the trading floor. He was successful and soon became the proud wearer of a gold-and-navy Barings Bank trading jacket. In his application for a trading licence, Leeson failed to declare that he had been turned down for a trading licence in London, and since there was no communication between the two regulatory authorities, nobody was the wiser.

This small lapse ultimately contributed massively to the collapse of Barings Bank. Leeson was in charge of the back office at Barings, monitoring the trades and accounting (in effect responsible for financial compliance). However, his trading licence allowed him to trade on the SIMEX, which he began doing. He was trading and at the same time monitoring his own trades. Leeson had, consciously or not, become a poacher as well as a gamekeeper, responsible for policing his own trading activity.

He began to make unauthorised speculative trades. Leeson was a natural at trading and initially did well, making huge profits for the bank. His bosses were very impressed with him and the revenue he generated.

What Leeson's bosses didn't know is that much of this profit came from his high-risk unauthorised transactions. He was gambling wildly with Barings' money and hiding these losses in a fake error account. Leeson was a high roller at the SIMEX casino, and as all high rollers know but usually ignore, the casino always wins in the end.

His losses built up, and by the end of 1994, they amounted to more than £208 million. This was almost half of the capital of Barings. Almost unbelievably, he managed to hide this massive loss from his bosses at the bank. No doubt this was due to a good knowledge of banking practices on Leeson's part, the fact that he was monitoring his own trading and a lot of cunning. However – and we will come to this later – there was also an unconscious collusion between Leeson and the bank's leaders that became the key factor in his activities being, let's say, 'overlooked'. Both Leeson and the leaders of Barings Bank desperately wanted him to be a success, and both were terrified of the prospect that his revenue might be in some way dodgy.

By the beginning of 1995, Leeson was becoming increasingly desperate to recover his losses. He was taking bigger and bigger risks, doubling his trades (bets). In one of these dodgy trades, he invested heavily in the Japanese stock exchange (the Nikkei). Unfortunately for Leeson and Barings, this was the day before the Kobe earthquake, which crashed the Japanese stock market. He desperately tried to recoup his losses by taking even riskier decisions, betting that the Nikkei Stock Exchange would recover quickly. It didn't and he lost.

By this time, he, or rather Barings, had lost $1.4 billion, which was more than double the bank's entire capital. Barings Bank went under.

Leeson fled Singapore, leaving a note which read 'my sincere apologies for the predicament that I have left you in. It was neither my intention or aim for this to happen… Apologies, Nick' (Rawnsley, 1995). He travelled to Malaysia, Thailand and finally Germany, where he was arrested and extradited back to Singapore. He was tried and sentenced to six and a half years in prison but was released early following a diagnosis of cancer.

The saboteur at Barings

What were the psychological forces that drove Nick Leeson to make riskier and riskier trades? What were the psychological forces that persuaded his bosses to turn a blind eye? The saboteur in Nick Leeson and the managers of Barings resulted in bankruptcy and the demise of this 300-year-old financial institution.

The story of Nick Leeson is interesting because it vividly illustrates how the saboteur can emerge in individuals, groups and organisations. When this happens, the outcome is usually catastrophic. In this story, Barings Bank was unable to survive the actions of the saboteur. It was unable to mitigate the power of the unconscious mind.

What do I mean by this? Well, a part of the unconscious mind sabotaged Leeson's desire to work with honesty and integrity. The saboteur was also at work in Barings Bank, encouraging senior managers to ignore Leeson's activities. Finally, in the wider political world, Margaret Thatcher's Conservative government favoured profit over financial circumspection, and the saboteur manoeuvred ministers to support deregulation of the financial services industry and markets, with the result that they avoided facing up to the possible consequences of such a policy.

This is a complex story, and so let's break the story of Nick Leeson and Barings Bank into more manageable chunks. I will look at Nick Leeson's individual history and personality, the nature of his job, the organisational culture of Barings and the political and economic situation.

The person

How did the saboteur emerge in Nick Leeson? What were the unconscious forces within him that drove his ultimately destructive behaviour?

Without doubt, Leeson was an outsider at Barings Bank. Remember, he was the son of a plasterer and with a comprehensive education who was working in an elite, blue-blooded financial institution (Gapper, 2011). We all have a strong need to be accepted and to fit in. Leeson was promoted on his merits because he was a good employee. He made lots of money for the bank. In that sense, he was accepted, but probably not as a social equal. There were many social, class and other points of difference between Leeson and his managers (and many of his peers) such as education, accent and etiquette, and these would have left him on the social periphery at Barings. Leeson wanted to join the Barings' inner circle, or ring.

Box 6.2: The inner ring

In 1944, C. S. Lewis, author, academic and religious writer, delivered a lecture at King's College London which he called 'The Inner Ring' (Lewis, 1949). In it, he discussed the natural human desire to be accepted within the 'inner ring' of whatever group matters to us at the time.

Lewis began his lecture with an extract from Tolstoy's *War and Peace* in which one of the characters, Boris, slowly begins to recognise two parallel systems within the Russian army. One of these systems was the official and sanctioned hierarchy of ranks and so on, and the other was a more subtle hierarchy that no one spoke of but everyone was all too aware of.

Lewis called this unofficial system the inner ring.

The desire to belong, to be accepted, is a strong and at times overwhelming need in all of us. Similarly, being excluded and rejected is one of the hardest pains to bear. So the desire to join the inner ring is one of the most fundamental motivations and a motivation that is largely emotional and thus at least partly unconscious.

Lewis points out that the inner ring has its own boundaries and its own culture which is separate from the observable culture of an organisation. He says that the inner ring is most often recognised by

---

people who are on the outside, and these people sometimes come up with a name for it, like 'the gang' or 'those'. In contrast, those who are members of the inner ring just think of it as 'us' or 'all the sensible people here'.

Lewis paints a vivid picture of the inner ring when he writes, 'The heads bent together, the fog of tobacco smoke, the delicious knowledge that we – we four or five all huddled together beside the stove – are the people who know' (Lewis, 1949).

It is not so much the inner ring that is dangerous, it is more the longing to join the inner ring that often causes problems. Lewis says: 'a thing may be morally neutral and yet the desire for that thing may be dangerous'. He is suggesting that the desire to join the inner ring has the power to seduce you into behaving in a way that you would not normally behave, perhaps in a way that lacks integrity. He goes on:

> And you will be drawn in, if you are drawn in, not by a desire for gain or ease, but simply because at that moment, when the cup was so near your lips, you cannot bear to be thrust back again into the cold outer world. It would be so terrible to see that other man's face—that genial, confidential, delightfully sophisticated face— turn suddenly cold and contemptuous, to know that you had been tried for the Inner Ring and rejected.

And this, argues Lewis, is where the danger lies:

> The choice which could lead to scoundrelism will come, when it does come, in no very dramatic colours. Obviously bad men, obviously threatening or bribing, will almost certainly not appear. Over a drink or a cup of coffee, disguised as triviality and sandwiched between two jokes, from the lips of a man, or woman, whom you have recently been getting to know rather better and whom you hope to know better still – just at the moment when you are most anxious not to appear crude, or naïve, or a prig – the hint will come. It will be the hint of something which the public, the ignorant romantic public, would never understand: something which even the outsiders in your own profession are apt to make fuss about: but something, says your new friend, which 'we' – and that the word 'we' you try not to blush for mere pleasure – something 'we always do.' And you will be drawn in, if you are drawn in, not by desire for gain or ease but simply because at that moment when the cup was so near your lips, you cannot be thrust back again into the cold outer world. It would be so terrible to see the other man's face – that genial, confidential, delightfully sophisticated face – turn suddenly cold and contemptuous, to know that you had been tried for the inner ring and rejected. And then, if you are drawn in, next week it will be something a little further from the rules, and next year something further still, but all in the jolliest,

friendliest spirit. It may end in a crash, scandal, and penal servitude; it may end in millions, a peerage and giving the prizes at your old school. But you will be a scoundrel.

Lewis makes the crucial point that the inner rings exist only on the basis that they exclude others. The fun and sense of power of being in the inner ring is knowing that there are other people who want to be but are excluded. Lewis says that there are positive inner rings, but people are included in these by virtue of being good at their job – they work hard and are competent and thus get included. Their desire isn't to be a member of the inner ring but simply to do a good job. Destructive inner rings are the opposite. Membership isn't dependent on competence but on desiring to be a member regardless of the cost.

Nick Leeson was an outsider desperate to join the inner ring at Barings. In her well-researched book on Leeson, the journalist Judith Rawnsley writes that we shouldn't feel too much sympathy for Nick Leeson, but equally we shouldn't regard him as an archvillain. She writes:

So what happened to Nick Leeson? I believe that his desire to please – his clients, fellow traders and managers – and his fear of displeasing them, was so great that he went to absurd lengths to achieve what he wanted. His desire, and proven ability, to please others may in turn have led to the realisation that he could also please himself. In the sunny, unreal cocoon of Singapore where he was King of the local exchange, it was easy for him to convince himself that he was doing nothing wrong, and just as there were very few around him who challenged him, there was almost no one in that puritanical city who imagined that he had indeed left the straight and narrow.

(Rawnsley, 1995)

One of the strongest factors in Nick Leeson's internal saboteur was this desire to please and to fit into the inner ring both at Barings Bank and on the trading floor. As C. S. Lewis argues, this need to be included, to belong, is a powerful motivator of behaviour, especially ignoble behaviour.

Interestingly, this feeling of being an outsider was a personality characteristic of other traders involved in subsequent financial scandals. For example, in 2012, Kweku Adoboli, a trader with UBS, lost the bank $2.3 billion through fraudulent trading, which earned him a sentence of seven years in prison. He was also an outsider. A Ghanian who moved to the UK and attended a comprehensive school, he made his way up to the trading floor via the back office (like Leeson). Another trader at UBS, Tom Hayes, was sentenced to 14 years in prison for manipulating the London Interbank Offered Rate (LIBOR). Again, Tom Hayes was an outsider. He had a diagnosis of Asperger's syndrome, something his colleagues teased him about, calling him 'Rain Man'[3] (Gapper, 2011).

In a sense, Barings Bank itself was an outsider, an old-fashioned, rather crusty British bank trying to break into the inner circle of the lucrative world of Wall Street investment banking.

Personality

To understand Nick Leeson's internal saboteur, we should also consider his personality. By personality I mean our individual, pervasive and enduring differences in thinking, feeling and behaving. Over the years, psychologists have come up with different models to explain personality. The most widely accepted model is the big five model, or more correctly, the five-factor model of personality (McCrae & Costa, 2006).

According to the big five model, our personality is made up of five factors:

- Extraversion
- Neuroticism
- Openness to experience
- Agreeableness
- Conscientiousness

Leeson's behaviour suggests that he was a strongly extroverted (affable) and agreeable (conflict averse) person who had low levels of neuroticism (tends not to worry):

- **Extraversion:** Leeson was good with other people. He would have gained a lot of energy and buzz from being around others. The two main factors that make up extraversion are enthusiasm and assertiveness. Looking at Leeson's biography, he comes across as a very enthusiastic and assertive person.
- **Agreeableness:** Leeson was very agreeable. Put simply, he was a people pleaser who really did not like conflict. At Barings, when a deal went wrong and he made a loss, rather than declare this, he avoided the consequences by hiding the loss. This established a pattern of behaviour, and as the losses grew, so did his avoidance. Leeson went extremes to create the fantasy of being hyper-effective. When the truth eventually came out, he ran off leaving a note apologising.

- **Neuroticism:** Leeson was low on the personality factor of neuroticism. People with high levels of neuroticism are life's worriers and tend to catastrophise. They are generally apprehensive, taking the view that if something can go wrong, it will go wrong. Leeson's behaviour suggests that his tendency to worry about the future and what might go wrong was pretty minimal. He didn't worry enough about the consequences of his behaviour and the probability that ultimately everything would go wrong. He was an optimist, but a deluded one. His saboteur had buried the anxiety and worry about the potential consequences of his actions deep in his unconscious mind where he could avoid thinking about it.

In summary, Nick Leeson was a bright, likeable, conflict-avoidant, cocksure man who wanted to please other people, impress other people and fit in. These are the factors that underpinned Leeson's internal saboteur and contributed to the demise of Barings Bank.

The role

A large and established group of people (for example, traders at an investment bank) is more than the individual constituent parts that make up the group. When people come together and, let's say, work together for any significant length of time, a group culture will inevitably emerge. As Leo Tolstoy observed above in the quote by C. S. Lewis, this group culture is partly visible, but much is below the surface and invisible unless you are part of the group. Formal and informal ways of relating to each other become established, and a shared language, which we call jargon, is constructed. A group saboteur can also emerge as a part of this culture.

For example, the saboteur on the trading floor might nudge the group to turn a blind eye when a trader bends the rules. The group saboteur might encourage drinking and drug taking, which sabotages the decision-making process. Nick Leeson's aberrant behaviour wasn't only an individual issue. He worked within a social group that, if not actually encouraging playing fast and loose with the rules, did little to actively discourage or oppose it.

The primary task of a trader in an investment bank is to make money. That's it. If you're good and make money for the bank, the financial rewards, paid in bonuses rather than salary, are spectacular.

The psychological and emotional rewards are equally as dramatic as the financial rewards. Successful traders not only make loadsamoney but are seen by their employer and colleagues as a superhero. The rewards are great, but (just like the investments they make) so are the risks. Once a trader stops making money, they can quickly go from hero to zero. Most traders tend not to remain at the top for very long. This isn't because they burn out but because ineffective traders are quickly fired, and the effective trader either retires to enjoy their wealth or moves up the bank hierarchy to manage more junior traders.

When a trader starts to lose money on trades, not only is their job and considerable income at risk, so is their ego and reputation. Traders who are having a bad streak of luck will be mocked and humiliated by their fellow traders and be acutely aware of the scrutiny that they are under from management.

This constant pressure results in a manic lifestyle, which is further reinforced by the rarefied and insular culture of the investment world. Most traders live in a bubble insulated from people in the 'real' world that most of us inhabit. They become completely absorbed in the markets because they have to be in order to do their job well. This preoccupation with the world of finance makes them somewhat boring company for the average person. Thus, most traders will end up spending their free time with other traders, obsessively discussing the financial markets, deals they have made and how much money they have (Gapper, 2011).

The average trader lives an isolated existence detached from most average people. Their emotional life is dominated by fear. Fear is the ubiquitous, destructive and dysfunctional way of controlling traders' behaviour. They are frightened of losing their job, their wealth and the respect of their peers – of being excluded from the inner ring of the City of London.

It is this manic, febrile and unthinking culture that nurtures the creation of groupthink and a group saboteur among traders. The fear leads traders to deny their vulnerability by pushing it 'underground'. They overcompensate and present themselves as being arrogant, entitled and macho (the stereotype of the red-braced, striped-shirted investment banker). This saboteur culture encourages denial of personal responsibility and projecting blame onto others when a trade goes wrong – which prevents the traders, either individually or as a group, from learning from their mistakes. In extreme cases, traders will hide their mistakes (their losses) from management and colleagues. This is how Nick Leeson began, and of course, the losses and his motivation to hide the losses dramatically escalated.

This chronic fear also disables the traders' ability to think rationally and exposes them to many cognitive biases such as confirmation bias (ignoring evidence that contradicts your opinion and magnifying evidence that supports it) and the sunk cost fallacy (also known as throwing good money after bad – 'I've invested a lot of money in this investment and so I need to invest more so I don't lose my original bet'). The culture of the trading floor is one that actively rewards risk-taking behaviour and punishes conscientious, thoughtful, cautious behaviour.

It is wrong, therefore, to see Leeson and other rogue traders as bad apples in an otherwise ethical environment. The saboteur manifests itself in groups as well as in individuals. The saboteur resided in the culture of the trading floor as well as within Leeson's personality. Leeson was just an extreme example, the tail end of the distribution, of the general manic risk-taking behaviour of traders as an occupational group.

The organisation/system

The saboteur was present in Nick Leeson's character, it was present in the culture of the group of people with whom he worked, and it was present in the wider organisational, economic and political culture of the early 1980s and early 1990s.

Prime Minister Margaret Thatcher's deregulation of the financial services industry, commonly known as the Big Bang, happened on the 27th of October 1986. This was the day that the London Stock Exchange (LSE) became a private limited company. The deregulation of the City of London had been a priority for Thatcher's Conservative government since 1983. For economic as well as doctrinal reasons, Thatcher was determined to introduce free-market competition and meritocracy to the financial markets, to destroy what Thatcher saw as bureaucratic overregulation and the old boys' networks of the City of London.

Her government introduced increased competition by allowing external corporations to enter the LSE's member firms. This included foreign companies. Overnight, American financial institutions became big players on the London market.

Before the Big Bang, trades had been carried out on the floor of the stock exchange with traders shouting offers as they had done for decades. The 1980s was the decade of the personal computer, and one of the most important and at the time revolutionary structural changes brought about by the Big Bang allowed the introduction of an electronic trading system. Orders were accepted by telephone and computer, which massively increased the speed and quantity of transactions. This also made automated price quotes possible, again making trading significantly faster and more efficient.

Before the Big Bang, the LSE was the poor relation of the major international stock exchanges. In the 1980s, the New York Stock Exchange (NYSE) was by far the biggest of the world's financial markets, with the LSE doing about a third of the transactions of New York. After the Big Bang, the City of London emerged as the most important global financial market.

Deregulation meant that the Bank of England's role of regulating the markets was taken over by the Securities and Investments Board (later the Financial Services Authority). The Big Bang generated a lot of money, but with this surge of activity and wealth came something dangerous. The saboteur began to emerge when the old boys' network changed and evolved into a dog-eat-dog culture. This was exacerbated by the practice of awarding enormous financial bonuses to successful traders, which encouraged short-term profit over long-term planning and prudence.

One BBC commentator wrote:

> David Willetts, who was then working in the No 10 policy unit but went on to be a Conservative minister, co-authored a paper for Mrs Thatcher on the likely impact of the Big Bang. He expressed concern about 'unethical behaviour' and that financial deregulation could lead to 'boom and bust'. But he concluded while there might be 'individual financial failures' he did not expect 'a systemic problem'. On this he was wrong.
>
> (Robertson, 2016)

The Big Bang stirred up two sets of conflicting, and ultimately destructive, emotions in the hearts of the normally prudent and conservative bankers who ran Barings Bank:

- **Fear:** The bankers looked around and saw these financial institutions, many of which had been bought up by big American investment banks, making cash hand over fist. They understood that they were now in this dog-eat-dog, sink-or-swim environment, and they were terrified that the bank could go under.
- **Mania:** They felt a compulsion to 'do something'. I picture the leaders of Barings rushing around their boardrooms shouting, in the manner of Private Jones of *Dad's Army*, 'Don't panic! Don't panic!'[4] Mania has three components: a denial of vulnerability, a sense of triumphalism and overactivity to distract from anxiety (Stein, 2011). Mania and panic are usually a defence against extreme anxiety.

This fearfulness and the consequent manic defence prompted the bankers at Barings to set up Barings Securities. This was a subsidiary of the bank, set up in a hurry, without the financial oversight and rigid management reporting structures that were the norm in the rest of the bank, with the hope this would allow Barings Securities to move more quickly and aggressively in the markets.

Barings Securities was the baby of Christopher Heath, who established its culture and ethical standards. Heath was an extroverted 'Wolf of Wall Street' character, straight out of central casting as a 1980s Loadsamoney banker. Heath was:

A Krug-drinking man who wore spit polished brogues and immacu-
late suits, with the charm, wit and joie de vivre to live up to this
image. He was a charismatic – some would say overbearing –
character, whose presence was ubiquitous.

(Rawnsley, 1995)

Spotting a potential acolyte, Christopher Heath nurtured and
promoted Nick Leeson at Barings Securities, and his career, along with
the organisation, grew rapidly. As we have already seen, Leeson knew
little about investment banking, was a risk taker and, to use another
1980s political catchphrase, tended to be 'economical with the truth'[5].
Leeson had been refused a trading licence in London, a fact that he
was able to bury very effectively.

Barings Securities began to generate massive, unbelievable profits for
Barings Bank. The leadership of the bank couldn't believe their good
fortune and avoided the inconvenient truth of what was happening
at Barings Securities, particularly in Singapore. Barings Securities had
circumvented many of its already minimal rules to support the activities of Leeson. Their fearfulness and mania had, in Nick Leeson, 'led
them to select as a "saviour" an opposite or "shadow" to themselves,
an extreme risk taker' (Stein, 2011).

The enormous amounts of money (often fictitious) being generated
by Leeson resulted in a dependency, and 'this dependence made it
unbearable to "see" what was in plain sight. Just ten days before the
bank's final collapse, the CEO visited Leeson, invited him to dinner
and appeared to still be considering awarding him a £450,000 bonus'
(Menon, 2019).

The story of Nick Leeson illustrates the complexity of unconscious
processes in organisations. It demonstrates the complexity of the saboteur at work.

People like Leeson have all kinds of unconscious and preconscious
psychological characteristics that predispose them to becoming organisational saboteurs. These characteristics include intelligence, ambition
and the need to be accepted, to be included in the inner ring whatever
the costs. Organisations need people who are willing to break the rules
in a manner that makes it easy for the organisation to turn a blind eye.
This is especially the case in organisations experiencing high levels of
anxiety, as was Barings in the 1980s.

In this high-pressure, high-anxiety situation, the individual, the
group and the organisation get caught up in a collusive spiral of a
manic denial of reality. The more Leeson took risks by breaking the
rules, the more revenue and profit he generated, and the more he was
rewarded and fêted by his managers at Barings Bank. These unconscious processes in the individual and the organisation resulted in a
collusive game of 'don't ask, don't tell'.

Unfortunately, for Barings Bank, 'the truth' that Nick Leeson and the leadership team collusively agreed not to examine too closely sabotaged the organisation: Barings Bank went under. Following the crash, the financial services industry explained this catastrophic event as being the result of a bad apple – a rogue trader. In some ways that's correct, but as we have seen, it's only part of the story. Nick Leeson was only one factor in a systemic process that resulted in the collapse of Barings. At this bank, the 'saboteur at work' was the destructive part of Nick Leeson but also the destructive parts of the senior leadership team. Finally, the motivation to act was provided by the high levels of anxiety resulting from the economic pressures triggered by the Big Bang. So, instead of seeing the collapse of Barings as being caused by a bad apple, we need to look at the rotten parts of the crate that contained the apple.

Box 6.3: The part we[6] play in this unconscious drama

There are strong social stereotypes about bankers – let's say we all have a fantasy of what a typical banker is like. The word 'banker' is often preceded by the adjective 'greedy'. We see bankers as being wealthy, selfish and greedy. This perception can serve a psychological purpose for society. In the late 1930s, Anna Freud identified a number of psychological defence mechanisms, one of which she termed 'projection'. This is where we deny shameful thoughts and feelings in ourselves and instead project them outwards onto another person or group – and then criticise and attack them (Freud, 1937). Money, especially lack of it, and a desire to be wealthy is a common feeling and for some a source of shame. Bankers are an easy target for our projections around money. We deny our shameful greed and avariciousness and project them onto the greedy banker, whom we then criticise.

Minimising the effects of the saboteur in your organisation

The saboteur operates at three levels in any organisation: the individual, the group and the organisation/system. To minimise the probability of your saboteur – your 'rogue trader' emerging to wreak havoc – you need to consider how to minimise the effects of the saboteur at the three levels in your organisation.

Ajit Menon (2019) argues that individual circumstances including background, identity and unconscious needs play a significant part in an employee's vulnerability to engaging in poor behaviour. Managers need to be aware of these personality characteristics, including high conscientiousness, high extroversion and high agreeableness, and how they might interact with the organisational culture.

Another way of addressing the problem at an individual level is to look at how organisations can recruit a more diverse and inclusive workforce. Demographic diversity often brings with it cognitive diversity, which makes phenomena such as groupthink and confirmation bias less likely to occur. Also, the more diverse an organisation is, the less likely that the inner ring will exert a malevolent influence, because the organisation will have many groups with which employees can identify and find an identity within, rather than just one dominant in a ring group.

One of the most important factors to combat rogue behaviour is an organisation that is characterised by psychological safety (Edmondson, 2019). In a psychologically safe workplace:

- People feel they can speak up, express their concerns and be heard.
- They are not full of fear and are not trying to cover their tracks to avoid being embarrassed or punished.
- People can offer suggestions and take sensible risks without provoking retaliation.
- Anxieties, risks and even risky possible solutions can be discussed openly, evaluated and either implemented or not.

This kind of organisational culture can help to prevent the anxieties that led to the collapse of Barings going underground, becoming unconscious saboteurs in the organisation. Psychological safety was conspicuously lacking at Barings Bank.

This chapter has been about Nick Leeson, Barings Bank and the financial services industry. What has it got to do with you if you don't work in financial services? Well, a lot, because the principles I have described in this chapter apply to all areas of human endeavour, especially work. Leeson and the collapse of Barings is an extreme example of how the saboteur can work to undermine individual people, groups and organisations. But ask yourself:

- Have you ever worked with someone who was likeable, who worked hard but would often cut corners?
- Have you worked in a team whose members demonstrated more loyalty to other team members than the organisation – even when one of those was doing something wrong?
- Have you ever had a manager who just wanted to get something done and wasn't concerned about how you did it?

All these situations are common in the workplace. They only result in significant organisational problems when all three are extreme and happen at the same time, and the thing that triggers this confluence of extreme behaviour is significant external economic or political pressure. This can occur in any industry and indeed has: for example, healthcare (South Staffordshire hospital scandal), entertainment (the BBC and Jimmy Saville) and car manufacture (VW emissions scandal). All these involved unconscious sabotage at an individual, group and systemic level. Rules, regulations and boundaries have evolved in organisations for good reason, and it is not advisable to turn a blind eye to them without a very good, well-thought-out reason.

Chapter takeaways

- The saboteur exists in individuals, groups and organisations/ systems.
- Significant organisational problems happen when all three interact, which is most likely to happen when an organisation is under significant external economic or political pressure.
- Organisations have an official social structure as well as below-the-surface, unofficial structures.
- All organisations have an inner ring of people with power, and a desire to join this inner ring often results in ignoble behaviour.

Notes

1 'If only there were evil people somewhere insidiously committing evil deeds, and it were necessary only to separate them from the rest of us and destroy them. But the line dividing good and evil cuts through the heart of every human being. And who is willing to destroy a piece of his own heart?' (Solzhenitsyn, 2003).
2 'Loadsamoney' is the brash 1980s comedy character created by Harry Enfield who would taunt audiences by aggressively waving a large wad of bank notes at them and proclaiming he didn't care about their opinion of him 'cos I got loadsamoney!'.
3 A reference to the character with an autistic spectrum disorder played by Dustin Hoffman in the film *Rain Man*.
4 Private Jones was a character in the 1970s sitcom *Dad's Army*, who would rush around shouting 'Don't panic!' in a stressful situation. You can see him in action here: https://www.youtube.com/watch?v=cJm0i4gEp8I&ab_channel=CoastlandsFamilyChurch
5 A phrase used by Sir Robert Armstrong, British cabinet secretary, in the 1986 'Spycatcher' trial 'It contains a misleading impression, not a lie. It was being economical with the truth.'
6 Here, I refer to 'we' as meaning you and me, but also 'we' in the sense of society as a whole.

References

Edmondson, A. C. (2019). *The Fearless Organization: Creating Psychological Safety in the Workplace for Learning, Innovation, and Growth*. Hoboken, NJ: Wiley.

Freud, A. (1937). *The Ego and the Mechanisms of Defense*. London: Hogarth Press and Institute of Psycho-Analysis.

Gapper, J. (2011). *How to Be a Rogue Trader*. Harmondsworth: Penguin UK.

Lewis, C. S. (2013, 1949). 'The Inner Ring'. In *The Weight of Glory* (p. 141). London: William Collins.

McCrae, R. R. & Costa, P. T. (2006). *Personality in Adulthood: A Five-factor Theory Perspective* (2nd ed.). New York: Guilford Press.

Menon, A. (2019). 'Beyond the Individual: Reframing Blame and Responsibility for "Rogue" Behaviour in the Financial Services Industry'. In A. Obholzer, & V. Z. Roberts (Eds.), *The Unconscious at Work* (pp. 229–40). Abingdon: Routledge.

Rawnsley, J. H. (1995). *Going for Broke: Nick Leeson and the Collapse of Barings Bank*. London: Harper Collins.

Robertson, J. (2016). 'How the Big Bang Changed the City of London For Ever'. *BBC*, 26 October. Retrieved from: https://www.bbc.co.uk/news/business-37751599.

Solzhenitsyn, A. I. (2003). *The Gulag Archipelago, 1918–56: An Experiment in Literary Investigation*. New York: Random House.

Stein, M. (2011). 'A Culture of Mania: A Psychoanalytic View of the Incubation of the 2008 Credit Crisis'. *Organization*, 18(2), 173–86.

7 The Saboteur in the Team

On 25th April 1986, engineers at Unit 4 of the Chernobyl nuclear power station in Ukraine were feeling anxious. They were preparing to shut down the reactor to test how long the turbines would continue to supply power to the main cooling pump in the event of an unplanned power failure.

The engineers had very good reason to be anxious, because this procedure always made the reactor dangerously unstable. The automatic shutdown safety mechanisms had been deliberately disabled so as not to interfere with the test. Although the engineers on duty were worried about how safe the test procedure was, Anatoly Dyatlov, deputy chief engineer, who was supervising the test, threatened to fire those engineers who refused to proceed. This was a culture that did not encourage independent thought or challenging authority.

As the reactor began to shut down, its energy output soared, and:

> runaway heat and pressure deep inside the core ruptured fuel channels, then water pipes, causing the pumps' automatic safety valves to close. This stopped the flow of coolant, increasing the rate at which steam was forming because of the diminishing water supply. The reactor's own safety valves attempted to vent the steam but the pressure was too great and they too ruptured.
>
> (Leatherbarrow, 2016)

This caused two explosions, and 50 tons of vaporised nuclear fuel was spewed into the sky, in a column that could be seen for miles. This poisonous cloud of highly toxic nuclear material was carried away in the wind and eventually spread across most of northern Europe. The explosion also dumped about 700 tons of nuclear-contaminated graphite on the city of Chernobyl and its surrounding area. It was a truly horrific accident.

Sasha Yuvchenko, a young engineer at the plant at the time, described the horror of the explosion:

> There was a heavy thud… a couple of seconds later, I felt a wave come through the room. The thick concrete walls were bent like

DOI: 10.4324/9781003188063-8

rubber. I thought war had broken out. We started to look for Khodenchuk, but he had been by the pumps and had been vaporised. Steam wrapped around everything; it was dark and there was a horrible hissing noise. There was no ceiling, only sky; a sky full of stars.

(Ibid.)

'Half the building had gone', Yuvchenko found when he went outside. 'There was nothing we could do', he said (Ibid.)

Thirty people, including six firefighters, died as a direct result of the explosion and consequent radiation sickness. A further 60 people died over the coming years from cancer caused by radiation. The World Health Organization (WHO) estimated that the total number of long-term deaths resulting from Chernobyl will be around 4,000 (WHO, 2006). As well as the fatalities, more than 300,000 people from the area surrounding Chernobyl experienced the upheaval and psychological trauma of being relocated and resettled.

Chernobyl was a disaster waiting to happen. Many at Chernobyl knew this, but few said anything. Those who did were ignored or silenced. Earlier accidents, one at a similar nuclear plant in Leningrad and another at Chernobyl itself, had revealed weaknesses in the reactor design and operation procedures. However, the potential lessons from these accidents were largely covered up or ignored, so as not to upset those higher up in the Soviet pecking order. Engineers at Chernobyl weren't even aware of the seriousness let alone causes of the Leningrad accident.

Those working in the Soviet nuclear industry were not empowered to speak up when they saw that something had the potential to go wrong. The global disaster that was Chernobyl was caused by frightened individuals caught up in a group dynamic of denying and avoiding reality and keeping their head down for fear of punishment. Of course, this reflected the experience of most other Soviet citizens at the time.

The Chernobyl catastrophe is a tragic real-life case study of the psychology of unconscious group dynamics and how these can affect decisions and behaviour in a positive or negative direction. The saboteur exists in groups as well as in individuals. A group is always more than the sum of the individuals who make up the group. Groups can unleash the potential for great creativity or great destructiveness. People behave differently in a large group compared with when they are alone. Groups generate conformity.

Confirmation bias flourishes in groups. Consequently, groups make more extreme decisions than individuals. The self-doubt, fearfulness and caution that we all experience is dissolved by the experience of being in a group, just as effectively as it is dissolved by alcohol.

The disaster at the Chernobyl nuclear power station is a powerful example of how the unconscious saboteur manifests at different levels in a system. It is present in individual human beings, in groups and teams, in organisations and in whole social systems. Many individual managers and engineers at Chernobyl were well aware of the potential for disaster but said nothing and hoped for the best. This culture of keeping your head down and not causing a fuss was strongly reinforced by the group culture, where speaking out would always end badly for the one blowing the whistle.

Box 7.1: Deviating from normal behaviour in a group

The group culture at Chernobyl was a reflection of the wider political and social culture of the Soviet Union. This culture of never being the one to stand out, speak out or be different from the crowd is chillingly described by Alexander Solzhenitsyn. He tells a darkly comic story in his famous and profound book *The Gulag Archipelago*. Solzhenitsyn describes a local communist party conference in Moscow. The conference is being chaired by a new secretary replacing the previous one who had been arrested in the purges. At the conclusion of the conference, the traditional tribute to Josef Stalin was proposed. Everyone leapt to their feet and began to applaud. The small conference hall was filled with the sound of rapturous applause. The ovation went on, and on; for three minutes, four minutes, five minutes. Hands were sore and arms began to ache, but no one dared be the first to stop clapping. Older party members began panting and slowed from exhaustion, but none would stop. I'll let Solzhenitsyn carry on and finish the story:

'And in that obscure, small hall, unknown to the Leader, the applause went on – six, seven, eight minutes! They were done for! Their goose was cooked! They couldn't stop now till they collapsed with heart attacks! At the rear of the hall, which was crowded, they could of course cheat a bit, clap less frequently, less vigorously, not so eagerly – but up there with the presidium where everyone could see them?

The director of the local paper factory, an independent and strong-minded man, stood with the presidium. Aware of all the falsity and all the impossibility of the situation, he still kept on applauding! Nine minutes! Ten! In anguish he watched the secretary of the District Party Committee, but the latter dared not stop. Insanity! To the last man! With make-believe enthusiasm on their faces, looking at each other with faint hope, the district leaders were just going to go on and on applauding till they fell where they stood, till they were carried out of the hall on stretchers! And even then those who were left would not falter...

Then, after eleven minutes, the director of the paper factory assumed a businesslike expression and sat down in his seat. And, oh, a miracle took place! Where had the universal, uninhibited, indescribable enthusiasm gone? To a man, everyone else stopped dead and sat down. They had been saved! The squirrel had been smart enough to jump off his revolving wheel.

That, however, was how they discovered who the independent people were. And that was how they went about eliminating them. That same night the factory director was arrested. They easily pasted ten years on him on the pretext of something quite different. But after he had signed Form 206, the final document of the interrogation, his interrogator reminded him: 'Don't ever be the first to stop applauding!'

(Solzhenitsyn, 2003)

These are terrifying examples of how being in a group changes normal behaviour. Speaking out at Chernobyl, raising concerns, would have been a bit like being the first to stop applauding Comrade Stalin at the party conference. If you were to behave differently than the crowd, then you would be 'punished' in one way or another.

However, human beings tend to conform to group pressure and to authority even in situations where there is no obvious political repression. Our tendency to obey those in authority and conform to the behaviour of the group that we are a part of is deeply ingrained and unconscious.

So how exactly does being in a group influence individual behaviour?

The Asch conformity study

Imagine for a moment you are a psychology student in 1950s America. You are asked to take part in an experiment on human vision. You agree and eventually find yourself sitting in a classroom with nine other participants. The experimenter shows you a piece of paper with several lines on it. Your task is simple: look at a comparison line on the left and then look at three other lines, labelled A, B and C, all of which are different lengths, and say which of those are the same length as the comparison line. It looks easy – it's obviously line B.

The experimenter then goes around the group asking which of the three lines is the same length as the comparison line and, as expected, everybody answers B.

This is repeated a couple of times with different pieces of paper. But on the third time around, something weird happens. The obvious answer is line C, but as the experimenter goes around asking people for their answer, everybody responds with B. That's just ridiculous; line B is much shorter than the comparison line – it's obvious. Then the experimenter comes to you and asks which line is the same length as a comparison line. What would you answer? By this time, eight other people have answered B. What do you say? Do you stick to your guns and say C, or do you begin to doubt yourself? In the end, you think, 'Well, eight people think the right answer is B. They can't all be wrong'. So you answer B.

If that had been you, back in the 1950s, you would have been taking part in one of Solomon Asch's now famous social psychology experiments on group conformity. Asch was interested in the power of groups to disable independent thought. He'd observed that people would often suppress their true opinion or feelings about the topic being discussed just in order to fit in with everybody else in a group. Asch came up with the 'vision test' to investigate this phenomenon. What you wouldn't have known had you been a student in the experiment was that all the other 'participants' in the room were actually colleagues of Asch who had been briefed to answer the questions in a particular way. They were told to answer correctly for a number of trials, but on the third trial give the same *incorrect* answer. The only person being experimented on was you! Asch wasn't interested in 'human vision', he was interested in whether you would go as far as to deny the evidence of your own senses in order to conform with the group. His results were surprising and fascinating. He found that about three quarters of all the participants chose to conform with the group rather than give the correct answer (Asch, 1956).

It's worth taking a moment to reflect on this. Three quarters of the people would rather deny the evidence of their own senses and consciously say something that they knew to be incorrect in order to fit in with a group. It's also interesting that the group that they wanted to fit in with was a group of strangers – people they would never see again and who probably meant very little to them. The desire to conform is so powerful, then, that you'll even do so with people you will never see again. The American psychotherapist Rollo May once said that the opposite of courage is not cowardice; it's conformity (May, 1953).

Just imagine how much more powerful this effect is if you are in a group of people who *are* important to you. A group of friends and colleagues whom you like and respect, or people who have power over your life in some way – who might decide whether you get a promotion, for example. Or a group you desperately want to be part of, like C. S. Lewis's *inner ring* (see Chapter 6).

We like to think of ourselves as autonomous individuals who make free choices, but we all greatly underestimate how much we are influenced and how much our decisions are constrained by the social context that surrounds us.

Obedience to authority: Stanley Milgram's electric-shock experiments

In the early 1960s, the atrocities of the Nazis were still fresh in people's minds. It troubled people, especially psychologists, how ordinary people, who made up the bulk of the German Armed Forces during World War II, could commit such atrocities. A young psychologist at Yale University named Stanley Milgram was particularly taken up with this question. In 1969, he wrote that 'the inhumane policies [of Nazi Germany] may have originated in the mind of a single person, but they could only have been carried out on a massive scale if a very large number of people obeyed orders' (Milgram, 1969). This idea led Milgram and his colleagues to develop what has become one of the most famous – and, frankly, chilling – experiments in the history of social psychology.

The standard defence of those who perpetrated the Holocaust and the many other Nazi atrocities was variations of the phrase, 'I was only obeying orders'. The political scientist Hannah Arendt reported on the trial of Adolf Eichmann in Jerusalem (Arendt, 1963). She expected Eichmann to be a monster, but instead concluded that he was a dull bureaucrat. This led her to coin her famous phrase, 'the banality of evil'. 'The trouble with Eichmann', she wrote, 'was precisely that so many were like him' (Ibid.).

Milgram was fascinated by what had happened during the war and wondered what factors cause people to either comply with or resist authority, particularly when the person is asked or told to do something that would ordinarily be morally repugnant.

Milgram came up with an ingenious idea to answer this question. He placed an ad in local papers inviting people to volunteer to take part in a psychology experiment on the effects of punishment on learning. All the people who applied were subjected to a battery of psychological tests to ensure that they were 'normal', emotionally stable individuals – in other words, average members of the general population.

At the start of the experiment, the participants were asked to play the role of teacher in the experiment on learning. The 'learner' was in fact a colleague of the experimenters, although the teacher did not know this. The teacher was told that the learner would be hooked up to an electric-shock generator that gave shocks increasing in small increments ranging from mild, through moderate, to severe. The teacher was instructed that each time a learner gave an incorrect response to their question, they had to give the learner an electric shock, then increase the severity of the shock by one level for the next incorrect answer. The fake shock-generator machine was labelled '15 volts: slight shock' for the lowest shock and '450 volts: danger – severe shock' for the highest.

The teacher was given a sample shock of 45 volts, which hurt – but not too much – so they knew (or thought they knew) what the learner was experiencing. Of course, the experiment was rigged and the learner did not receive any shocks at all. The teacher was told that participation in the experiment was entirely voluntary and they could withdraw at any time.

Two rooms were used, one for the learner and another for the teacher and experimenter with the fake electric-shock generator. The learner was strapped to an electric chair with electrodes and given a list of paired words and asked to learn them. After this, the teacher was told to test the learner by reading out one of the words in each pair and asking the learner to recall the matching word.

The learner responded with mainly incorrect answers, or sometimes silence, and when this happened, the teacher would give them increasingly severe electric shocks, moving up in 15-volt increments. The learner was instructed to grunt in pain at 75 volts; protest and loudly complain at 120 volts; ask to leave the experiment at 150 volts; protest and then plead to be released at 220 volts; and eventually, when the shocks reached 285 volts, scream in agony and complain of chest pain. At this, some teachers began to show signs of stress, including sweating, crying and nervous laughter.

Finally, at 330 volts, the learner fell totally silent, but the teacher was asked to continue administering potentially lethal electric shocks to this silent (presumably unconscious or dead) learner.

Let's pause for a moment while you consider some questions. How many people in the experiment would you expect to obey the bland command, 'The experiment requires that you continue...'? What do you imagine you would do if you believed you were administering a potentially lethal electric shock to another person who was begging you not to? Would you carry on administering electric shocks to a person who wasn't responding? No? Well, think again, because according to Milgram's results, you probably would.

Twenty-six of the 40 subjects (65 per cent) obeyed the experimenter right to the end and administered shocks of 450 volts to the learner, who by that point was unresponsive (remember: 450 volts was labelled 'danger – severe shock'). The remaining 14 subjects (35 per cent) only refused to continue when the shocks reached 330 volts, which was when the learner fell silent after previously screaming in agony and complaining of chest pain (Milgram, 1963).

You might say, 'Yes, well, okay, but that was the 1960s. People wouldn't behave like that now, would they?' Well, the answer is that they probably would. In 2007, Jerry Burger, a psychologist at the University of Santa Clara, set out to answer this question by replicating, as best he could, the Milgram experiments. Of course, university ethics committees are considerably stricter than they were in the 1960s, and so some aspects of Milgram's original experiment design had to be toned down. Nevertheless, Burger concluded that people today – his experimental subjects – obeyed the experimenter at about the same rate as Milgram's subjects did back in the early 1960s (Burger, 2007).

Solomon Asch's experiment showed how people conform to group pressure. Stanley Milgram significantly built on this finding by demonstrating how people also conform to pressure from authority. In addition, he raised the bar, because the results of this conformity were not trivial (as in determining the length of the line) but were very profound in that it involved what amounted to torture.

Milgram's work replicated the horrors of the Holocaust by showing that ordinary people – people like you and me – can be persuaded to torture and even kill for the flimsiest of reasons (experimental learning) when told to do so by someone with minimal authority. Those who perpetrate atrocities are not monsters, they are people like us (Goldhagan, 1996).

Here again we see the saboteur at work: the dark, unconscious parts of ourselves that have the capacity to be destructive. What terrible things might happen if group conformity and obedience to authority were combined and our unconscious saboteur was given free rein? The psychologist Philip Zimbardo was to find out when he built a pretend prison at Stanford University in the US.

The Stanford Prison experiment

Have you seen the film *The Green Mile*, which tells the story of a death row prison guard during the Great Depression? One of the characters in this film is a sadistic guard called Percy Wetmore who takes great pleasure in making the prisoners' lives miserable. Imagine for a moment you were a guard in an American prison. How do you think you'd behave? I'm guessing you think that you'd be a kind and fair prison guard. Well, very possibly not. The research I'm about to describe suggests that even with all your education, good intentions and general stability, you could still end up behaving like Percy Wetmore.

Palo Alto, California, is a quiet, middle-class, academic city in the San Francisco Bay Area of California. The city is the home of Stanford University, one of the most prestigious Ivy League universities in the USA.

On Sunday 14th August 1971, residents of this quiet city were woken up by the sound of police sirens. This was unusual in Palo Alto, which was neither New York City nor the 'Streets of San Francisco'. The residents witnessed the mass arrest of nine Stanford students. Police officers banged on doors and young men were dragged out of middle-class homes and bundled into black-and-white squad cars. They were driven to Palo Alto police station, where they were fingerprinted and charged. The suspects were blindfolded before being taken to prison.

The arrests were nothing to do with the current protests against the Vietnam War, the emerging Black Panther movement or the militant women's liberation movement. This idea led Milgram and his colleagues to develop what has become one of the most famous – and, frankly, chilling – experiments in the history of social psychology.

At the prison, which had been built in the basement of the psychology department of Stanford University, the 'prisoners' met their 'guards'. The 'prisoners' and 'guards' were drawn from a group of volunteers who'd applied to take part in a social psychology study on the effects of prison life. Earlier that month, they had answered this advert, placed in local newspapers: 'Male college students needed for psychological study of prison life. $15 per day for one–two weeks, beginning August 14. For further information and applications come to room 248 Jordan Hall, Stanford University' (Haney et al., 1973).

Seventy-five young men applied to take part in the study – after all, the money was good; the equivalent of about 100 dollars a day in 2021 money. The applicants were screened for psychological stability. Twenty-four made it through the screening and were selected to participate in the study. All were psychologically robust, emotionally stable, physically fit young men who reported happy, stable backgrounds with no history of law breaking. All were nice young men, or so you might think. Each of the participants was then randomly assigned to play the role of either a guard or a prisoner during the experiment.

Students assigned the role of guard were kitted out with a khaki paramilitary uniform including a nightstick (a truncheon, which the experimenters had to borrow from the police department), a whistle and large mirrored '*Easy Rider*' sunglasses, which prevented eye contact with the prisoners. The uniforms were designed to strip as much individuality from the guards as possible. The experimenters gave them some basic training, telling the guards that their job was to maintain order as best they could without inflicting violence on the prisoners or withholding food or drink.

The following day, the prisoners were 'arrested' by the ever-helpful Palo Alto Police. They were charged with 'armed robbery' and taken to the pretend prison at Stanford University. On arrival, the prisoners were stripped naked, de-loused and issued with a prison uniform: a smock with no underwear and a tight nylon cap to hide their hair. The uniform had a large number on it and they were instructed to only refer to themselves by this prison number and not their name. Finally, a chain was attached to the ankle of each prisoner to allow them to be restrained and to act as a constant physical reminder of the oppressiveness of their environment.

As the first day of the experiment wore on, both prisoners and guards settled into their roles. Then, something strange began to happen. Some of the guards began to behave in a mildly sadistic fashion. They started to harass the prisoners.

On the first night, the prisoners were woken up at half past two in the morning by the guards blowing whistles. The guards working the night shift wanted to count the prisoners to 'make sure no one had escaped'. This was the first example of the descent into cruelty and sadism of many of the guards. They seemed compelled to exercise their authority even when there was no real need to do so.

This emerging culture of cruelty also began to affect the prisoners. Their heads dropped and they eased into a passive and submissive manner. Not all, though: some rebelled, refusing to obey the guards' instructions and to leave their cells to be counted. In response to this rebellious behaviour, the guards sprayed them with fire extinguishers. They also strip-searched the rebels and removed their clothes and mattresses from the cells. The ringleader was sent to solitary confinement ('the hole'). The guards divided the 'good' prisoners from the 'bad' prisoners and rewarded the good prisoners and punished the bad. Some of the punishments included preventing the bad prisoners from using the toilet, instead ordering them to use a bucket in their cell.

Things went from bad to worse. The guards began taunting the prisoners with insults and imposing arbitrary punishments like demanding that they do push-ups. One of the guards would step on the prisoners' backs while they were doing these push-ups. Most of the prisoners became even more passive and dependent on the guards. Some began to experience mental health problems. Some were observed sobbing and screaming in their cells. One prisoner in particular suffered very badly. As the prisoners became increasingly passive, the guards' brutality and sadism escalated.

Just pause for a moment and reflect that these were normal, average, well-educated, middle-class college boys a few days into a psychology experiment. Zimbardo had planned for the experiment to run for two weeks, but he had to end it on the sixth day, so dramatic was the impact on the participants' personalities, mental well-being and behaviour.

The Stanford Prison Experiment demonstrated very dramatically how our behaviour is influenced far more than we suspect by the social setting in which we exist. It showed that we all have the capacity to become passive slaves or sadistic, cruel tyrants given the right circumstances. A corrupting environment can very quickly turn us – you and me – into people capable of evil.

After the experiment had ended, Zimbardo interviewed the participants. Here's what one 'guard' said:

> I was surprised at myself. I made them call each other names and clean the toilets out with their bare hands. I practically considered the prisoners cattle and I kept thinking I had to watch out for them in case they tried something.
>
> (Zimbardo, 1973)

Summing up the study, Zimbardo wrote:

> When we began our experiment, we had a sample of individuals who did not deviate from the normal range of the general educated population on any of the dimensions we had pre-measured. Those randomly assigned to the role of 'prisoner' were interchangeable with those in the 'guard' role. Neither group had any history of crime, emotional or physical disability, or even intellectual or social disadvantage that might typically differentiate prisoners from guards and prisoners from the rest of society... At the start of this experiment, there were no differences between the two groups; less than a week later, there were no similarities between them. It is reasonable, therefore, to conclude that the pathologies were elicited by the set of situational forces constantly impinging upon them in this prison-like setting... Neither the guards nor the prisoners could be considered 'bad apples' prior to the time when they were so powerfully impacted by being embedded in a 'bad barrel.' The complex features within that barrel constitute the situational forces in operation in this behavioural context – the roles, rules, norms, anonymity of person in place, dehumanising processes, conformity pressures, group identity and more.
>
> (Zimbardo, 2007)

There have been criticisms of the Stanford Prison Experiment for both ethical and methodological flaws (for example, Le Texier, 2019). However, the consensus is that although far from perfect, the experiment provides solid evidence of how powerful social contexts and social forces compel human behaviour.

Abu Ghraib

In late 2004, horrific photographs of US soldiers torturing and abusing Iraqi prisoners at Abu Ghraib prison in Iraq began to appear in the world's media. The pictures showed naked, hooded prisoners smeared in faeces watched over by armed guards who were grinning and giving the thumbs-up gesture. Other photographs showed naked prisoners crawling on all fours on leashes and having guns pointed at their genitals by grinning guards. One showed a fresh-faced female soldier standing over the dead body of a prisoner, she too with a big smile and a thumbs-up. The most horrifyingly memorable image was of a prisoner wearing a black hood and standing on a box, with electrodes on his fingertips and his arms stretched out in a Christ-like pose. The pictures looked like scenes from a particularly nasty horror movie. They combined terror, torture, filth and evident pleasure on the faces of the soldiers perpetuating the abuse. These were trophy photos taken by the soldiers at the time, who were presumably proud of their actions.

Thirty years on, the social, group and psychological processes uncovered by Philip Zimbardo in the Stanford Prison Experiment were replicated in real life at Abu Ghraib. This wasn't an experiment, though: it was real. Real people were tortured, raped and abused; at least one prisoner lost his life. Unlike in the Stanford Prison Experiment, the prisoner abuse at Abu Ghraib wasn't ended after six days but continued, and the horror escalated as the guards became more and more desensitised.

The parallels between the Stanford Prison Experiment and Abu Ghraib are striking. The 'guards' at Stanford and the guards at Abu Ghraib weren't monsters but normal, average people. For example, Ivan 'Chip' Frederick was the reservist sergeant who came up with the idea to stand the man on a box with electrodes attached to his fingers. Philip Zimbardo wrote: 'He put electrodes on his fingers, he put him on a box, and said, "You get tired, you fall off, you get electrocuted." Imagine the terror?' (Zimbardo, 2007) Just like the students in the Stanford Prison Experiment and the participants in Milgram's electric-shock experiment, Chip Frederick was your typical, all-American boy with a distinguished military record and a normal, settled upbringing and family life. Yet he could do that to a fellow human being.

The US government and military sought to explain the horrors of Abu Ghraib as being the actions of a few 'bad apples'. In other words, a dispositional explanation. However, there is no evidence that the guards initially approached their mission with evil or sadistic intent. There was no evidence that they were psychopaths or sadists. Rather, it was the 'bad barrel' of the organisation and of the war that transformed previously good people into people who perpetrated evil.

Here is what Chip Frederick wrote to a relative, Mimi Frederick on 22 January 2004:

Dear Mimi,

I am feeling so bad at how the army has come down on me. They always said that shit rolls downhill and guess who is at the bottom? I have asked for help and warned of this and nobody would listen. I told the battalion commander that I didn't like the way it was going and his reply was 'Don't worry about it. I give you permission to do it'. I just wish I could talk to someone about what is going on but I was ordered not to talk to anyone besides my attorney and CID. As far as trusting someone, DON'T.

(*Guardian*, 2004)

Frederick received an eight-year custodial sentence for his actions at Abu Ghraib.

This systemic 'bad barrel' explanation does not absolve people of responsibility for bad behaviour. However, if we can begin to understand the systems that enable our unconscious capacity for evil, we can understand how to build systems that prevent or at least minimise the risk of abuses in the future. Individuals like Chip Frederick have, as we all do, an innate unconscious capacity for evil. This unconscious destructiveness also resides in the group dynamics and structures that oversee people like Chip Frederick. For all those involved in the horror and tragedy of Abu Ghraib, this was the culture and structures of the US military and the Bush administration, who turned a blind eye to and even implicitly encouraged the abuses at Abu Ghraib. The all-American boy Chip Frederick tortured people.

Winterbourne view

A woman with learning disabilities cowers on the floor, soaking wet, and a man throws a bucket of cold water over her and laughs. Another man slaps a young man with learning disabilities across the cheek, saying, 'Do you want a scrap? Do you want a fight? Go on and I will bite your bloody face off' (Hill, 2012). These incidents didn't take place at Abu Ghraib or as part of some gruesome 1970s social psychology experiment. No, they took place in 2011 at Winterbourne View, Gloucestershire, a residential care home for people with learning disabilities.

The abuse came to light as a result of an undercover BBC *Panorama* investigation. One of the nurses at the unit, Terry Bryan, repeatedly 'blew the whistle' on the abuse at Winterbourne View, but was ignored both by his employer and the Care Quality Commission, the organisation that regulated the home. Eventually, in desperation, he approached an investigative journalist at *Panorama*.

The *Panorama* documentary was screened in May 2011 and made for shocking viewing. Staff were shown slapping the vulnerable learning-disabled residents, soaking them in water, pinning them to the ground with chairs, taunting and swearing at them, pulling their hair and poking their eyes. The documentary led to a judicial review into Winterbourne View and its owner, Castlebeck Limited. It also resulted in the prosecution of 11 care workers who admitted 38 charges of neglect and ill-treatment. The abuse was that bad that six were given custodial sentences. Addressing one of the perpetrators, the trial judge said:

> I have read the pre-sentence report in which you say you were originally shocked by the ill-treatment of residents at the hospital but that you became desensitised to it over time. You consider that you were completely out of your depth. For a considerable time you minimised your responsibility for your conduct but now accept that your behaviour was wholly inappropriate… You suggested it was born of boredom during long shifts and that you had viewed patients as playthings.
>
> (Ibid.)

Just as at Stanford and Abu Ghraib, the events at Winterbourne View show the emergence of the saboteur in a group and organisation context.

Conclusion

I began this chapter with the story of the disaster at Chernobyl. However, I could have begun with lots of other examples – less serious examples – of how unconscious psychological processes influence group behaviour, resulting in catastrophe. These psychological processes were present in the Jimmy Savile and BBC child abuse scandal (see Chapter 1), the 2010 BP Deepwater Horizon oil spill in the Gulf of Mexico and the VW emissions scandal of 2015. A whole book could be written about the evil of the child sexual abuse perpetrated and covered up in the Roman Catholic Church.

These terrible events had one thing in common. While the wrongdoing (the evil, in the Jimmy Savile case) was being perpetrated, many people in the organisation, including leaders and senior managers, were aware of what was going on but decided to turn a blind eye. When some did raise concerns, as did Terry Bryan, the nurse at Winterbourne View, they were ignored or told to be quiet by people higher up in the pecking order.

In this chapter, I have reviewed psychological literature on obedience to authority and our innate predisposition to conform. This shows that when most people are told to do something by someone in authority, they will obey, even when they are told to do something wrong. Similarly, when put under pressure by their peers to do something wrong (or in the case of the Asch experiments, contradict the evidence of their own eyes), most people will conform. Remember, as Rollo May wrote: the opposite of courage in society is not cowardice; it is conformity (May, 1953). This is a profoundly true statement.

One of the biggest challenges for leaders today is how to create a culture where people feel safe to speak out when they see wrongdoing (or even evil) in the organisations in which they work. As we have seen, this is not an easy or straightforward task.

It's a task that needs to be addressed at the three levels: the person, the role and the system. In other words, we need to understand the unconscious psychological processes – the saboteur – which exist in all of us. That means really working to understand our own personal saboteur, to listen to the part of us that urges us to turn a blind eye when we see something that shouldn't be happening in a group, team or organisation that we are a part of. It means looking at the primary task of our organisation and not getting sidetracked. It means looking at the culture of our organisation and the external pressures on culture. There is an old Native American saying that goes something like this: 'If you don't hear the whispers, you will soon hear the screams'.

Like with anything, the best place to start in this process is with yourself. It's very easy to criticise people who are 'out there' without first looking at your own internal saboteur. Carl Jung wrote:

> The acceptance of oneself is the essence of the whole moral problem and the epitome of a whole outlook on life. That I feed the hungry, that I forgive an insult, that I love my enemy in the name of Christ – all these are undoubtedly great virtues. What I do unto the least of my brethren, that I do unto Christ. But what if I should discover that the least among them all, the poorest of all the beggars, the most impudent of all the offenders, the very enemy himself – that these are within me, and that I myself stand in need of the alms of my own kindness – that I myself am the enemy who must be loved – what then?
>
> (Jung, 1963)

Begin by recognising and understanding your own saboteur, your own vulnerability to turning a blind eye to evil. Jung called this your shadow. All of the 'actors' in the dramas of evil that I've described in this chapter were not, for the most part, evil people (with the exception of Jimmy Savile, who undoubtedly was). They were people who were caught up in a system that brought out and nurtured their potential for evil – their saboteur. To paraphrase Philip Zimbardo, they weren't 'bad apples', they were simply apples in a 'rotten barrel'. And like all apples, they had the potential to go bad.

Think about you and your organisation. Do people feel safe to speak up if they see wrongdoing? If not, why not?

Usually, if something does go wrong, then you and/or your organisation will be subjected to some form of investigation and scrutiny. When we think of scrutiny, we think of it as something being done to us by an external person or body. It happens when something has gone wrong – usually, badly wrong. Why not change your mindset a little and think about how you can scrutinise your organisation and yourself in a proactive way, in a preventative rather than reactive manner?

Chapter takeaways

- A group can sabotage just as much as an individual – and the consequences can be extremely damaging.
- Unconscious dynamics in a group affect decisions and behaviour. We all tend to conform to a group's culture and to authority, and this can lead us badly astray.
- Awareness of the saboteur is essential, at an individual, group and organisational level. Are you self-aware enough to ensure you're not turning a blind eye to wrongdoing in your team and organisation? Is your organisation a safe place where people can speak up? Are you doing all you can to recognise and disempower the saboteur *before* it can do damage?

References

Arendt, H. (1963 [1994]). *Eichmann in Jerusalem: A Report on the Banality of Evil*. Harmondsworth: Penguin Books.

Asch, S. E. (1956). 'Studies of Independence and Conformity: I. A Minority of One against a Unanimous Majority'. *Psychological Monographs: General and Applied*, 70(9), 1–70.

Burger, J. (2007). 'Replicating Milgram'. *Association for Psychological Science Observer*, 20(11), n.p. Retrieved from: https://www.psychologicalscience.org/observer/replicating-milgram

Guardian. (2004). 'I Asked for Help and Warned of This but Nobody Would Listen'. *Guardian*, 1 May. Retrieved from: http://www.theguardian.com/world/2004/may/01/iraq1.

Haney, C., Banks, W. C. & Zimbardo, P. G. (1973). 'Interpersonal Dynamics in a Simulated Prison'. *International Journal of Criminology and Penology*, 1, 69–97.

Hill, A. (2012). 'Winterbourne View Care Home Staff Jailed for Abusing Residents'. *Guardian*, 26 October. Retrieved from: http://www.theguardian.com/society/2012/oct/26/winterbourne-view-care-staff-jailed.

Jung, C. G. (1963). *Memories, Dreams, Reflections*. London: Vintage.

Leatherbarrow, A. (2016). *Chernobyl 01: 23:40: The Incredible True Story of the World's Worst Nuclear Disaster*. London: Andrew Leatherbarrow.

Le Texier, T. (2019). 'Debunking the Stanford Prison Experiment'. *American Psychologist*, 74(7), 823–39.

May, R. (1953). *Man's Search for Himself*. New York: W. W. Norton & Company.

Milgram, S. (1963). 'Behavioral Study of Obedience'. *Journal of Abnormal and Social Psychology*, 67(4), 371–8.

Milgram, S. (1969). *Obedience to Authority: An Experimental View*. New York: Harper and Row.

Solzhenitsyn, A. I. (2003). *The Gulag Archipelago, 1918–56: An Experiment in Literary Investigation*. New York: Random House.

World Health Organization. (2006). *Health Effects of the Chernobyl Accident and Special Health Care Programmes*. Report of the UN Chernobyl Forum Expert Group 'Health'. Geneva: World Health Organization.

Zimbardo, P. G (1973). 'The Mind Is a Formidable Jailer'. *New York Times*, 8 April. Retrieved from: https://www.nytimes.com/1973/04/08/archives/a-pirandellian-prison-the-mind-is-a-formidable-jailer.html.

Zimbardo, P. G. (2007). *The Lucifer Effect: Understanding How Good People Turn Evil*. London: Random House, p. 551.

8   Global Saboteurs: Self-Destructive Societies

In May 1944, Major Wilhelm Trapp found himself in Poland as the officer in charge of the Nazi's Reserve Police Battalion 101. He was a 53-year-old career police officer, tired of the war and looking forward to retirement. Trapp was a jovial and kindly man, well liked by his men, who had nicknamed him 'Papa Trapp'. In the early hours of 13th July 1942, he roused his men from their bunks in the old school that was their temporary home in the remote Polish village where they were billeted.

Theirs was a reserve battalion made up of middle-aged family men. Before the war, these men were the sort who had been greengrocers, factory workers and schoolteachers – ordinary men, not Nazi zealots. Most were new recruits with little or no military experience. They had arrived in Poland only three weeks earlier, and for many of them, this was their first trip abroad. Reserve Police Battalion 101 was a bit like a Nazi version of the TV show *Dad's Army*, with Major Trapp cast in the role of Captain Mainwaring.

After coffee and a quick breakfast, the men climbed into military trucks and drove for two hours to their destination, Jozefow, another small Polish village. It was dark and very quiet. The men climbed down from the trucks and assembled for a briefing by Major Trapp. As he began to speak, the men stared at him with an increasing sense of unease. Trapp was welling up with tears as he explained that the task they were required to carry out was terribly unpleasant and distasteful. Trapp said it wasn't to his liking, but he had been given strict orders from the highest authority.

Major Trapp explained that the village where they now stood was full of Jews, many of whom had been involved with the partisans. He then went on to tell his men what exactly their unpleasant and distasteful task was. The male Jews of working age were to be separated from their families and transported to a work camp. The remaining women, children and old people were to be executed – shot in the head.

Trapp then made an extraordinary offer. If any of the men felt unable or unwilling to do this, they could be excused by stepping forward. He assured them that there would be no recriminations and nobody

DOI: 10.4324/9781003188063-9

would think any less of them should they choose not to participate in the executions. A dozen did, but the rest – the former greengrocers, factory workers and schoolteachers – carried out their task efficiently, brutally and without complaint (Browning, 1998).

How is it possible that these previously normal, decent and respectable men behaved like monsters? How could a man who a few months previously had been a village postman willingly put a bullet through the head of a pregnant woman?

The actions and motivations of the men of Police Battalion 101 are described and analysed in Christopher Browning's book *Ordinary Men: Reserve Police Battalion 101 and the Final Solution in Poland* (Browning, 1998). Browning attributes their dramatically out-of-character behaviour to a mixture of comradeship, peer pressure and a perverted sense of honour. The ordinary men of Reserve Police Battalion 101 felt a strong sense of duty and a need to follow orders. They supported each other and knew that if they declined to carry out the murders, then one of their comrades would have to, and that would not be right or fair. The positive characteristics of comradeship, loyalty and self-sacrifice were perverted by the evil of the situation.

The electric shock experiments of Stanley Milgram and Philip Zimbardo's Stanford Prison Experiment, described in Chapter 7, go some way in answering the question of how good people can enact evil. In fact, it was the actions of people like Major Trapp's reserve police battalion that inspired (if that is the right word) their research in the first place. Another writer of the Holocaust, Hannah Arendt, said of Adolf Eichmann (the architect of the Final Solution), 'the problem with Eichmann was that there were so many others just like him' (Arendt, 1963). And this is precisely the point. Adolf Eichmann and Major Trapp and his men were all normal people, not monsters. Or rather, they all contained the potential to become monsters, and this was set free by the social and political situation in which they found themselves. They all embodied the saboteur.

The story of Police Battalion 101 is an example of how the saboteur tends to emerge in mass social and political movements – in this case, the ideology of Hitler's Third Reich determining the actions of individual, ordinary people. In this chapter, I will explore how the saboteur can grip not just individuals and groups but also entire nations and how the saboteur can shape large-scale social and political movements. Our subject will be a grim one: the role played by the saboteur in the rise of Hitler, the Third Reich and the Holocaust.

Why this chapter matters to *you*

You may be wondering: how is understanding the saboteur in society helpful?

First, it's important to remember that corporate cultures are not immune to the saboteur unleashed by social and political movements. As I explain later in this chapter, big companies actively participated in the movement that resulted in the Holocaust: Hugo Boss dressed the SS in their infamous black uniforms, Volkswagen used slave labour from the concentration camps for their wartime workforce, and IG Farben made Zyklon B, the poison gas used to murder an estimated one million Jews at Auschwitz and other death camps.

Second, knowing how the saboteur takes hold of social and political movements might just help you to understand and resist contemporary political movements that are socially destructive. For tyrannies to develop and prosper, they need millions of people to support or at the very least to collude with them.

For every SS trooper dropping the canisters of Zyklon B into the tubes in the roof of the gas chamber of Auschwitz, there were hundreds of workers at IG Farben manufacturing that murderous gas. Somebody had to make those well-tailored, iconic SS uniforms and death's head insignia, and that somebody was working for Hugo Boss. The historian James Holland convincingly argues that the role of the corporate world in producing the stuff needed to win wars (arms, uniforms, transport and so on) has been badly neglected in military history (Holland, 2015).

So far, we have seen how the saboteur can emerge in individuals and small groups. But what about large corporate organisations and even governments and the machinery of the state? It is easy to understand how unconscious forces – the saboteur – can take hold of individual people and small groups. But surely, you would think, very large organisations have structures in place to impose rationality and prevent or restrain the unconscious destructive influence of the saboteur? Surely big corporations and governments employ armies of managers and lawyers to oversee operations? In particular, lawyers are known for their risk aversion and ability to say no to anything that might make an organisation vulnerable to criticism and legal action. Well, even the most rational corporate lawyer possesses an unconscious saboteur which when put under stress will find a way to justify the unjustifiable.

Hitler's willing executioners

In his book *Hitler's Willing Executioners*, Daniel Goldhagen demonstrates how most ordinary German citizens were active participants in the events that culminated in the Holocaust (Goldhagen, 1996). He cites extensive testimony to show that ordinary Germans were not compelled to act as they did (they knew they could refuse without retribution), yet, with a few notable exceptions, they participated in the persecution, the rounding-up and ultimately the murder of Jews and other minority groups disliked by the Nazis, willingly and zealously. How can we even begin to understand this? A good start might be to consider how the group dynamics in mass movements create the conditions for the emergence of the saboteur in individuals. In the grip of mass social movements, people (you and I) are prone to behaving in ways that would, in normal circumstances, horrify us. It is also much easier to turn a blind eye to evil because everybody is turning a blind eye (remember the story of Kitty Genovese?).

Victims of their environment?

Imagine five friends, all in their early twenties, living in Berlin in the 1940s. The group are all young, middle class, well educated and likeable. And like most young people, they are wrapped up in their own lives and hopes for the future.

There is Viktor, who is Jewish, the son of a successful tailor; Greta, a self-centred cabaret singer; Charlotte, a serious and traditional German girl; and finally Wilhelm and his younger brother, Friedhelm. Wilhelm is a soldier in the German army, and Friedhelm has just been conscripted into the army.

These are the main characters in the 2013 German TV mini-series *Generation War*. (The original German title is *Unsere Mütter, Unsere Väter*, translated as *Our Mothers, Our Fathers*.) I can describe the historical research that illustrates how the saboteur can influence ordinarily decent people to behave like monsters, but *Generation War* brings this process to life very vividly in a realistic, moving and shocking drama.

The story begins in 1941 with the five friends meeting in a bar and vowing to meet up again at Christmas, believing the war will be over by then. The characters are all ordinary people at this point, but they end up as active participants in the brutality of the Nazis. The most striking transformation is in Friedhelm, the idealistic and artistic young man who towards the end of the war carries out brutal and sadistic atrocities against civilians.

The underlying assumption of *Generation War* is the same as that of Christopher Browning in his book on Police Battalion 101: that people who are basically decent can be corrupted when they are put in a corrupt and evil authoritarian environment. This assumption is also consistent with the social psychology research discussed in the previous chapter.

Is this assumption entirely accurate – or, to ask the question in a more nuanced way, does it tell the whole story? Does it account for all the factors that unleashed the evil buried in ordinarily decent people?

Anti-Semitism in Germany

Daniel Goldhagen argues that the nature and extent of the Holocaust cannot be explained by individual or group social psychological processes alone. In *Hitler's Willing Executioners*, he challenges the assumptions we make about the German people before and during the Second World War: that most German people were essentially victims of their environment, were not particularly anti-Semitic and were passive rather than active supporters of Hitler and the Nazis.

Goldhagen argues that when we try to understand the behaviour of the people in the past, we have a tendency to make two fundamental errors of thinking:

- We judge past belief systems based on our current way of seeing the world. To us, the beliefs people held many years ago can seem very odd, irrational and perhaps evil. But to those people at that time, their beliefs were entirely normal and self-evidently true.
- Some beliefs that seem bizarre or evil to us are held mainly by a few cranks or lunatics in our modern society, and thus we assume that the same was true in the past. But it may well not have been so.

Anti-Semitism is a belief that we find irrational and evil today. Thus, it's easy to think that German anti-Semitism was located in just a few Nazi zealots, and everybody else was a bit like us and viewed those with anti-Semitic beliefs as nasty, extreme and unhinged. We make the assumption that most average Germans couldn't possibly have shared Hitler's beliefs about Jewish people being less than human. German society in the 1930s consisted of mostly educated, decent – let's say – civilised people. Looking back, it seems utterly absurd that the majority of Germans could believe that Jews were parasitic, mal-evolent and devilishly cunning, a race apart that would eventually destroy German society. Yet they did.

The term 'anti-Semitism' had a different meaning and flavour in 1930s Germany than it has today. When we think of anti-Semitism, we might think of it as a crude stereotype of Jewish people being mean with money, having big noses and being a bit anxious and whiny (think of Woody Allen). According to Goldhagen, though, the Nazis and most of the German people didn't believe that the Jews were a bit of a joke. Their anti-Semitism cast the Jewish people as being the root cause of all evil and corruption in the world.

Goldhagen presents much historical evidence to show that for centuries German society had been rife with the most extreme anti-Semitism. One of the reasons that Hitler and his ideas were so popular was because they reflected the private beliefs of most German citizens at the time. According to Goldhagen, the majority of people in 1930s

Germany knew in their heart of hearts that Jewish people were bad, in the same way that today we know in our heart of hearts that stealing is bad or democracy is good. Anti-Semitism was a belief that was so ingrained, fundamental and obvious, it simply wasn't open for discussion or examination. Anti-Semitism had been a fundamental part of German society since the Middle Ages.

This strong political, social and, most importantly, cultural tendency to blame the Jews for all of the misfortunes of German society was greatly exacerbated by the hardships the German people experienced because of reparations following the First World War. A popular phrase at the time, usually muttered with a sigh and rolled eyes, was 'the Jews are our misfortune' (Goldhagen, 1998).

The National Socialist Party – a profoundly anti-Semitic institution built on a deep hatred of Jewish people – offered Germans a solution to the 'Jewish problem'. The Nazis advocated eliminationist anti-Semitism: the elimination of the Jews as a race from German society. This is horrifying to us – but that wasn't the case for most Germans.

According to Goldhagen, the German people who supported Hitler (the majority of German citizens) and eventually perpetrated the Holocaust were not robots, but thinking and feeling human beings who made what was for them, in that historical context, an entirely rational choice. Their choice was not strange or extreme to them; it was based on the deep-seated, culturally accepted belief held by most German people that Jews were malevolent. The same German people had a view about whether it was a good thing or a bad thing to exterminate Jews. Most felt that it was a good thing, and it was this strongly held belief that informed their willingness to act. Thus, Adolf Hitler simply put into action what many German citizens privately thought and felt. He embodied the anti-Semitic belief in men who marched through the streets wearing brown shirts and jack boots.

Meanwhile, alongside expressing extreme eliminationist anti-Semitic views, Hitler and the Nazis ruthlessly suppressed the expression of alternative opinions. Opinions weren't just dismissed; those who expressed such views were demonised. They weren't just seen as people who held different and opposing views; they were seen as being evil and worthy of being fired, beaten and sometimes murdered. This was the era of book burning. Anti-Nazi ideas and the people who held them weren't argued with – they were destroyed. One of those who spoke out was Dietrich Bonhoeffer.

Dietrich Bonhoeffer and the stupidity of crowds

If you glance up as you enter the west entrance of Westminster Abbey, you will see a statue of a German pastor and theologian called Dietrich Bonhoeffer. His statue is there because Bonhoeffer died a martyr to

Christianity when he was executed for speaking out against Hitler and the Nazis and taking part in the German resistance movement against the Nazis.

Bonhoeffer was arrested in April 1943 for helping Jews escape to Switzerland. Following his arrest, the Gestapo connected him with a group of high-ranking Nazi officers planning to assassinate Hitler. He was imprisoned, first in Berlin and eventually in Flossenburg concentration camp, where, three weeks before the end of the Second World War, he was executed by hanging (Metaxas, 2020).

Bonhoeffer famously wrote, 'If you board the wrong train, it is no use running along the corridor in the other direction' (Bonhoeffer et al., 2017). Unlike many German citizens, Bonhoeffer got off the train. In *Letters and Papers from Prison* (ibid.), a collection of his writing while he awaited execution, is an essay called 'On Stupidity' in which he writes:

> Upon closer observation, it becomes apparent that every strong upsurge of power in the public sphere, be it of a political or a religious nature, infects a large part of humankind with stupidity. … The power of the one needs the stupidity of the other.

By 'stupidity', he wasn't referring to people's intellectual capacity but rather *their capacity to think independently*. Bonhoeffer said that in the face of the overwhelming social forces associated with rising power, humans are deprived of their sense of themselves as separate from the group.

> The fact that the stupid person is often stubborn must not blind us to the fact that he is not independent. In conversation with him, one virtually feels that one is dealing not at all with a person, but with slogans, catchwords and the like that have taken possession of him. He is under a spell, blinded, misused, and abused in his very being. Having thus become a mindless tool, the stupid person will also be capable of any evil and at the same time incapable of seeing that it is evil. This is where the danger of diabolical misuse lurks, for it is this that can once and for all destroy human beings.

From his prison cell in 1940s Germany – well before the social psychology research of the 1960s and 1970s – Dietrich Bonhoeffer identified the power that authority and being part of a group exerts over people's ability to think clearly and act ethically. He added that this effect was intensified by overwhelming social forces. In other words, it wasn't just internal psychological characteristics that resulted in people enacting evil; it was external social, political and economic forces.

What Dietrich Bonhoeffer called 'stupidity' is caused by the saboteur. The saboteur has the power to, as Dietrich Bonhoeffer put it, take possession of the mind and put it under a spell where the person turns a blind eye to objective reality. This is what happened to the participants in the social psychology experiments, the soldiers at Abu Ghraib and the care workers at Winterbourne View (see Chapter 7). The saboteur took possession of their minds and in doing so anaesthetises the parts that realised their behaviour was wrong. They became less than their normal selves.

The business of supporting the Nazis

Just as normal, respectable, kind people can behave like monsters when in the grip of the saboteur, normal, respectable, kind businesses can also perpetrate evil. The saboteur hides evil behind the screen of the desire for profit and shareholder returns. Leaders know what they are doing but don't look too closely at the second-order consequences of their corporate behaviour, as you will see. IBM produces card index systems, but is not interested in the information to be put on those cards. Ford builds trucks but is not interested in who will drive their truck and what cargo they carry.

All of the many ordinary people who were enthusiastic supporters of the Nazis had to eat, pay bills and occasionally go to the cinema to watch Leni Riefenstahl films. They needed to earn a living – they needed jobs. Most would have been in day jobs, like the elderly police reservists described earlier. Many, however, would have been in professional, management and leadership roles. Their beliefs and their saboteur would have found expression and guided the business decisions they made.

Most German businesses enthusiastically supported Hitler's policies and discriminated against, fired and prosecuted their Jewish workforce. (I say 'most', because there were some honourable exceptions. The most famous of these was probably Oskar Schindler, immortalised in Steven Spielberg's magnificent film *Schindler's List*.) From the perspective of German business leaders, it made sense to support Hitler and the Nazis in the Germany of the 1930s. After all, why not? They were making good money, and supporting the chancellor, Adolf Hitler, wasn't a crime, was it?

How German business bailed out the Nazis

In 1932, the Nazi Party was practically bankrupt. At the time, Joseph Goebbels wrote, 'We are all very discouraged, particularly in the face of the present danger that the entire party may collapse... The financial situation of the Berlin organisation is hopeless. Nothing but debts and obligations' (Manchester, 2003). Hitler's dream (and humanity's nightmare) very nearly died in infancy.

So how did the Nazis move from being almost broke to governing Germany less than a year later? They managed this feat because they were bailed out and then financed by German big business.

In late 1932, Hermann Goering made contact with 25 of Germany's wealthiest and most powerful industrialists. He invited them to a confidential meeting with Hitler and the top brass of the Nazi party to discuss areas of mutual interest. The meeting took place in Berlin on 20th February 1933. Four directors of the enormous pharmaceutical company IG Farben attended, but the star guest was Gustav Krupp, CEO of the monolithic German arms manufacturer that bore his name.

Hitler spoke first and mesmerised the group with his passion, his oratory skills and what he had to say. He told the group that democracy wasn't any good for private enterprise and promised them that when he gained power the first thing he would do was get rid of the trade unions and communists. This was music to their ears. Hitler concluded by asking these uber-wealthy businessmen to support him politically and, most important of all, financially. These early leaders of corporate Germany were so enthusiastic that they raised three million Reichsmarks – over £20 million in today's money – for Hitler and the Nazi party (Manchester, 2003).

We can only speculate about the direction world history might have taken if these huge corporations hadn't bailed Hitler out. Nevertheless, they did, and their investment, at least in the short term, turned out to be very lucrative. Krupp made millions arming the German military. IG Farben made similar profits supplying the Third Reich with everything from aspirin to the infamous Zyklon B poisonous gas that was released into the fake shower blocks at Auschwitz.

And with the rise of the Nazis came growth for other big businesses too.

Hugo Boss and SS uniforms

When I was a child watching war films, I remember having a grudging respect for how well dressed the German villains were. Those smart, well-cut uniforms with their death's head and lightning insignia looked so much more stylish than the baggy, crumpled olive-green uniforms favoured by the British.

Those smart and stylish black SS uniforms were manufactured by none other than Hugo Boss. As well as owning the eponymous high-end clothing company, Hugo Boss was a committed member of the Nazi party, having joined in the early days of 1931. He quickly became a sponsoring member of the elite Schutzstaffel (German: 'Protective Echelon'), better known as the SS. Like many businesses at the time, Hugo Boss was struggling financially. However, by the end of 1932, Hugo Boss was manufacturing those all-black SS uniforms and doing very well financially. The business's profits increased as the Third Reich expanded, and during the war, its profits really took off because it began using slave labour – conditions at the Hugo Boss factory were grim (BBC News, 2011).

The Ford Motor Company and Nazi vehicles

These smartly dressed Nazis needed transport. You won't be surprised to learn that many of the Third Reich's cars and trucks were built by VW and Mercedes. However, it may surprise you to learn that a third of all the vehicles used by the Wehrmacht (the German army) were actually built by the Ford Motor Company.

Ford made huge profits by producing military transport for the Third Reich. Robert Hans Schmidt, the head of Ford Werke, Ford's German subsidiary, was an enthusiastic Nazi, and Ford's production for the Third Reich was done with the knowledge and support of the company's US executive team (Billstein et al., 2000). Ford's cooperation with the Nazis continued for a full eight months after the US had declared war on Nazi Germany following Pearl Harbour.

Ford's eponymous founder, Henry Ford, was a committed anti-Semite. In the early 1920s, he had published a pamphlet entitled 'The International Jew: The World's Foremost Problem', which Hitler commented on. In *Mein Kampf*, Hitler sang the praises of Ford. In 1938, Henry Ford accepted the Grand Cross of the German Eagle, the Nazi regime's highest honour for foreigners.

The Ford Werke operation contributed enormously to the Nazi war effort, and to the profits of the Ford Motor Company. Between 1938 and 1943, revenue went through the roof and the value of the Ford Werke more than doubled. Ford made millions by actively helping Hitler prepare for and then wage war. By 1942, three years into the war, Ford Werke had manufactured more than one-third of the 350,000 cars and trucks used by the German military (Billstein et al., 2000).

IBM and the Holocaust

One of the many terrible images that emerged from the Holocaust is the concentration camp tattoo: the five-digit number tattooed on the arm of those entering Hitler's death camps. Have you ever wondered what that sinister number was for? It was an IBM Hollerith prisoner identification number, and it was used to keep track of the personal characteristics, whereabouts and skills of the slave labourers in the concentration camp system. Each number corresponded to an IBM Hollerith punch card containing information about the prisoner.

The Hollerith punch card system was invented in the late 19th century by an American, Herman Hollerith. It was an early version of a computer and became one of IBM's most successful products. In its day, the Hollerith machine represented the most advanced information technology system available, and IBM (to be clear, a US company) made this technology available to the Nazis from the beginning to the end of the Third Reich.

Edwin Black, who wrote the history of IBM's involvement with the Nazis, described the concentration camp number as 'a nineteenth-century bar code for human beings' (Black, 2012). If you were tattooed when you arrived at a camp, you were one of the lucky ones, because not to be tattooed meant you were to be sent straight to the gas chambers.

The IBM Hollerith system gave the Nazis the logistical capability to facilitate the Holocaust. Hollerith cards made it easier and more efficient to steal people's money and possessions (the card contained bank account numbers), organise deportations (matching people to train departures) and manage slave labour requirements (matching people's skills/profession with labour demand). Ultimately, the cards kept track of the efficiency of the extermination process.

This horrific business took place with the knowledge of the leaders of IBM in the US:

> executives at the firm's New York headquarters directly controlled a Polish subsidiary which leased punch-card machines used to 'calculate exactly how many Jews should be emptied out of the ghettos each day' and to transport them efficiently on railways leading to the camps.
>
> (Burkeman, 2002)

Just like Ford, IBM made a great deal of money working with the Nazis in wartime Europe. IBM was one of the very few US companies to expand during the Great Depression (1929–41), and the decade between 1933 and 1945 was IBM's most profitable ever, largely because of its German operation.

Mass suicides following Germany's defeat

Let's think for a moment about all of the hundreds of thousands of ordinary German citizens working for companies such as the ones described in the preceding sections – doing ordinary jobs and believing that they were contributing to the war effort, which in their minds was contributing to the greater good. They believed in Hitler, they believed that the Nazis were a positive force in Germany, and they believed in their heart of hearts that they were doing the right thing.

What happens to these people when they realise that they have been taken in? When they realise that, in the words of Dietrich Bonhoeffer, an alien force had taken over their minds and sabotaged their ability to think critically and see reality objectively? What happens to them when they understand that an unconscious part of the mind – the saboteur – has been driving their behaviour? What happens to people who thought that they had been following God when all the time they had been following Satan?

Well, many of them took their own life. In the final weeks of the Second World War, thousands of ordinary Germans died in a wave of mass suicides that swept the country.

One such ordinary German was Paul Kittel, a 46-year-old clerk who lived with his wife and two teenage children in the small town of Malchin, just north of Berlin. On 1st May 1945, as the Red Army was advancing towards the town, he took a gun from the body of a neighbour who had already killed himself and he shot dead his wife and two children: Ullrich, 13, and Joachim, 14. He then put the gun to his head and pulled the trigger. But nothing happened, just a loud click. The gun had run out of bullets, and Paul survived.

He was found, with the bodies of his wife and children, by Red Army troops. Mr Kittel spent ten years in a detention camp before eventually being tried for the murder of his family by a West German court. According to statements read out in court, all three members of Paul Kittell's family had begged him to shoot them. He was acquitted, in part because his actions weren't at all unparalleled. At that time, such terrible scenes were taking place throughout Germany.

About twenty miles from Malchin, where Paul Kittel killed his wife and children, is the town of Demmin. In the last weeks of the Second World War, Demmin was the scene of the largest mass suicide in German history. Between late April and early May 1945, more than 600 people in the town took their own life. These were people from all walks of life: pensioners and teenagers, middle-aged married couples and parents with young children and babies. The suicides crossed class boundaries: doctors, pharmacists, labourers, academics, policemen, accountants and teachers. The deaths represented a cross-section of the town and of German society. Entire families died.

Paul Kittel's story and the epidemic of suicides are described movingly by the German historian Florian Huber in his book, *Promise Me You'll Shoot Yourself: The Downfall of Ordinary Germans, 1945* (Huber, 2019). He tells us that when the battle-hardened troops of the Red Army arrived in Demmin, even they were shocked by the scenes that greeted them:

> There were dead bodies all over the place – hanging in houses and streets, green spaces, floating anywhere there was water... One woman who tried to hang herself in a tree after poisoning her three children and burying them in the countryside was cut down three

times by Soviet soldiers. Elsewhere, the enemy soldiers rescued people from rivers or bandaged bleeding wrists.

(Huber, 2019)

Box 8.1: Almost forgotten

The victims of the mass suicide in Demmin were buried in mass graves by the Red Army. These soon became overgrown and neglected; some even became farmland and were cultivated. This was because after the war Demmin became part of the communist German Democratic Republic. It was common knowledge that as the Red Army had advanced through Germany in the dying days of the Second World War, they had committed atrocities including arbitrary executions, rapes and the burning down of towns. The East German government was by and large controlled by Moscow. Unsurprisingly, the East German authorities did all they could to suppress this unsavoury history of the Soviet RED Army in Germany. The mass suicide in Demmin was just lumped in with all the other terrible things that had occurred in Germany. The state simply turned a blind eye. Consequently, the history of Demmin was almost forgotten.

Until the early 1990s, German society as a whole had ignored the fact that one of the greatest mass suicides in European history had taken place in a provincial town two hours north of Berlin. According to Huber:

The dead of Deming, Berlin, Leipzig, and Siefersheim have no place in the German tableau of history, with its focus on culprits, victims and the occasional hero or heroine. They don't fit the accepted narratives, so the suicides have remained private tragedies. But, every one of the deaths is proof of the depth of the abyss that had opened up before the Germans during the Nazis rule.

(Huber, 2019)

The causes of these mass suicides are complex and multi-factorial. At one level, people were terrified of what the Soviet troops would do to them. This terror had been encouraged and exacerbated by Nazi propaganda about stories of the savagery of the Red Army, in particular mass rapes. However, there were also more nuanced and deeper psychological factors at work. Huber wrote:

Our philosophy is a matter of the heart. Feeling is more to us than reason.' This simple Hitler Youth principal helps to explain the power of the Nazi movement. When the German's world came to an end in 1945, they had spent 12 years being driven from one extreme emotion to the next: The hope of upturn, the joy of belonging, the pride of being special, the euphoria of success, the arrogance of

power, the rage of destruction. They had been in a state of per-
manent intoxication with never a moment to sober up; there was no
respite in those densely packed years, no time to reflect, and when
everything ended in collapse, the overblown emotions collapsed
too. What remained was the beginnings of other, less exhilarating
feelings that had sprouted in the shadow of success: guilt at having
taken part, shame at having looked away, hatred and self-hatred,
fear of revenge and violence, despair at the emptiness that now
faced them.

(Huber, 2019)

The saboteur can wreak destruction on other people, on organisations
and on countries. Ultimately, though, its biggest victim is the self, and
the events at Demmin are the starkest, most extreme example of how
the saboteur is always self-destructive.

The saboteur can exert a powerful influence over how we perceive
reality and, consequently, how we act. However, it's only possible to
deny reality for so long. The majority of subjects in Stanley Milgram's
electric shock experiments were (forgive the pun) shocked when they
realised what they had been seduced into doing. But the Milgram
experiments were just that: experiments carried out in a university
psychology department. Nobody was really hurt and no one died, and
so the subjects eventually came to terms with their actions. The US
soldiers at Abu Ghraib caused real harm to people, as did the care
workers at Winterbourne View, and they faced prison. Many German
people colluded with the atrocities of the Nazis either actively or pas-
sively. How could people do that? Well, it comes down to the saboteur
turning a blind eye. The people in Demmin, and many other German
towns, were frightened of the Red Army, but they also had to face the
horror of what they had participated in as a result of the saboteur.
Some people can live with that, but other people can't.

Conclusion

We think of the saboteur as something that exists within individual
people, and in a sense that's true. We all have our own saboteur that
manifests in different ways. However, it's more than just an individual phenomenon. When individual people form groups, the group
becomes more than just the aggregation of the individuals involved in
that group. Groups take on a life of their own. And along with this
group identity comes a group saboteur. As Solomon Asch found in his
group conformity studies (see Chapter 7), individual people will distort their perception of reality by turning a blind eye to wrongdoing
in order not to stand out in a social or corporate group. We tell lies
to ourselves, and after a while we begin to believe those lies. We do

so because our own sense of our self as being a good person becomes dependent on the lies we have told.

When you tell the story of your life and explain why you acted in the way you did, you cast yourself in the role of hero. If in reality you are not a hero – if you are a member of the Reserve Police Battalion 101, the senior executive at IBM who negotiated the sale of Hollerith machines to the SS or an executive at the Ford Motor Company signing off the delivery of a 1,000 Ford trucks that get used to round up Jews for the concentration camps – how then do you live with that unpleasant reality? Your saboteur takes over and transforms your perception of that reality. Your saboteur transforms evil into good. If you did anything bad, you can always blame the person who gave the orders. This was the defence of most SS officers when they were brought to trial after the end of the war. It was the defence of Adolf Eichmann: he was just a good soldier obeying orders and thus should not be held responsible for his actions. As Stanley Milgram found in his electric shock experiments, we readily defer to authority. If that authority turns out to be corrupt or evil, then we will, on the whole, end up behaving in a corrupt and evil manner – we will do as we are told. That is the lesson from decades of social psychology research into obedience to authority.

In some cases, the saboteur can fail in its task of hiding the horror of our behaviour from us. This is perhaps what happened in Demmin in the final days of the war. Many people were confronted with the reality of their collusion with the Nazis and many felt overwhelmed with guilt and anger. These feelings came together with terror at what the Red Army might do to them, and the only way out they could see was suicide.

When we see evil being committed, we have an essential choice: to oppose that evil (as did Dietrich Bonhoeffer) or to turn a blind eye and go along with it as most people do. It is very difficult to accept the reality that we are colluding with something evil, because such acceptance brings with it the risk of destroying our self-image as a good and decent person. How many of us can live with that? The biggest and most convincing lies are those that we tell ourselves.

In our ongoing work to understand and disempower the saboteur, we need to think carefully about our behaviour and its consequences. To look at reality as it is, not as we hope it is. This is very difficult because it can mean standing up to the crowd, standing up to authority and putting ourselves at risk by speaking out. This is what Terry Bryan, the lead nurse at Winterbourne View, courageously did. He reported the abuse to his bosses, and to the government agency responsible for the quality of care at Winterbourne. He was ignored, though, and it wasn't until he spoke to an investigative journalist at *Panorama* that the scandal was exposed.

One of the biggest, if not the biggest, leadership challenges today is: how can corporate leaders encourage people to speak out when they see wrongdoing? This is what we will examine in the following chapters.

Chapter takeaways

- Social and political movements can set loose the saboteur.
- The saboteur exists in individuals and small groups – but also in large organisations, governments and societies as a whole.
- The saboteur causes 'stupidity': a lack of capacity to think independently. It can make us turn a blind eye to wrongdoing.
- The saboteur can blind us to the second-order consequences of our decisions.
- Awareness of the saboteur enables us to see reality as it is, not as we hope it is or have been told it is.

References

Arendt, H. (1963 (1994)). *Eichmann in Jerusalem: A Report on the Banality of Evil*. Harmondsworth: Penguin Books.

BBC News. (2011). 'Hugo Boss Apology for Nazi Past as Book Is Published'. *BBC*, 21 September. Retrieved from: https://www.bbc.co.uk/news/world-europe-15008682.

Billstein, R., Fings, K., Kugler, A. & Levis, N. (2000). *Working for the Enemy: Ford, General Motors and Forced Labor in Germany during the Second World War*. New York: Berghahn Books, Incorporated.

Black, E. (2012). *IBM and the Holocaust: The Strategic Alliance between Nazi Germany and America's Most Powerful Corporation* (expanded edition). Washington, DC: Dialog Press.

Bonhoeffer, D., Bowden, J. & Wells, S. (2017). *Letters and Papers from Prison* (new edition). London: SCM Press.

Browning, C. R. (1998). *Ordinary Men: Reserve Police Battalion 101 and the Final Solution in Poland* (illustrated edition). New York: Harper Perennial.

Burkeman, O. (2002). 'IBM "Dealt Directly with Holocaust Organisers"'. *Guardian*, 29 March. Retrieved from: http://www.theguardian.com/world/2002/mar/29/highereducation.

Goldhagen, D. J. (1996). *Hitler's Willing Executioners: Ordinary Germans and the Holocaust*. New York: Little Brown. p. 634.

Holland, J. (2015). *The War in the West – A New History, Volume 1: Germany Ascendant 1939–1941*. London: Corgi.

Huber, F. (2019). *Promise Me You'll Shoot Yourself: The Downfall of Ordinary Germans in 1945*. Harmondsworth: Penguin UK.

Manchester, W. (2003). *The Arms of Krupp: The Rise and Fall of the Industrial Dynasty That Armed Germany at War* (new edition). New York: Back Bay Books.

Metaxas, E. (2020). *Bonhoeffer: Pastor, Martyr, Prophet, Spy* (revised, updated edition). Nashville, TN: Nelson Books.

9 Learning to Manage Your Saboteur

After reading the preceding chapters, you may be feeling quite hostile towards the saboteur. It seems to be involved in everything bad that can happen to people, from vandalising a car, to bankrupting a bank, to participating in the Holocaust. The saboteur can be enormously destructive for sure. But it can also serve as a very efficient early-warning system for potential trouble.

The problem with the saboteur isn't the saboteur itself; the problem is our own stubborn resistance to listening critically to our saboteur and reflecting on its demands and its messages.

When the saboteur fills you with feelings (usually anxiety), you may well feel compelled to behave in a manner that under normal circumstances would appal you – just like Rabbi Levy (see the Introduction), Nick Leeson (Chapter 6) or the participants in Stanley Milgram's electric shock experiments (Chapter 7).

These strong feelings are messages from your unconscious mind, and if you are able to pause and reflect on them rather than impulsively acting on them, you may be able to choose how you act. More than this, your saboteur will be telling you something very important about your situation and probably your values and your life. Far from being your enemy, the saboteur is really your ally – and so in this chapter, I will describe how you can make friends with your saboteur and transform it into your most trusted advisor.

You can't get rid of your saboteur because it is a part of you. It is one of the many sub-personalities that make up your whole self. The saboteur is the sub-personality that has evolved to protect you by acting quickly in response to potential threats. Because it needs to act very quickly, it communicates using feelings rather than thoughts. As Daniel Kahneman has written, emotion compels action and thought follows along later. We act on emotion, and later our mind makes up post-hoc rationalisations to justify our behaviour (Kahneman, 2011).

Everyone's saboteur is different. Your saboteur will tend to reflect your personality. If you're a quiet, introverted person, your saboteur might compel avoidance, whereas if you're a loud, outgoing extrovert, your saboteur might compel pushy and aggressive behaviour. In this chapter, I will describe the different forms that your saboteur can

DOI: 10.4324/9781003188063-10

assume. It might be helpful to give your saboteur a label to make it more real and tangible – I will come on to that later.

Once you understand your saboteur and recognise it in yourself, you can begin to listen to it. That can be tricky because the saboteur communicates mainly with feelings, not words. To help you listen to your saboteur, I draw on psychoanalysis and cognitive behavioural therapy. My approach involves looking not so much at the feeling itself but at the meaning or thought behind that feeling.

When you figure out what message your saboteur is trying to give you, you shouldn't ignore the message but rather consciously tell your saboteur that it has been heard. This will gentle-down the anxiety and thus the compulsion to act. Only then can you combine the message from the saboteur with all the other data you have and decide what you should do. It sounds a lot easier than it is!

Finally in this chapter, I will talk about adult personality development, sometimes known as ego development. The higher you are on this developmental ladder, the easier it will be to manage your saboteur. I will describe how the way in which we understand ourselves, others and the world (our ego) develops through different stages. Most people get stuck at one stage. I will explain how you might be able to make it to the highest stage. Then, your saboteur won't sabotage you any longer but will be your best friend.

Getting to know your saboteur

Think of your feelings as data

The first step in getting to know your saboteur is to treat any strong feelings you have at work (or indeed anywhere) as data – useful information that tells you what's going on beneath the surface of the particular situation you're in. The saboteur communicates predominantly through feelings, not thoughts, so if you want to start listening to your saboteur, you need to start listening to your feelings – in other words, striving to become more consciously aware of your emotions and the meanings that might lie behind them.

In my experience, people have an ambivalent attitude to thinking about feelings in the workplace. Outside of work, emotions play a central role in our lives. We love our families and get cross with them. We go to a football match and cheer on our team with passion and enthusiasm or again get cross with them. We listen to a piece of music or watch a film and feel emotionally moved.

In contrast, our emotional lives at work are often hidden or tightly controlled. If we feel angry or annoyed or frustrated – or maybe excited and enthusiastic – we learn to minimise, hide or even, over time, repress those feelings. For most of the time, when we're at work, we carry on as if everything is fine. We put on a mask that hides our emotions and sends the message that everything is OK and we don't feel that strongly about anything much in particular. It's only when we get home and offload on our spouse, partner or significant other that the strength of our work-related feelings begins to emerge. If we've had a rotten day at work, sometimes that tension and anger build up and we come home and metaphorically kick the cat – or pick a fight with those we live with.

At work, whatever is going on inside, we tend to be mild-mannered and even-tempered most of the time. Of course, there is nothing wrong with that. We can't be emoting at work all the time. I am suggesting, however, that if we can start to become a bit more aware of our strong feelings and acknowledge and think about them without necessarily acting them out, then they're far less likely to get bottled up – only to emerge later when we get home.

The other side of the coin to this reluctance to treat emotions at work seriously is Daniel Goleman's famous idea of emotional intelligence (Goleman, 2005). Most, if not all, books or articles on leadership or management suggest that any good leader needs to be able to demonstrate high levels of emotional intelligence. An excellent leader should be self-aware, empathetic, expert at managing emotions both in themselves and in others, skilled in persuading and inspiring others and somehow able to 'use' emotion at work to improve rather than sabotage performance. Like many things in life, this is easier said than done.

An underlying assumption of Goleman's concept of emotional intelligence is that emotions are almost like commodities. Our feelings at work become assets or deficits, things that are either valuable or toxic. Seeing emotions in this way separates the emotion from ourselves. It conceptualises emotion as being something that is outside of us rather than an essential living part of us. This way of thinking about our feelings results in us wanting to either exploit, defuse or sanitise them, rather than experience them and reflect on them and try our best to understand them (Trainor, 2019).

When we understand emotions as being a part of us, we can then stay with them and be curious about their meaning. What happened that caused us to feel so anxious or angry or hurt? What happened to trigger that emotion? When we experience a strong emotion, it tells us just as much about what is happening in the system as a whole – in the organisation – as what is happening within ourselves. If we understand our feelings at work not just as an individual experience but as valuable data about what is going on in the organisation as a whole, then this can provide incredibly useful information about what might be going on beneath the surface.

Box 9.1: The triangle of thinking, feeling and doing

Think of a triangle with the words 'thinking', 'feeling' and 'doing' at each point of the triangle. In difficult, stressful situations, most people tend to focus their energy on one of these points of the triangle while withdrawing energy from the other two points. For example:

- When we are filled with *feeling*, it's difficult to think clearly and get anything done.
- If we're on the verge of burnout and just working, *doing*, too much, we feel emotionally numb and find it difficult to think.
- If we're bombarded with complex contradictory information that requires deep *thinking*, we might feel emotionally numb, overwhelmed or bored and find it difficult to act on the information. This is commonly called 'paralysis by analysis'.

If we find ourselves *thinking* too much, *doing* too much or *feeling* too much, we should pause to reflect on what is actually going on both in ourselves and in the system. If we're just *doing*, what thoughts and feelings might we be avoiding? If we're overwhelmed with *feeling*, what could we do to understand the feeling and what could we do about it?

This is the first step in learning to communicate with our saboteur. When there is an imbalance in this triangle of thinking, feeling and doing, the saboteur is often the cause.

Leading our internal psychological team

As soon as we start to reflect on our emotional state, we become more aware of the internal dialogue that chatters away in our mind. One part of you says, 'do this', while another part says, 'no, that's way too risky; just keep quiet'.

Think of these voices as a cast of internal characters. Each one gives a voice to a different part of the self – to the internal cast of sub-personalities that make up your sense of who you are. One of these characters is your saboteur. Your saboteur might argue passionately and strongly for you to pursue a particular course. Your saboteur's voice is usually very loud and very powerful and overwhelming in this internal debate.

We all have these internal voices – some arguing for change, others urging restraint. All these voices have a strong emotion attached to them. This community of voices in our head is a bit like an inner leadership team (Wickremasinghe, 2021) – a bit like a leadership team in an organisation. Every workplace team has conflicts and competing views; it has positive members, negative members, eccentric creative members and destructive members. It's the same with our internal psychological team. There are parts that are optimistic, pessimistic, creative and destructive. The trick of good leadership in an organisation is to listen to all these competing voices, acknowledge their views, reflect on their contributions and eventually come to a decision on how to act. It's exactly the same with our internal team. We need to carefully listen to our team of internal voices, including our saboteur's voice. In a sense, the conscious thinking part of you – your ego – has to act as the CEO of your internal psychological team and make the final decision. In many of the examples I have written about in this book, the final decision was determined not by this CEO but by the voice shouting the loudest: that of the saboteur.

The masks the saboteur wears

Our saboteur can take different forms. If we think of the examples from early in the book, we see that the saboteur can urge us to act impulsively, like Nick Leeson or Rabbi Levy. Alternatively, the saboteur can urge us to turn a blind eye to wrongdoing, as in the participants in Stanley Milgram's electric shock experiments. Our saboteur comes in different forms. Which form of the saboteur gets triggered will depend on the situation.

Another way of thinking about this is that we have one saboteur, but that saboteur will wear a different mask depending on what is happening in our life at that particular point.

To understand our saboteur better, we can label it, personalise it. Doing so makes it much easier to engage in a dialogue with the saboteur, which means we make its demands conscious rather than unconscious. Then we have a chance of negotiating with it, rather than blindly feeling compelled to act on the saboteur's demands.

Our saboteur will appear to us in one of the following 'masks' (Chamine, 2012):

- **The judge** is the most common saboteur and the one that we can all immediately identify with. The judge compels you to constantly find fault with yourself, other people and the world. The judge is harsh, critical and, of course, judgemental. It's another word for Freud's concept of the superego.

  Think back to the story of Andrea Dunbar, the playwright who grew up in poverty in Bradford (see Chapter 1). Despite being objectively a great success, she remained unconvinced of her talent. Her internal judge saboteur was constantly evaluating her and finding her wanting. Because her judge saboteur was unconscious, it was very difficult for Andrea to consciously dispute its messages. She *felt* like a failure although she *knew* she was a success. Feelings always trump thoughts. She coped with these feelings of failure in an impulsive unconscious manner by drinking heavily to try to block them out – and, tragically, this is probably what eventually killed her.

- **The stickler** is the perfectionist, slightly obsessional part of you. The stickler saboteur is an exaggeration of the personality factor of conscientiousness. If something isn't absolutely perfect, the stickler, in a rather black-and-white way, regards it as worthless.

  Claude Monet was one of the most famous, respected and influential painters of the French Impressionist movement. And he was a terrible perfectionist, which is another way of saying that he was vulnerable to the internal saboteur we call the stickler. In 1908, after three years of working on a new set of paintings of the water lilies in his famous garden in Giverny – and right before they were to be taken to Paris for the opening of an exhibition – Monet decided that at least 15 of his precious canvases weren't good enough. In a fit of despondency and rage, he used a knife to destroy these masterpieces. His stickler saboteur took over and compelled this act of destruction. Even in 1908, the canvases were worth a fortune – now, 15 paintings by Monet would be priceless.

- **The pleaser** is an exaggeration of the personality factor of agreeableness. It compels you to avoid conflict at all costs and seek other people's approval, again at all costs. The worst catastrophe that can befall the pleaser is conflict resulting in rejection. Avoiding rejection is what motivates the pleaser saboteur.

  Remember the example of Nick Leeson in Chapter 6? One of the factors that led to his aberrant behaviour was his desire to please others, particularly those above him in the dominance hierarchy. Financial journalist Judith Rawnsley wrote of Leeson, 'So what happened to Nick Leeson? I believe that his desire to please – his clients, fellow traders and managers – and his fear of displeasing them, was so great that he went to absurd lengths to achieve what he wanted' (Rawnsley, 1996). His compulsion to please overrode his sense of probity and integrity.

  Just like the judge, the influence of the pleaser saboteur can be seen in many instances of wrongdoing. The participants in Milgram's electric shock experiments, the prison guards at Abu Ghraib (see Chapter 7) and even Tony Blair (Chapter 3) abdicated their sense of personal responsibility in their desire to please other people. The pleaser saboteur is also a major player in our compulsion to be included in the inner ring, which I described in Chapter 6.

- **The hyper-achiever** believes that your self-worth is entirely dependent on your achievements. You are compelled to do more, to apply for more senior jobs, to obtain more degrees, not because you're interested in the jobs or education but because you never feel quite good enough without ever-increasing external validation.

- **The victim** member of your internal team will constantly remind you of your status as the victim of other people's malevolence. The victim saboteur will also tell you that attempting to compete with other people or other groups as an equal is bound to fail because those other people not only look down on you but actively oppress you because of your social class, gender, race or religious group. Your victim saboteur compels you to feel put upon, angry and resentful – the victim of other people's prejudice or malevolence. You become a failure, not because of your incompetence but because of the oppressed group to which you belong: 'I've failed at my job not because I'm incompetent but because people are prejudiced against me'. That lets you off the hook. Also, your victim saboteur will generate some secondary gain in the form of attention, sympathy and practical assistance.

  Real objective victimisation does exist. I discussed in Chapter 8 the victimisation of Jews – that is all too real. Racism is real, as is misogyny. However, the victim saboteur is an internal, psychological and largely destructive defence mechanism that protects some people from the anxiety of situations in which they might fail. It's right for people to struggle against the victimisation of, let's say, racism or misogyny, by actively calling it out and pushing back. The victim saboteur is different because it advocates for a passive, helpless, whining attitude – it compels a 'poor me' way of relating rather than an 'empowered me'.

  A dramatic example of the victim saboteur is the case of the American actor Jussie Smollett. Mr Smollett, who is black and gay, reported to the Chicago police in January 2019 that three years earlier he had been the victim of a racist, homophobic attack. This became big news and he was inundated with support and sympathy from both celebrities and the public. He described being assaulted on a dark and deserted street by two masked men who roughed him up and put a noose around his neck while yelling racist and homophobic insults. Following their investigation of the assault, the Chicago police made an arrest – not of the 'two masked men', though. They arrested Jussie Smollett for faking the attack. They cited overwhelming evidence that he had paid two acquaintances $3,500 to stage the assault. Smollett was found guilty of faking the assault as a strategy to boost his career in show business (Yang, 2021).
- **The hyper-rational saboteur** member of your internal team helps you to avoid anxiety by focusing your attention on facts. Your perception of the world is data driven, and emotion is not considered as being data. This includes relationships. When you are under the influence of the hyper-rational saboteur, you come across as cold,

distant – and sometimes hostile and critical. When the hyper-rational saboteur is in charge, you turn into a mini Mr Spock. The hyper-rational saboteur often produces 'paralysis by analysis', which is common in the corporate world. Somebody will come up with a great idea which then gets analysed ad infinitum, in numerous committees, until the idea is strangled – never implemented.

These descriptions aren't of separate individual sub-personalities, but rather of the form that our individual saboteur can take. At times, you will experience your saboteur as being the judge, and maybe at other times, it will be the victim. The form your saboteur takes will largely be influenced by the environment and situation you find yourself in. The saboteur will wear a different mask to adapt to the situation you are in.

How to manage your masked saboteur

There are four steps you can take to manage your saboteur. These steps will help you to understand your saboteur, lessen its control over your inner psychological team and use your saboteur's wisdom to help you make the right decision or behave in the right way.

1. **See feelings as evidence.** When you start to experience a strong emotional reaction to a person or situation, pause, take a breath and reflect on that feeling. Are you feeling judged, like a victim, or desperate to avoid something?
2. **Label the saboteur.** The type of feeling that you're having will give you a strong clue about your saboteur and what mask your saboteur is wearing at that time. Even an absence of feeling is relevant; it might suggest that you're under the influence of the hyper-rational saboteur.
3. **Understand your saboteur.** Spend a few moments reflecting on the saboteur you're experiencing. Remember that the saboteur evolved in a particular phase of your life to protect you. At one point in life, it was highly adaptive. The problem is that people's circumstances change dramatically but often the saboteur stubbornly remains the same.

   Think about the form of the saboteur you're experiencing currently and then ask if there was a time in your life when that type of reaction would have helped you. How might that saboteur have protected you from danger? Try to really understand your saboteur and view it as a misguided friend rather than an enemy.
4. **Integrate your saboteur.** Reflect on what the saboteur is urging you to do. Do your best to think about what your rational mind

is telling you and what your saboteur is urging you to do. Then make an informed decision. If you can do this, you'll find that the strong, 'compulsive' desire to behave as the saboteur is urging you to behave will disappear. This is because your saboteur has been listened to and taken seriously.

When you follow these steps, what you're doing is accepting your saboteur as a valid part of your internal psychological team. You're giving your saboteur a voice and taking that voice seriously. Of course, you might choose not to act on the advice of your saboteur. But then again, you might choose to accept the advice, because sometimes the saboteur will be right. The situation might contain a risk for you, or being circumspect in keeping your head down might be safer than speaking out. The situation might call for you to 'choose your battles', where you might overlook bad behaviour in the short term in favour of intervening later, when you have more evidence or support.

By listening to your saboteur, you not only defuse its emotional intensity but you can access potentially useful data/information about the situation. You can then choose what to do with that information. This is far better than being either unconscious of that information or turning a blind eye, or being emotionally compelled to act on the feeling that you haven't properly processed or thought through.

Earlier in the chapter, I described your mind as being like an internal team of people. If we stay with that metaphor and think about a real-life team of people, we see the same approach applies. Imagine that you're a team leader and a member of your team is constantly pointing out risks and dangers or urging you to ignore potential risks or dangers or urging you to 'act now'. How do you deal with that sort of person?

Well, it would be a mistake to ignore them, because if you do that, they'll push even harder and clamour for your attention. In that situation, that difficult team member will feel ignored and possibly angry and resentful. At the same time, it would be a mistake to blindly accept what that person says.

An experienced leader would calm the team member down, listen to them in a thoughtful and respectful manner, consider their views and thank them for their input. Then the leader would make a decision and inform the team member of that decision. If you've had any experience of managing people, you know that when you explain to someone why you've decided not to go along with their suggestion, they're usually quite all right with it. What infuriates people is a sense of being ignored and not taken seriously, rather than being disagreed with.

It's the same with your internal psychological team. If you acknowledge the worries of your psychological saboteur and think about the best course of action, your saboteur will be happy with that.

Taking it to the next level: personality, ego development and the saboteur

Very occasionally, you'll meet hyper-competent people who seem to be able to manage themselves and others with aplomb. Not only are they self-aware and have insight into their own strengths and weaknesses, but they have the ability to see the world from other people's perspective and combine the different views. They are flexible and adaptable, can make authoritative decisions, can admit it when they are wrong and can change their mind. When you encounter such a person, you would probably describe them as being wise.

At the other extreme, you will have come across people who are very intelligent and competent but struggle to see the world from anyone else's perspective but their own. The world revolves around them. Sometimes, they seem unaware of their emotional life and find it hard to manage their emotions. They can easily fly into a rage or, conversely, a trivial slight provokes waves of self-doubt. This lack of empathy and lack of emotional control isn't, I emphasise, anything to do with intelligence or ability; you would probably describe it as being part of their personality – just how they are.

We all know that children have distinct developmental stages; for example, the 'terrible twos'. You wouldn't expect a seven-year-old to manage their emotions, or see the world the same way as a 12-year-old. You wouldn't berate your two-year-old for having a tantrum and accuse them of being immature. That's because we have different expectations of behaviour and attitude depending on the age of the child. We understand that as children get older, they mature and understand the world and their place in the world differently. We also know that this developmental journey is different from intelligence. A three-year-old child does not behave like a three-year-old child because they lack intelligence – and children learn far more than any adult ever would. They have plenty of intelligence; they're simply at a particular developmental stage.

Adults are the same. Our ego – our sense of self and our place in the world – doesn't just stop developing when we're 18 or 21. Adults, like children, go through distinct developmental changes. This explains why one adult can be highly intelligent but behave like a teenager, while another adult might not be quite as smart intellectually but is sensible, mature and successful.

Box 9.2: Immature ego development in action

Brad was an extremely wealthy, powerful and bright investment banker from the US. He held a master's degree in international finance from a top US university.

Brad was in London on business and desperately wanted to experience a typical London pub. We went to a pub, and he decided he wanted to order a pint of beer at the bar. The bar was busy, and there were a couple of people in front of him waiting to be served. The barmaid served these two people and then, rather than serving Brad, she served someone who was behind him in the queue.

Brad eventually got served and came back to the table. He was furious and seemed obsessed with the idea that the barmaid ignored him on purpose. The poor barmaid was rushed off her feet and probably just made a mistake, but Brad took it very personally and experienced her mistake as a personal slight. For the rest of the evening, he could talk of nothing else but the barmaid who didn't serve him in turn. He seemed to find it impossible to see it as something trivial and let it go.

Brad was an intelligent man. He wasn't arrogant or discourteous (it's easy to make that assumption, reading the anecdote). He was a nice guy and socially skilled. Yet he wasn't able to see the situation from the perspective of the barmaid, who was rushed and trying to keep everybody happy. He was only able to see it from his perspective, and that's the essence of someone at one of the lower stages of ego development. Brad's immature ego development enabled his saboteur, spoiling his evening.

Brad's difficulty in seeing the world from other people's perspective was also an obstacle in his business life. Although he was successful, his success came from just doing things as he wanted and either ignoring other people or steamrolling his views over theirs. Although he made money, his future at the bank was insecure. He was a good trader but an incompetent leader. He understood the markets but didn't understand himself or others. His interaction with the London barmaid was a microcosm of his interactions with other people in both his business and personal lives.

Had Brad been at a higher stage of ego development, he would have been able, without consciously thinking about it, to understand the situation from the perspective of the barmaid. He would have seen his failure to be served as trivial and unimportant. He would not have become upset and preoccupied, and his behaviour would have been more positive. His saboteur would not have been in command of his internal psychological team.

Child ego development

Before we explore adult ego development, it's helpful for you to understand how your mind developed in childhood.

The person who has contributed most to our understanding of children's minds is the Swiss psychologist Jean Piaget. Before Piaget, most of us would have regarded children as mini adults who hadn't learnt enough – in other words, the same as adults just a bit smaller and less educated. Piaget understood that children were qualitatively different to adults. The difference was not in how big they were or how much they knew but in *how they thought about* the world.

He observed that children go through a number of distinct developmental stages. A 12-year-old knows more than a six-year-old but also understands the world in a completely different way. For example, Piaget demonstrated that younger children interact with the world based on *doing*, whereas older children are able to interact with the world based on their abstract mental representations of the world. Older children are able to construct an internal map of the world and use this to try out different strategies, whereas these internal maps are simply not available to the younger child. If you show a baby a ball and then hide the ball under a cloth, the baby will think the ball has disappeared. Do the same with an older child, and they understand perfectly well that the ball continues to exist but is under the cloth. Piaget called this object permanence.

According to Piaget, there are at least four distinct stages of child development (Piaget & Cook, 1952; Piaget, 1957):

- **The sensorimotor stage (birth to two years):** At this stage, the child interacts with the world purely through movements and sensations. As the child gets older, they start to develop a sense of agency – in other words, they understand that their actions can cause things to happen. This stage is one of the most dramatic and important periods in human development.
- **The preoperational stage (two to seven years):** From about the age of two, children begin to develop the skill of thinking symbolically about the world. They begin to develop mental representations, or mental maps of the world, and include themselves at the centre of the maps. For toddlers and young children, the world revolves around them. People and objects are either good or bad. This is reflected in the literature children begin to engage with. Fairy tales with wicked witches and good fairies are a fair representation of the internal world of a small child.
- **The concrete operational stage (seven to eleven years):** By the time the child reaches the age of seven, they are able to think more logically and rationally about the external world. A simple example of this is that the child understands perfectly well that the amount of water in a tall, thin glass is the same as the amount of water in a short, stumpy glass. Children at this stage can think far more abstractly about the world, albeit in quite a rigid way.
- **The formal operational stage (12 to adulthood):** It's at this stage that our ability to think about the world in a far more sophisticated and less rigid way begins to rapidly emerge. The young adult begins to wonder about moral, political and social issues and to use

inductive and deductive logic to understand the world. They can see the world from the perspective of others and realise there are multiple solutions to the same problem. They become less egocentric and see that the world in general does not revolve around them.

The stages of adult ego development

It may have occurred to you as you read the preceding section that many adults seem to be stuck at some of the child development stages. We've all met adults who feel the world revolves around them (a clinical psychologist may refer to them as having a narcissistic personality). It's also common to encounter others who struggle to see the world from another person's perspective. Again, these people might be highly intelligent but at the same time emotionally immature.

The developmental psychologist Robert Kegan has shown that to reach our full potential as adults we have to negotiate distinct developmental stages (Kegan, 1982, 1998). We will explore those stages, but first we need to understand what Kegan calls Subject and Object.

Moving from Subject to Object

Kegan's idea of Subject and Object helps us understand how people see the world. By *Subject* he means everything we know to be 'true', everything that is unquestioned and uncritically accepted as being 'just the way things are', just as we accept gravity or that the sun will rise every morning. *Object* is the opposite of Subject. Things that are Object can be just the same as Subject, but they're experienced as something separate from the self. Things that are Object are up for question and aren't just accepted uncritically. They can be thought about and manipulated in the mind.

For example, it's often very easy to see other people's faults and be completely blind to our own. Our faults are Subject, and other people's faults are Object. So you may believe that you're a failure and can't change (Subject). Your friend tells you that they also feel a failure, but you observe their potential and start to suggest things they can do to be a success (Object). You can't see or change things that are Subject, but with Objects you can see them and also see the possibility of change.

Strong political beliefs are a good example of this. At one stage of ego development, a person's political beliefs might be Subject. For example, Pete might say, 'I *am* a socialist'. In this case, the person, Pete, is indistinguishable from the belief. A second person, Ben, might say, 'I am a person who believes socialism is right'. Ben is more developed in his ego because his political view is more Object. It is separate from him. Pete *is* the belief. Ben *has* a belief. Ben can recognise that other people have contradictory beliefs that are also separate from them as individual human beings. This opens up the possibility of discussion, debate and growth. If you're talking to Pete and criticising socialism, you're also criticising Pete as a person, because in his mind he's indistinguishable from the belief in socialism. This might lead to offence and possibly conflict. However, if you're talking to Ben and you criticise socialism, not criticising him personally just criticising his belief, he can then defend his belief without getting too upset and in the process can listen to your belief.

Ego development is the journey from seeing most things in life as Subject (taken for granted and invisible to us) to Object (things we can observe, understand, influence and even change). The more you're able to see yourself and the world as Object, the more sophisticated your world view becomes.

Like Piaget, Kegan identified a number of stages in our journey to ego development and to fulfilling our human potential, as outlined in the following sections. Generally, we can move up the stages in our adult life, but it is possible to regress to a lower stage, such as when you're under stress or with certain people or in certain situations.

Stage 1: The self-sovereign mind

To understand the self-sovereign mind, think of a teenager stuck at Piaget's formal operational stage. Adults who haven't moved much beyond the self-sovereign mind are preoccupied with their own needs and view of the world. Their relationships tend to be transactional; in other words, they see other people as existing mainly to meet their needs. They struggle to see others as independent human beings with feelings, thoughts and desires that are separate from their own. They are low on empathy and high on entitlement. People at this stage of ego development follow rules or refrain from lying or stealing because they fear getting caught or some other retaliation, not because these behaviours transgress their moral or ethical values. According to Kegan's research, about 6 per cent of people remain stuck at this level of ego development.

Stage 2: The socialised mind

Most people, about 60 per cent, never make it past the socialised mind level of development. They have insight into their own emotional life and understand that other people are different to them and can experience different feelings, beliefs and desires. Relationships are reciprocal rather than simply transactional.

People at this stage are preoccupied with the beliefs, feelings and behaviour of others in their social group. It's very important that they fit in with others and conform to the norms of their social group. Because of this need, they will take on (often uncritically) the beliefs of the social group with whom they most strongly identify or want to be accepted by. Theirs is a world of black and white – my side (my group) is wholly right and any other group is wholly wrong. They will spout the 'clichés and slogans' that Dietrich Bonhoeffer described in his essay on the stupidity of crowds (see Chapter 8).

To understand the socialised mind, think of a football fan or the leavers and remainers during Brexit. For people at this stage, all the value and 'goodness' is obtained from being a member of their group. Often, this group is built around an occupation, like doctor, lawyer or teacher. Or it might be based on political or religious beliefs; for example, 'I am a liberal' or 'I am a Christian' or 'I am a Muslim'.

At this stage of development, a person's sense of self, particularly their self-worth is very dependent on how other people in their group react to them. If someone is dismissive of them in some way, they internalise that and feel bad about themselves. Similarly, they will go out of their way to avoid conflict because of the possibility of upsetting the other person. An example would be the manager who in order to feel effective has to be popular with everyone, including their direct reports as well as their own manager. It's as if they look into the person's eyes and see their self-worth reflected back.

People at the socialised mind stage of development find it hard to make decisions because a firm decision runs the risk of displeasing another person in their social group. They struggle to know what they want in life because they're preoccupied with other people's needs and what others think of them.

The difference between the stages becomes most apparent in moral behaviour. The person with the self-sovereign mind follows the rules simply because they're scared of getting caught should they break the rules. If they were in a situation where they were certain that they could, let's say, steal something and not get caught, they would and would feel good about it. In contrast, the person at the socialised mind stage follows the rules because these rules are consistent with their moral values. As a part of their development, they have internalised society's moral rules and values, and those values have become a part of them. If they were to break the rules, they would be troubled by strong feelings of guilt and remorse, rather than fear of getting caught.

Stage 3: Self-authored mind

The main leap forward at this next developmental stage is that we begin to understand that we're independent beings with our own beliefs, feelings and values. We're part of society, social groups, but we're not defined by them. You might work as a doctor, for example, but being a doctor doesn't define your whole identity. Doctors who are in the socialised mind state of development will tend to socialise with other doctors. Doctors at this stage have a wide group of friends from different occupations and social groups.

At this stage, we define ourselves and can form our own views rather than being defined by our social group and simply taking on the ready-made values and beliefs of that social group. We can confidently argue our own opinions and listen, with an open mind and curiosity, to the opinions of others.

People at the self-authoring mind stage have a stable sense of self. They have a clear set of values and the confidence to hold on to them when put under pressure to conform to the views of others. They also have a sense of direction in life and are not easily distracted by other people or circumstances. People at this stage are able to take responsibility for their own feelings and behaviour without experiencing the need to blame bad outcomes on others or difficult circumstances. According to Kegan, about 35 per cent of people you meet are at the self-authoring mind stage of ego development.

Stage 4: Self-transforming mind

The self-transforming mind is the highest level of ego development, and according to Kegan, only about 1 per cent of the population make it to this stage. People at the self-transforming mind stage are constantly evolving and reinventing themselves. They aren't tied to a particular occupation, set of religious or political beliefs, or the approval of others. They are flexible, and their sense of self is constantly adapting to the changing environment. Their profile on the big five model of personality (see Chapter 6) would be high openness and high conscientiousness. People at this stage find it easy and natural to really listen to others and, without any sense of discomfort, either change their own mind or hang on to their own views.

People at the self-transforming mind stage have little difficulty in taking up their authority as well as feeling confident to challenge the authority of others if they think they're wrong. Similarly, they'll question and challenge their own attitudes and behaviours. They're good at dealing with the complexity of modern life. They perceive other people as complex beings – neither black nor white – who contain the capacity for great good and evil. Their defining belief is that the only constant in life is change, and people at this stage of ego development have the flexibility to change and adapt to new events and challenges.

Steps to develop your ego

Is it then possible to accelerate your own ego development? Yes, it certainly is – but it is difficult. Like any change, you'll find it stressful and exhausting, but well worth it.

Jennifer Garvey Berger and Keith Johnson have written about this process of change (2015). They describe three practical steps that you can take to develop your ego. These steps will help you to manage your internal psychological team and understand, learn from and happily coexist with your saboteur.

The three techniques that follow will force you to think and behave at a higher stage of development than you currently are. They create self-reinforcing feedback loops that over time will shift your level of ego development upwards. This particularly applies for those of you at the socialised mind stage who want to move up to the self-authored mind stage.

Asking different questions

When you think about the world or encounter another person, your perceptions and understanding will be pretty much determined by your level of ego development. If you're at the self-sovereign mind stage, you might approach a situation with the question: 'What's in it for me?' Someone with a socialised mind might be wondering: 'What do people think of me?' These questions don't come from genuine curiosity about the world but rather from a need to confirm our own perception. Any facts that come along and seem to confirm that perception feel right, and anything that seems at odds with our perception just feels wrong, and because it feels wrong, we reject it. But the fact that feels wrong might actually be correct, and because of our saboteur urging us to turn a blind eye, we miss it.

Here's a question for you: How do you feel when you're wrong? You might reply, 'I feel stupid. I feel bad'. Well, that might be how you feel *after* you've found out you were wrong, but how did you feel in the five minutes before you realised you were wrong? You probably felt great. You don't know you're wrong until you know you're wrong; until then, you know you're right.

As part of the Subject to Object journey, think of your perceptions of the world as being hypotheses – as beliefs you hold rather than objective truths (this is hard but possible). Here are some awkward questions you can ask yourself that will help you achieve this:

- What do I believe about this situation?
- What evidence do I have for my belief?
- In what way could I be wrong?

Taking multiple perspectives

Being able to see the world as other people see the world – taking the perspective of others – is an enormously helpful skill to develop. In negotiation theory, this is described as being able to 'go to the balcony'. This means viewing the negotiation (or, indeed, the situation) as being like a dance that you're involved in. If you're able to take yourself away from the dance and metaphorically climb the stairs to the balcony and look down on the dance, you have a much more useful and powerful perspective than if you were part of events.

Whenever you're in a difficult situation, make a conscious effort to describe that situation from the multiple perspectives of others involved. Try to reflect on how they might feel. We tend to see ourselves as being the hero of our story. Try to drop this for a moment and realise that you're just another character in a story that has somebody else as the hero.

Similarly, think of your own internal psychological team. Try to separate out the competing voices. Listen to the enthusiastic part of yourself, the sceptical part of yourself and the fearful part of yourself. Maybe even write down a few sentences that sum up how these different parts of you feel. Then reflect on those thoughts and remember that you are the CEO of your internal organisation.

Here are some questions that might help you to do this:

- What am I feeling and thinking?
- What are the different parts of me feeling and thinking?
- Who are the other people involved in this situation feeling and thinking?
- When I look at this situation from the balcony, what do I observe?
- If I disagree with someone, in what way is that person right?
- If I feel supportive of someone, in what way is that person wrong?

Seeing systems

We're all part of a system that we're often blind to. We experience conflict with a colleague, feel overworked or feel pressure to do something we feel is wrong. That is what we see, but we don't see all the factors that lie behind that.

For example, Nick Leeson behaved badly only partly because of his individual and internal personality characteristics. Other drivers of his bad behaviour included increased competition; relaxed scrutiny/compliance in the financial markets as a result of Mrs Thatcher's Big Bang; and intense fear of being left behind in the senior leadership team of Barings Bank, which encouraged an organisational culture of turning a blind eye to practices that previously would have been unacceptable.

Nick Leeson was described as a 'bad apple', but that's not true because it puts all the responsibility on him and disregards the other systemic factors that fuelled his behaviour.

Another example is burnout. The World Health Organization describes burnout as an occupational phenomenon. In other words, we can only experience burnout in a workplace context. The big mistake that most organisations make is to see burnout as the result of individual weakness or a lack of resilience. That is usually how the person who is burnt out experiences it. They blame themselves. The solution to burnout, if you take that view, is therapy or resilience training or some other individual solution. However, burnout isn't caused by individual weakness; it's caused by poorly managed chronic workplace stress. People burn out because organisations pile too much work onto them and they can't cope. Attributing burnout to individual weakness is a bit like attributing the shellshock experienced by a soldier in the trenches of the Somme to their individual weakness. Soldiers developed shellshock (or PTSD as we would call it now) because of the trauma of being in the trenches, not because of any individual psychological characteristics.

Therefore, when you find yourself in a particular situation where you're experiencing strong feelings and an urge to behave in a way that you wouldn't normally behave, think about all the other systemic factors that are involved. You are an individual person, but you're also part of a much larger system. We find it easy to see individual people because they're there and in front of us. We often find it much more difficult to see the system and the systemic factors involved in the way we behave at work. If you want to develop your ego functioning, then whenever you feel any strong emotion, think about the system that you're a part of and what this emotion you're experiencing says about that system.

Ask yourself:

- What do I bring to this situation?
- What aspects of my personal history, personality and current psychological state might contribute to this situation?
- What are the current demands of my role, and how do these demands add value to the business?
- What are the politics of the organisation, and have these changed?
- What is happening in the larger economic and political world that might be influencing this situation?

If you are able to use this technique, and the previous ones, in situations you face in your organisation and indeed your life, you'll notice two things. First, your ability to respond wisely will improve; in other words, your ego will develop. Second, your saboteur will have less and less influence over your actions. The demands of your saboteur will move from the unconscious mind to the conscious mind, and you'll be able to make an informed decision on how you respond to those demands. You'll find the aspects of your life that were previously Subject become Object. This will give you more insight and control of your life.

Chapter takeaways

- The saboteur serves an important purpose, and it can actually help rather than hinder you.
- Feelings from the saboteur can compel you to behave unusually – perhaps even badly. But when you learn to stop, listen and reflect on what your saboteur is trying to communicate, you gain control over your actions.
- Noticing and reflecting on your feelings gives you lots of very useful information you can learn from.
- We all have an inner psychological team, and each character on that team needs to be heard. Then your internal CEO can make an informed decision about whether and how to act.
- The saboteur has a collection of masks. It's important to recognise when the saboteur is at play in your life and use strategies to manage it.
- Working on 'levelling up' your ego will help you to build a better relationship with your saboteur.

References

Berger, J. G. (2011). *Changing on the Job: Developing Leaders for a Complex World* (1st ed.). Redwood, CA: Stanford Business Books.

Berger, J. G. & Johnston, K. (2015). *Simple Habits for Complex Times*. Redwood City, CA: Stanford University Press.

Chamine, S. (2012). *Positive Intelligence: Why Only 20 Per Cent of Teams and Individuals Achieve Their True Potential and How You Can Achieve Yours*. Austin, TX: Greenleaf Book Group Press.

Goleman, D. (2005). *Emotional Intelligence*. London: Bloomsbury Publishing.

Kahneman, D. (2011). *Thinking, Fast and Slow*. London: Penguin Books, p. 499.

Kegan, R. (1982). *The Evolving Self*. Cambridge, MA: Harvard University Press.

Kegan, R. (1998). *In Over Our Heads: The Mental Demands of Modern Life*. Cambridge, MA: Harvard University Press.

Piaget, J. (1957). *Construction of Reality in the Child*. London: Routledge & Kegan Paul.

Piaget, J., & Cook, M. T. (1952). *The Origins of Intelligence in Children*. New York: International University Press.

Rawnsley, J. H. (1996). *Going for Broke: Nick Leeson and the Collapse of Barings Bank*. London: Harper Collins.

Trainor, K. (2019). 'Feelings as Data'. In A. Obholzer & V. Z. Roberts (Eds.), *The Unconscious at Work*, pp. 196–204. Abingdon: Routledge.

Wickremasinghe, N. (2021). 'Characterful Leadership'. *The Dialogue Space Review*, September. Retrieved from: https://www.triarchypress.net/uploads/1/4/0/0/14002490/characterful_leadership__4___002_.pdf.

Yang, M. (2021). 'Jussie Smollett Found Guilty of Faking Hate Crime Against Himself'. *Guardian*, 10 December. Retrieved from: https://www.theguardian.com/us-news/2021/dec/09/jussie-smollett-found-guilty-faking-hate-crime-against-himself.

10 Managing the Saboteur at Work

In the previous chapter, I discussed how to manage the saboteur within us all – within individuals. This chapter will explore the far more complex problem of tackling the saboteur in organisations. I have already, briefly, discussed how the saboteur manifested in IBM and the Ford Motor Company supporting the Third Reich (see Chapter 8).

I'll begin this chapter by telling you about how the saboteur in the Boeing Corporation contributed to two serious plane crashes and the deaths of 346 people. The story of the Boeing 737 Max scandal is told graphically in the 2021 Netflix documentary *Downfall: The Case Against Boeing*. I'll contrast this with another organisational culture, one that was very successful, shortening the Second World War and saving millions of lives. This organisation was Bletchley Park, the war intelligence department that cracked the German Enigma code. The organisational culture at Bletchley Park was characterised by two factors that made it very difficult for the saboteur to operate: cognitive diversity and psychological safety. I'll then go on to unpack the various factors that create a culture that will inhibit the unconscious destructive parts of our mind – in other words, our individual and collective saboteur.

How organisational culture killed people: what really brought down the Boeing 737 Max

It was a pleasant sunny morning in Jakarta on 29 October 2018 as Lion Air Flight 610 taxied down the runway heading for Pangkal Pinang. The gleaming brand-new Boeing 737 Max was carrying 189 passengers and crew. Soon after take-off, the pilot reported problems in the plane's handling. About five minutes later, the plane crashed into the sea, killing all on board. In the ensuing investigation, Boeing blamed the accident on pilot error and a poorly run airline 'there was a public narrative, the one advanced by Boeing chief executive officer Dennis Muilenburg, his top engineers, and the FAA officials to convince airline pilots and passengers – and maybe even themselves – that the plane was safe. The problem (as they all but said) was one badly run airline from Indonesia' (Robison, 2021).

DOI: 10.4324/9781003188063-11

Less than six months later, on 10 March 2019, Ethiopian Airlines Flight 302, again a new Boeing 737 Max, took off from Addis Ababa airport en route to Kenya. The same thing happened. The pilot reported handling problems, and soon after the 737 Max crashed, killing all 157 passengers and crew.

It was only after this second accident that Boeing grounded all of its 737 Max aeroplanes. A total of 346 people had died as a result of these two air crashes. In the subsequent investigation, Boeing was damned because it became clear that in their rush to get the 737 Max in the air, they had ignored multiple warnings that the plane wasn't safe. Despite introducing a new safety system that required pilot training to manage malfunctions (it was such malfunctions that had caused the crashes), Boeing knowingly hid the new system and reassured airlines that pilots needed no further training for the new aircraft (pilot training is very costly to both Boeing and the airlines).

Boeing paid out over $2.5 billion in fines and reparations to the bereaved families (Robison, 2021). Executives at Boeing were charged with fraud, and the previously respected Boeing Corporation suffered catastrophic reputational damage at a level that is difficult to overstate.

The saboteur at Boeing

What were the organisational factors that sabotaged Boeing's previously high level of integrity and commitment to good engineering and passenger safety? What factors led to this tragedy?

There were at least two: first, the dramatic change in organisational culture at Boeing following its merger with McDonnell Douglas; and second, the economic pressure that Boeing was under in the global airline market from its main competitor, Airbus.

Before the merger, Boeing was proud to call itself a traditional high-quality engineering firm that regarded staff as family. This was accurate in a tangible way because it was the sort of company where sons had followed fathers and grandfathers to work there. One writer described the Boeing culture as follows: 'For about 80 years, Boeing basically functioned as an association of engineers. Its executives held patents, designed wings and spoke the language of engineering and safety as a mother tongue. Finance wasn't a primary language' (Useem, 2019). The company had been based in Seattle for decades. Boeing was:

> An engineers' company that made planes to make its engineers proud, whatever the cost. Employees enjoyed watertight contracts, thanks to an assertive, family-like union, and an attitude to aviation that put design and quality above all else. In the process, it produced some of the world's greatest planes.
>
> (Frost, 2020)

McDonnell Douglas had a rather different corporate culture. It was a hard-nosed US corporation motivated by the desire to maximise profit and exceed shareholder expectations. Engineering and passenger safety took a back seat for the corporate executives at McDonnell Douglas.

The man who emerged as CEO of the merged company was a man straight out of the McDonnell Douglas organisational culture mould – Harry Stonecipher.

> he had a mien you'd call Trumpian if such a thing had existed then: a kind of deep-seated need for alpha displays, public humiliation, and conflict… In Stonecipher's first appearance at Boeing's annual management retreat at a hotel in Palm Springs in January 1998, he asked the managers in charge of commercial aircraft production, among the 200 attendees, to stand-up. 'They should apologise,' he told the group, for falling behind in their commitments and therefore causing the entire company to miss its financial goals. The only threat to Boeing comes from within – the failure to execute, he told them.
>
> (Robison, 2021)

This change of culture manifested itself in a dramatic move away from safety and innovation towards cut-throat management that emphasised cost-cutting and upgrading older models rather than developing and building new ones. The other dramatic move was a physical one: relocating the senior leadership team to a new corporate headquarters in Chicago, 2,000 miles away from the influence of the engineers who continued to build the planes in Seattle. This further broke down and degraded the channels of communication between the engineers who built the 737 Max and who were aware of its faults and the managers who made the commercial decisions to sell the aeroplane.

In effect, the organisational culture at Boeing effectively sabotaged,

> the ability to comfortably interact with an engineer who in turn feels comfortable telling you their reservations, versus calling a manager [more than] 1,500 miles away who you know has a reputation for wanting to take your pension away. It's a very different dynamic. As a recipe for disempowering engineers in particular, you couldn't come up with a better format.
>
> (Useem, 2019)

The culture at Boeing became almost unrecognisable from its pre-merger culture. Boeing was transformed from a safety-first engineering culture to a hard-nosed commercial operation. 'McDonnell Douglas executives, headed by Stonecipher, introduced a cost-cutting, profit-at-all-costs, shareholder-pleasing mentality. That led, under subsequent Boeing leaders, to a disregard for passenger safety that culminated in the most catastrophic events in Boeing's more than century-long history' (Skapinker, 2021). This culture was exacerbated by pressure from Airbus, which in less than a decade had more than doubled its annual sales. Boeing executives felt threatened by Airbus and feared they would be overtaken as the leading and most successful commercial plane manufacturer in the world.

This was the organisational context in which warnings about the faults in the 737 Max were not just ignored but actively suppressed.

Boeing's culture had evolved into one that turned a blind eye to safety and this led directly to the deaths of 346 people. The change in culture sabotaged the organisation's collective ability to think about, and act on, warnings that the 737 Max was dangerous. The ability to think was confined to Boeing's engineers, who had been systematically disempowered and isolated from those who made the decisions.

From a culture that resulted in loss of lives, let's now look at a culture that saved lives –millions of lives.

How organisational culture saved lives: the creative chaos of Bletchley Park

You might have heard of Bletchley Park. The work conducted here was famously dramatised in the 2014 film *The Imitation Game*.

Bletchley Park is a Victorian mansion house about 50 miles north of London. It was the centre of Britain's signals intelligence (codebreaking) service during the Second World War. It was an enormously successful organisation.

Bletchley Park was equidistant and on direct rail routes between London, Oxford and Cambridge. The location was important because many of its star codebreakers were mathematicians and other academics from the two universities. The codebreakers included experts in modern and ancient languages, crossword fanatics and post office engineers. It was the post office engineers who built the famous Bletchley Park bombe machine, an early mechanical computer which allowed the thousands of calculations that enabled the Germans' code to be decrypted relatively quickly. This, the modern computer, was not born in Silicon Valley, as many think; it was born in a large Victorian house in the Buckinghamshire countryside. The development of the bombe machine established Bletchley Park as the birthplace of the computer and computer science.

Bletchley Park was where Alan Turing and his colleagues broke the unbelievably complex Enigma code, which the German military were absolutely convinced was unbreakable. The work done at Bletchley Park saved the lives of so many people. Winston Churchill and many respectable military historians have estimated that the achievements of Bletchley Park shortened the war by somewhere between two and four years (Hinsley & Stripp, 1993). Just think of how many more lives would have been lost in those years – millions.

How was Bletchley Park so successful?

One reason for the achievements of Bletchley Park is that a particular organisational structure enabled its effectiveness, a structure that put firm scaffolding in place to support the less tangible intellectual work that went on there. Say the organisational structure at Bletchley Park had resembled that of Boeing 40 years later: then the post office engineers who built the bombe mechanical computer would probably have been located 500 miles away from the codebreakers, and the collaboration that produced the bombe just would not have been possible. The leadership, research and engineering at Bletchley Park were centralised rather than disconnected.

But beyond the organisational structure, it was the organisational culture that really fired up the intellectual firepower – the genius – of the people who worked there. There was a particular culture at Bletchley Park of intellectual curiosity driven by the emotional intensity of wartime.

Christopher Grey and Andrew Sturdy have written that there were at least three unique (for the time) characteristics that contributed to the success of Bletchley Park (Grey & Sturdy, 2010). They describe Bletchley Park's culture as 'a chaos that worked'. To make the chaos work at least three factors were required:

- **Shared social capital** between the people who worked there. People at Bletchley had a strong sense of meaning and purpose.
- **Mix of skills**: it was a hybrid organisation that included sections of highly intellectual Oxford and Cambridge academics, sections employing the practical engineering and mechanical skills of post office engineers, and the factory-like, production-line departments that gathered the intelligence and, after it was decrypted, disseminated the processed intelligence to military and government customers.
- **Centralisation**, which supported knowledge sharing and discouraged silos. The other factor that enabled centralisation was a very high level of secrecy at Bletchley Park. The existence of Station X (Bletchley's codename) was kept secret even from other members of the Allied Intelligence Community, as well as senior military officers and politicians. The work of Bletchley Park was very much kept in-house with minimal contact with the outside world.

To add to this complexity, Bletchley Park was a constantly and rapidly expanding organisation, growing from about 200 people in 1939 to more than 10,000 in 1944.

Bletchley Park had a unique, creative and exceptionally effective culture, which made it very difficult for individual, group and organisational psychological saboteurs to do damage. It was a culture that managed volatility, uncertainty, complexity and ambiguity extremely well. It was a culture that we can learn a great deal from today.

Cognitive diversity and psychological safety at Bletchley Park

The organisational culture at Bletchley Park was strong in terms of cognitive diversity. Bletchley Park was a place where people from different backgrounds, with different ways of conceptualising the world and solving problems and a strong sense of purpose and meaning, came together in an organisation that supported direct communication and the sharing of ideas.

In addition, the presence of psychological safety, or the ability to speak out if you see something bad happening, or something particularly good happening, was a prominent factor in Bletchley's organisational culture. This further magnified the impact of cognitive diversity. People who saw problems from different perspectives were encouraged to discuss and debate their understanding of and ideas of how to solve hard problems.

This quote from Michael Smith's book on Bletchley Park describes how the codebreaking teams in the 'Huts' were organised:

> you might readily find a Major working under a Lieutenant or under a civilian, somewhat younger. Whoever was in charge was the person who had been judged to be more effective at doing it. It was meritocracy in spades and without regard to where you came from or whether you were a man or a woman...'
>
> (Smith, 1988)

An account from an anonymous official internal history of Bletchley Park paints a similar picture:

> Here [Hut 3] over five hundred and fifty individuals of widely differing ages, gifts, and characters, men and women, Service and civilian, British and American, yet formed with all their variety one welded whole; working – often overworking – together, year by year, with unpretentious skill and pertinacity, gaiety and irony, and with less time wasted in intrigue than one could easily have thought possible in this too human world. Not everyone doubtless overworked. Not everyone was always angelic. This is not a fairy-tale. Not everyone was always content. There were grumbles... but we were 'a happy ship'.
>
> (Grey & Sturdy, 2010)

And:

> Ours... was an exceptional freedom. Those who did their work well were left, within the inevitable limits, to do it their own way. (By their nature, that freedom was particularly felt in the Research Sections). It was the exact reverse of the HITLER principle of the greatest possible meddling with the greatest possible number. That trust was repaid. And if mistakes were made (as of course they were) by ignorance or negligence, the remedy was found not nearly so much in reprimands, or witch-hunts for the delinquent, as in the mortification decent persons felt at having let things down.
>
> (Grey & Sturdy, 2010, emphasis in original)

In other words, a great mixture of people who had very different life experiences, views of the world and ways of solving problems were brought together at Bletchley Park. Over half the staff were women and many staff were what we would call nowadays neurodiverse (on the autistic spectrum). Esoteric academic mathematicians would be working with and socialising with linguists, including experts in ancient languages. They would work on ciphers with people who could solve *The Times* crossword in minutes. These very clever, but rather diffident and unworldly people worked alongside intensely practical post office engineers and together they built the first computer.

The academics and engineers worked with the military to understand the real-world significance of the intelligence on the German war effort that their combined genius had discovered. In other words, '[Bletchley] encouraged everyone from intercept personnel to the top cryptanalysts to collaborate and brainstorm for improvements. Initiative was assumed' (Ratcliff, 2006). This very diverse group of people were united by a common set of values and a strongly desired outcome – to win the war.

Centralisation of information

British signals intelligence (known as SIGINT) was centralised at Bletchley Park. This is in contrast to equivalent services in Germany and the USA, which were spread over many sites. This centralisation of function discouraged a silo mentality. People at Bletchley Park had a shared sense of identity and purpose. This shared identity more or less eliminated professional and service rivalry and one-upmanship, which is often seen in organisations that are spread over different functions and sites.

The culture at Bletchley Park also actively encouraged people to collaborate, brainstorm and, in short, talk to each other. Because of the high level of secrecy and consequent security, Bletchley Park was a very centralised, enclosed environment that was isolated from the normal, day-to-day world. The people at Bletchley not only worked together but by necessity also socialised together. Staff enjoyed the many on-site recreational activities including an amateur drama society, concerts, chess clubs, language classes, debating groups and so on. This in-house social activity further enhanced collaboration and the building of shared social capital between people from very diverse backgrounds. The culture at Bletchley Park led to the centralisation of information and also high levels of communication and collaboration. Contrast this with the professional and social isolation that we saw at Boeing.

Comparing Boeing and Bletchley Park

The organisational culture at Boeing couldn't have been more different. There was very little cognitive diversity at Boeing, and the organisational culture under CEO Harry Stonecipher was toxic rather than psychologically safe. Finally, there was a dramatic divergence of values and desired outcomes between management and engineers. The leadership and management valued shareholder profit and wanted a cheap but functional 737 Max. The engineers valued safety and wanted a well-engineered, safe 737 Max. These values were incompatible and, as is so often the case, the leadership team won.

What made Bletchley Park such a success was its potent combination of psychological safety and cognitive diversity. Conversely, it was the absence of these two factors that led to the Boeing tragedy.

The presence of psychological safety, or the ability to speak out if you see something bad happening, or something particularly good happening, is the antidote to the organisational saboteur. This effect is emphasised in an organisation that has a high level of cognitive diversity – in other words, people who can see situations and problems from different perspectives, in an organisation where they are encouraged to share their views, will disable even the strongest organisational saboteur.

Box 10.1: Defining structure and culture

The examples of Boeing and Bletchley Park show the interplay between structure and culture in creating a workplace that minimises the impact of our saboteur. There is a symbiotic or dialectical relationship between the structure and culture of an organisation.

By *structure* I mean the way work is organised and the tangible things you can see and touch in an organisation. For example, structure includes how the workplace is laid out. Is it open plan or do people have individual offices? Are the leadership team on the top floors of the building or even (as in the case of Boeing) in a different building altogether? Does the building have spaces where people can meet and talk informally?

> Edgar Schein provided the simplest, most helpful and most accepted definition of organisational *culture*. He wrote:
>
> Organisational culture is the pattern of basic assumptions that a given group has invented, discovered, or developed in learning to cope with its problems of external adaptation and internal integration, and that have worked well enough to be considered valid, and, therefore, to be taught to new members as the correct way to perceive, think, and feel in relation to those problems.
>
> (Schein, 1984)

Psychological safety

The records of Bletchley Park certainly suggest a culture of psychological safety. Amy Edmondson, Professor of Leadership and Management at Harvard Business School, writes that a sense of psychological safety is the essential characteristic of a high-performance organisational culture (Edmondson, 2019). Conversely, a lack of psychological safety results in a toxic organisation, such as Boeing prior to the tragedies discussed earlier.

She describes a culture of psychological safety as one in which people feel they can speak up and discuss and debate issues at work. They feel comfortable to express their concerns and be heard. In a psychologically safe organisation, people are not frightened to express their opinions. They don't talk about having to cover their backs. They don't have to self-censor because they are worried about saying the 'wrong' thing or offending somebody. They are allowed to make mistakes without being embarrassed or punished.

This is a workplace where people can offer suggestions and take sensible risks without provoking retaliation.

Charles Duhigg, a business journalist, wrote about the culture of psychological safety at the tech giant Google. He described research carried out by Google to understand why some teams performed better than others. This research project was called Project Aristotle. According to Duhigg, Project Aristotle found that psychological safety was *by far* the single most important factor driving success. He wrote:

> Individuals on teams with higher psychological safety are less likely to leave Google, they're more likely to harness the power of diverse ideas from their teammates, they bring in more revenue, and they're rated as effective twice as often by executives.
>
> (Duhigg, 2016)

Cognitive diversity

The other factor, aside from psychological safety, that made Bletchley Park such a success was the great degree of cognitive diversity among the people who worked there. There was a diversity of professional skills, social class, gender and thinking style that was unusual for 1940s Britain.

Cognitive diversity means the diversity in the way in which different groups of people think about problems, the environment and the world in general. When we think about diversity, we often think of demographic diversity – in other words, differences in gender, race, sexual orientation, age and religion and so on. The real power of demographic diversity doesn't lie in skin hues, genitalia or years lived on the planet, though; it is the different life experiences those diverse groups of people have had that lead to different ways of thinking about and perceiving the world.

There is often an overlap between cognitive diversity and demographic diversity – but not always. An upper-middle-class, Eton-educated white lawyer is likely to think very similarly to a British-born, upper-middle-class, Eton-educated lawyer of Nigerian heritage. However, that upper-middle-class, Eton-educated white lawyer is likely to think very differently about life than a working-class woman or a gay working-class man or a second-generation son of Jamaican immigrant parents brought up in inner-city Birmingham. People who look and sound the same can be very diverse in their world view. Matthew Syed put this very well when he wrote:

> Now take two white, middle-aged, bespectacled economists, who have the same number of children and like the same TV programmes. They may seem homogenous and, from a demographic perspective, they are. But suppose that one of them is a monetarist and the other a Keynesian. These are two different ways of making sense of the economy; two very different models. Their collective prediction will, over time, be significantly better than either alone. The two economists may look the same but they are diverse in the way that they think about the problem.
>
> (Syed, 2019)

Cognitive diversity, especially when combined with a culture of psychological safety, will minimise the risk of unconscious sabotage in groups and organisations. This is because a group or organisation will have a much more nuanced and comprehensive perception of the reality that they are facing. The following section provides a simple but elegant illustration of this from the world of social psychology.

How culture makes us blind to our environment

Two social psychologists from the University of Michigan, Takahiko Masuda and Richard Nisbett, wondered whether cultural differences affect the way people see the world – not 'see' in the abstract sense, but what they tangibly perceive. Can culture make us blind to what is happening in front of our eyes? The researchers decided to compare two groups from very different cultures: Americans and Japanese.

They showed each group animated video clips of scenes of tropical fish swimming around in the sea. When the Americans were asked to describe what they saw, they tended to describe the characteristics of the individual fish. However, when the Japanese participants were asked the same question, they described the environment and the group of fish – in other words, the context. Both groups were shown the same scene, but their descriptions (reflecting their perceptions) of the scene were radically different, as if they were describing completely different scenes. Americans saw individuals, and Japanese saw groups and context.

This experiment was replicated, this time with images of animal wildlife. The American subjects were sensitive to changes in individual animals but almost blind to changes in the environment, whereas Japanese subjects were almost blind to changes in individuals but were very attuned to the environment and context (Masuda & Nisbett, 2001).

This fascinating experiment shows just how profoundly our perception of the real world is influenced by the culture in which we grow up. The American subjects, who grew up in a very individualistic culture, naturally saw individuals in the scenes. The Japanese participants, whose culture is far more centred on groups and communities, saw groups – the context in which the individuals existed, rather than just the individuals. The study also effectively shows the value of cognitive diversity. The Japanese were able to see things that the Americans were blind to, and vice versa. Just think: if this were applied in a business context, then the value would be astounding.

In his excellent book on cognitive diversity, *Rebel Ideas*, Matthew Syed, also discusses this point:

> suppose you were to combine a Japanese and an American in a 'team'. Alone, they might perceive only a partial picture. Alone, they each miss aspects of the scene. Together, however, they are able to recount both objects and context. By combining two partial frames of reference, the overall picture snaps into focus. They now have a more comprehensive grasp of reality.
>
> (Syed, 2019)

It is precisely this comprehensive grasp of reality that makes it very difficult for our internal and group saboteur to operate. The saboteur works by showing us just one perception of reality, which is usually a distorted, extreme, 'black-or-white' perception. The saboteur also works by hiding different aspects of reality for us – encouraging us to turn a blind eye to things that don't fit with our distorted perception. When you have people in the team who can see the world from multiple perspectives and they are able to voice these perspectives, the saboteur has a much harder task.

Box 10.2: Business outcomes with cognitive diversity and psychological safety

A business environment that is diverse and minimises the risk of psychological sabotage has impressive performance outcomes. Chad Sparber (2009) found that performance and productivity increased over 25 per cent when organisations increased the racial diversity of their staff by just one standard deviation.

However, this dramatic effect only applied in organisations whose success is dependent upon creative thinking, problem-solving and human interaction, such as law, healthcare and finance. Diversity made absolutely no impact on performance and productivity in industries that relied on production-line type work, for example making aeroplane parts. This is because the experience of being black, gay or a woman contributes little, if anything, when you are doing routine production-line type work.

Building psychological safety and cognitive diversity

It's no good having different views, perceptions and opinions about the world and solving problems if people are too frightened to voice those diverse opinions. This is where psychological safety comes in. Here are a few really practical things that you can do, as a leader, to foster both psychological safety and cognitive diversity.

- **Inclusivity – solicit people's opinions:** Clearly and explicitly tell the people in your team that you want them to be honest with you about the good things and the bad things in the organisation. You should emphasise that doing this requires courage on their part. Give them the clear message that if they want to say something to you and are frightened that you won't want to hear it, they should absolutely speak up. Explain that you won't be cross with them and you will listen to them. They need to know that you might not necessarily agree with them, but you'll take their views seriously and treat them with respect.

- **Engagement:** If somebody does have the courage to talk to you in an honest and straightforward manner, be present and focus on the conversation – close your laptop during the meeting. Make eye contact, listen and don't interrupt. At the end of the conversation, tell the person, 'Thank you, I appreciate you telling me that'. Don't be defensive or start telling the person why they are wrong – just say thank you.
- **Feedback:** Think about what the person has told you, and when you've decided what you're going to do about it, tell them. You don't have to necessarily agree with them or implement their ideas, but tell them what your thoughts are. There's nothing worse than telling the boss something important and then your ideas just seem to disappear and get forgotten. Catch up with the person and say, 'Your idea is very thoughtful, but for various reasons we can't implement it right now. But thanks so much for discussing it with me'. Most people won't mind that you don't use their ideas but will feel pleased to know that you've taken them seriously and given them serious consideration.

These very simple techniques are easy to implement and make a massive difference to team and organisational culture if they're put into practice with a degree of thoughtfulness and compassion.

Destroyers, equalisers and creators

Having said all this, diversity isn't always a good thing in teams. Some diverse teams are terrible and spend more time arguing than getting on with the job. Diversity without psychological safety doesn't add much value at all. In teams that aren't particularly psychologically safe, diversity produces friction and can result in mediocrity and disengagement.

Joe DiStefano and Martha Maznevski, psychologists at the Institute for Management Development in Switzerland, found that when diverse business teams are managed badly, they underperform when compared with similar homogeneous teams (DiStefano & Maznevski, 2000). They wondered why this was and what the characteristics of a high-performing diverse team actually were. They found that poorly performing diverse teams tend to fall into one of these three categories:

- **Destroyers:** Some diverse teams are disasters. Their members mistrust each other, guard information jealously and take every opportunity to criticise each other. The energy that could be channelled into effective work ends up being drained into office politics, conflict and negative stereotyping. This 'team' destroys value rather than creating it.
- **Equalisers:** Some teams manage diversity by pretending that it doesn't exist. Team members, particularly management, tend to

actively suppress differences to smooth over any potential conflict. Unfortunately, though, this also suppresses any creativity and differences in ideas and perspectives. Most diverse teams that think of themselves as 'doing well' are really equalisers. They aren't bad, but they're dull and mediocre.

- **Creators:** Some diverse teams, of course, do perform exceptionally well. In these teams, differences are explicitly recognised and accepted, even nurtured. People talk to each other about the different opinions and find a way of integrating these different ideas into the work. These are the teams that create value.

Creator teams do three things well: (1) they explicitly recognise the differences in the team; (2) they figure out an effective way to communicate the different ideas; and (3) they are able to convert the diverse ideas into practical methods of generating value.

There are three steps to enabling a diverse team to excel, overcome their saboteur and create value from their diversity.

Stage 1: Mapping to understand differences

It is important to actively and explicitly recognise and understand your team's diversity. This goes way beyond a tokenistic celebration of diversity for diversity's sake, which leads to the mindset of being superficially different but thinking that deep down we are all the same. Such a mindset has the result of subtly suppressing diverse thinking, creating what DiStefano and Maznevski call the equaliser mindset. Similarly, if teams just focus on the differences – on what divides them to the exclusion of what unites them – then this creates a destroyer team, where value is actively sabotaged.

Rather than just saying, 'Aren't we all great', try to actively and assertively bring the different ways of thinking out into the open. Consciously recognise people's talents – that some team members are better at some tasks than others. Adopt the mindset that some conflict (conflict around ideas) is creative tension and not disharmony.

This might sound simple – and it is, but that doesn't mean that it's trivial. We are all different, we know that, but the important factor is to identify which differences will make a difference in which situation. Which differences are important in helping the team fulfil its primary task to create value? Conversely, which are the differences that might lead to destructive conflict or turning a blind eye to something bad? In other words, how might differences sabotage the work of the team?

Diversity in personality, thinking style, gender, race or profession will impact the team's dynamics in lots of ways that the team can be blind to. In order to mitigate this sabotage and fully realise the team's creative potential, its members must fully understand these differences.

Stage 2: Bridging to communicate across differences

If we understand the differences in a team, then it follows that different people have different preferences in the way they communicate. This means simply sending and receiving meaning as it was intended. In diverse teams, there is a heightened potential for miscommunication and misunderstanding when compared with homogeneous teams.

When we are in a team, we want others to understand us, but we are often much less anxious to understand others. To prepare the ground for effective communication, our team needs to encourage and nurture three mindsets:

- A mindset of active listening. A simple but very meaningful explanation of active listening is, 'first seek to understand, before being understood' (Covey, 2013).
- The motivation to actively communicate your opinions, and a belief that individual opinions, even if they dissent from the prevailing consensus, are important.
- A confidence in the team that dissent is well intentioned and that any conflict can be overcome – become a team that can argue assertively about ideas but is respectful of people.

Stage 3: Integrating to leverage differences

Good communication, particularly good listening, is important in making the best of diversity, but it doesn't guarantee that the team will use that diversity to make good decisions and convert those decisions into higher performance. In order to convert diversity into high performance, the team has to integrate the differing perspectives into the way they make decisions and implement those decisions. To achieve this, we need to give some serious thought to two things: group participation and conflict management.

Manage and encourage participation

If we accept that people have different communication preferences (some people prefer an informal chat, others might prefer to communicate by email, etc.), then the team needs to figure out how all members of the team can be actively involved in communicating their ideas and contribute to decision-making and planning. Managers of high-functioning teams actively and assertively encourage every member of the team to participate.

Here are some ideas for managers to encourage participation during a meeting:

- Go around the room and ask people for their thoughts in turn. The most senior person in the room should always speak last. When the most powerful person speaks first, those people beneath them in the dominance hierarchy will consciously or unconsciously alter their views to fit in with those of the boss.
- Give people the message that when somebody is speaking, the task of all the other participants in the meeting is to listen, rather than think of what their response might be or what they are planning to say. Interruptions are banned. This helps to create what the psychologist Nancy Kline describes as a 'thinking environment': in other words, a social environment that supports effective thinking (Kline, 1999).
- Pause the meeting periodically to give people time to think, reflect and write down their thoughts.

Address and resolve disagreements

The biggest factor that will sabotage the implementation of ideas in diverse teams is disagreement. Therefore, it's important for the team to figure out a team strategy for resolving conflict. This is much easier in homogenous teams because they will already have in place culturally accepted ways of managing conflict. By their very nature, diverse teams are made up of people from different backgrounds who have evolved different ways of managing conflict. An American is likely to attempt to resolve conflict in a very different way than a Japanese team member or even a Russian team member. A team member who has had the benefits of an Oxbridge education will approach disagreement and conflict far differently than a team member who has grown up in South London the child of second-generation immigrants. Resolving conflict becomes much harder when the team members have different opinions on the best way to resolve conflict in the first place.

The first step in effective conflict management is to reframe conflict from diversity of opinion as creative and desirable rather than destructive. The fact that there is conflict in the team shows that people care and have an emotional attachment to the outcome, and that's good because that's what drives behaviour. Managing participation will really help team members to depersonalise the conflict. This is because everybody will have a say and will be seriously listened to. This helps enormously to promote the idea of arguing about ideas rather than people. Team members should be encouraged to be curious about conflicting ideas and ask, 'How can this intelligent person sitting opposite me hold a view that is so different to mine?' In a very polarised discussion, the manager can pause and ask each side to accurately summarise the opposing side's ideas.

Another technique I have used is to draw a line on a flipchart with one idea at one end and the opposing idea at the other. Each team member is then asked to put a cross on the line to represent where they are on the continuum between the two extremes. Often what is expected is polarisation with groupings of crosses at each end of the line. In practice, what usually happens is that most crosses are towards the centre, on either side of the midpoint. So, if we put numbers on the line, most crosses don't group around 1 or 100, but around, say, 40 and 60. This shows graphically that members are often far closer together in their views than they might initially have thought.

It takes time and skill to build and manage a diverse team, but the reward will be increased performance and added value. The team will also evolve in its ability to be creative and innovative. This requires effort to sustain: for example, examining processes regularly and making a special effort to integrate new members into the team's way of working.

Psychological safety and cancel culture

As I have written, psychological safety is important to mitigate the malign effects of the saboteur. The biggest threat to psychological safety in organisations is the emergence of 'cancel culture'. Many leaders now frequently and actively self-censor their speech because they are worried about saying the wrong thing or 'causing offence'. This is the kiss of death for psychological safety and cognitive diversity – and, indeed, innovation.

The term 'psychological safety' is sometimes confused with the term 'safe space'. According to the Merriam-Webster dictionary, a safe space is 'a place (as on a college campus) intended to be free of bias, conflict, criticism, or potentially threatening actions, ideas, or conversations' (Merriam-Webster, n.d.). The concept of safe spaces is the opposite of that of psychological safety. A psychologically safe space is one where people can listen to and debate ideas that are potentially threatening, critical or even biased (of course, the person expressing the opinion doesn't think that they are biased!). This is an environment of creative conflict where new ideas can emerge and stupid or destructive ideas can be actively challenged.

Of course, we have to be courteous, polite and professional in our organisations. It's important to be sensitive to other people and not go out of our way to upset our colleagues. Bob Sutton, professor of organisational design at Stanford, wrote convincingly of the value of respect and courtesy in his imaginatively titled book *The No Asshole Rule: Building a Civilized Workplace and Surviving One That Isn't* (Sutton, 2007). It can seem like a difficult balance at times between being straightforward and honest in your comments and being what Bob Sutton would call 'an asshole'.

However, there is a continuum between being overzealous in policing what people say and being too permissive and excusing poor behaviour. The middle ground should be not turning a blind eye to egregiously discriminatory, discourteous and disrespectful behaviour. But if someone makes a genuine mistake in their words or behaviour that lacks obvious malicious intent and the person is genuinely apologetic, then it is probably best to forgive and learn from the experience rather than punish and 'cancel' the individual concerned. The more people are cancelled, the more psychological safety is eroded – and the more the saboteur can emerge. Remember the Boeing tragedy, and the Bletchley Park triumph: of course, we want to build organisations like the latter, not the former.

Chapter takeaways

- Although the saboteur is an individual phenomenon, it can also emerge and take over large groups like companies and organisations.
- When there are no shared values, no centralisation, no ability to speak up and be heard, and no room for different opinions to shape decisions and processes, the saboteur can wreak havoc.
- The best way to mitigate the effects of the saboteur is through creating a culture of cognitive diversity and psychological safety.
- Teams need to be made up of a diverse group of people who see situations and problems from different perspectives.
- People must be safe to share their views; they must be genuinely heard and their opinions must be respected.
- Managers need to build creator teams where differences are accepted and different ideas are integrated into decision-making and work.

References

Covey, S. R. (2013). *The 7 Habits of Highly Effective People: Powerful Lessons in Personal Change*. New York: Simon and Schuster.

DiStefano, J. J. & Maznevski, M. L. (2000). 'Creating Value with Diverse Teams in Global Management'. *Organizational Dynamics*, 29(1), 45–63.

Duhigg, C. (2016). 'What Google Learned from Its Quest to Build the Perfect Team'. *New York Times Sunday Magazine*, 16 February, p. 20. Retrieved from: https://www.nytimes.com/2016/02/28/magazine/what-google-learned-from-its-quest-to-build-the-perfect-team.html.

Edmondson, A. C. (2019). *The Fearless Organization: Creating Psychological Safety in the Workplace for Learning, Innovation, and Growth*. New York: Wiley.

Frost, N. (2020). 'The 1997 Merger That Paved the Way for the Boeing 737 Max Crisis'. *Yahoo Finance*, 3 January. Originally published by Quartz. Retrieved from: https://finance.yahoo.com/news/1997-merger-paved-way-boeing-090042193.html.

Grey, C. & Sturdy, A. (2010). 'A Chaos That Worked: Organizing Bletchley Park'. *Public Policy and Administration*, 25(1), 47–66.

Hinsley, H. & Stripp, A. (Eds) (1993). *Codebreakers*. Oxford: Oxford University Press.

Kline, N. (1999). *Time to Think: Listening to Ignite the Human Mind*. London: Hachette UK.

Masuda, T. & Nisbett, R. E. (2001). 'Attending Holistically Versus Analytically: Comparing the Context Sensitivity of Japanese and Americans'. *Journal of Personality and Social Psychology*, 81(5), 922–34.

Merriam-Webster. (n.d.). 'Safe Space'. Retrieved from: https://www.merriam-webster.com/dictionary/safe%20space.

Ratcliff, R. (2006). *Delusions of Intelligence: Enigma, Ultra and the End of Secure Ciphers*. Cambridge: Cambridge University Press.

Robison, P. (2021). *Flying Blind: The 737 MAX Tragedy and the Fall of Boeing*. Harmondsworth: Penguin Business.

Schein, E. H. (1984). 'Coming to a New Awareness of Organizational Culture'. *MIT Sloan Management Review*, Winter. Retrieved from: https://sloanreview.mit.edu/article/coming-to-a-new-awareness-of-organizational-culture.

Skapinker, M. (2021). 'The 737 Max Tragedy and the Fall of Boeing – What Have We Learnt?' *Financial Times*, 14 December. Retrieved from: https://www.ft.com/content/dcd39dc6-ae3b-4203-9210-c321eac8f5e5.

Smith, M. (1988). *The Secrets of Station X: How the Bletchley Park Codebreakers Helped Win the War*. Basingstoke: Macmillan.

Sparber, C. (2009). 'Racial Diversity and Aggregate Productivity in U.S. Industries: 1980–2000'. *Southern Economic Journal*, 75(3), 829–56.

Sutton, R. I. (2007). *The No Asshole Rule: Building a Civilized Workplace and Surviving One That Isn't*. London: Sphere.

Syed, M. (2019). *Rebel Ideas: The Power of Diverse Thinking*. London: John Murray.

Useem, J. (2019). 'The Long-Forgotten Flight That Sent Boeing Off Course'. *The Atlantic*, 20 November. Retrieved from: https://www.theatlantic.com/ideas/archive/2019/11/how-boeing-lost-its-bearings/602188.

Conclusion: Knowledge Is Power

The philosopher and statesman Sir Francis Bacon coined the phrase 'knowledge itself is power' in his *Meditationes Sacrae* of 1597. It's easy to see why the aphorism has endured: its meaning is so simple and yet so profound and fundamentally true across many aspects of life.

'Knowledge is power' has underpinned the writing in this book. The saboteur that can damage individuals, groups or even whole nations is unconscious, hidden. If you don't know of its existence, how can you hope to minimise its influence? To stop it causing terrible damage to your life and the lives of others.

And as we have seen, the saboteur really can cause havoc. It caused Rabbi Levy to 'snap' and behave in a most uncharacteristic way; it made Andrea Dunbar, a successful playwright, end her days alone and in a fog of alcohol; it led Hungarian MEP Jozsef Szajer to ruin his career at a sex party. The saboteur was behind the collapse of Barings Bank, the failings of the Boeing Corporation and the disaster at Chernobyl. It was the psychological force behind the terrible atrocities committed at Abu Ghraib and at Auschwitz.

I could go on and on, because there are so many examples of the saboteur in action at an individual, organisational and national level. Evidently, the saboteur is a powerful force, and it can be a very dangerous one. Therefore, we must be prepared to both recognise it and, through informed thinking and actions, disempower it.

In this concluding chapter, I will pull together the threads of the book to give you a clear overview of how and why the saboteur operates and how you can build a workplace that's as 'sabotage proof' as possible.

Uncloaking the saboteur

Here's another famous quote, this time from *The Art of War* by Sun Tzu, a general from ancient China: 'If you know the enemy and know yourself, you need not fear the result of a 100 battles'. Now, I wouldn't quite class the saboteur as an enemy – after all, it works hard to protect us. But certainly, it can *act* like an enemy in the way it sabotages us and the groups and organisations to which we belong. So, we need to know about this psychological force that exists in ourselves and in others.

DOI: 10.4324/9781003188063-12

The saboteur is part of the unconscious, which itself is a huge part of the mind and is hugely influential in shaping our thoughts, feelings and actions. Quite often when we think we're in charge, it is in fact the unconscious that's in control. We're sure we want to get that promotion at work, and yet somehow, we miss important deadlines and fumble our way through a presentation: the saboteur has sabotaged us.

Uncloak the saboteur and you'll find fear, anxiety, anger, shame and desire. Remember, this is all in the subconscious, way below the tip of the iceberg represented by the conscious mind. These kinds of feelings can be difficult to experience, and so we have defence mechanisms to protect us – we have the saboteur. Its intentions, in fact, are good, but it constantly leads us astray. We have the saboteur to thank for:

- Imposter syndrome: feeling not good enough despite achievements
- Denial: thinking that we're right when we're not
- Cognitive dissonance: misinterpreting facts to support beliefs
- Confirmation bias: looking for evidence to confirm our beliefs and rejecting any that contradicts
- Our oversensitive burglar alarm: seeing threats where there are no threats, and reacting quickly from a place of anxiety
- Chronic stress: the result of the saboteur jumping in to 'save' us over and over again
- Sabotaging stories: stories we tell in the unconscious that distort reality and can become self-fulfilling prophecies.

Evidently, then, the saboteur is the source of a great deal of unhappiness at a personal level and a vast number of problems at a group and organisational level. We need to know how to manage the saboteur as we manage so many things in the workplace.

Managing the saboteur

I suggest *managing* the saboteur at work because it is not something you can simply boot out of the door. The saboteur exists in every one of us and it always will do, so we can't simply eradicate it. What we need to do is recognise when the saboteur is at work and employ strategies to disempower it. This means working at an individual and organisational level.

Listening to your saboteur

Returning to the *Art of War* quote, Sun Tzu advised that you should know *yourself*. The saboteur is a part of you, and you need to recognise how it works in you and notice when it's in action. A good clue that the saboteur has risen up is that you're feeling a strong emotion and a strong compulsion to act.

Managing the saboteur is more of an emotional challenge than a cognitive/intellectual challenge. If you have read so far, you understand, at an intellectual level, what the saboteur is, it can be a friend, or how it can influence us to commit great evil. You also know that the saboteur works at an unconscious and emotional level. It compels us to act. To manager our saboteur we have to first pay attention to our feelings and then resist the compulsion to go straight from feeling to behaviour. In situations where the saboteur is active, that will feel very stressful and exhausting, and that's the challenge. The challenge is a behavioural one rather than an intellectual one.

Here's what to do. Once you identify that the saboteur is at work, stop. Take a pause. Don't act – even if the saboteur is clamouring for you to do something (probably something unhelpful). Just stop and listen. What is it trying to tell you? How can you respond without sabotaging yourself? Take a step back and challenge yourself. Are you seeing things as they really are, or how you want them to be? Ask yourself:

- How do I feel? (Remember, feelings aren't facts.)
- What do I believe about this situation?
- Is there evidence to support my belief?
- Is there a different way to look at this situation?
- Are any opposing viewpoints valid?
- Am I thinking logically and rationally?
- Is my saboteur trying to protect me right now?

The saboteur needn't be your enemy; it can be your ally. It gives you really valuable information, data if you like. You can carefully consider these data and then integrate them with your decision-making. Then, once heard, the saboteur will settle right down, and you'll have made a balanced, considered decision.

The more you stop and listen to your saboteur, the easier it gets. This means when you want to get that promotion at work, you won't somehow miss important deadlines and fumble your way through a presentation: the saboteur won't have the power to sabotage you.

Protecting the organisation

The examples in this book have shown that the saboteur at work in a group of people can have extremely damaging consequences. At the very least, the saboteur can create a depressing work environment and poor performance, affecting the bottom line. At its worst, the saboteur can cause the collapse of companies – and even, as in the case of Boeing, loss of lives.

Rather than laying out the welcome mat for the saboteur, then, organisations should be building a culture that protects people from this destructive force. That means organisations need to:

- Create cognitive diversity by employing people with diverse views and perspectives. Encourage people to think independently, not follow the herd.
- Encourage people to share their views, and genuinely listen to them. Use these views to make changes: factor them into decision-making and work.
- Make the company a psychologically safe space where people can share any concerns or wrongdoing they see. Ensure that these views are taken seriously and, where appropriate, acted upon.

At a glance, perhaps the work required to combat the saboteur at work seems fairly straightforward, and in a sense, it is: welcome different views, listen and integrate diverse opinions. But establishing such a culture takes a lot of hard work, and this work is ongoing: keeping the saboteur in check requires constant management. All the effort is well worth it, however, when your organisation is operating effectively, not sabotaged by an invisible force.

When you know all about the saboteur – why it exists, in yourself and in your organisation, and how it operates – you can ensure it doesn't undermine all of your hard work. Knowledge is power.

Index

Note: page numbers followed by "n" denote endnotes.

Ingram Content Group UK Ltd.
Milton Keynes UK
UKHW022252140423
420216UK00012B/91